CW00811761

Sitting Ducks

by

~Sam Newman~

Sitting Ducks

Sam Newman

Copyright © Sam Newman 2013

All rights reserved. No part of this publication may be reproduced, stored in or introduced into a retrieval system, or transmitted, in any form, or by any means (electronic, mechanical, photocopying, recording or otherwise) without the prior written permission of the publisher. Any person who does any unauthorised act in relation to this publication may be liable to criminal prosecution and civil claims for damages.

~Chapter 1~

Rebecca Beresford drooped against the mottled pink granite of the kitchen counter, arms clutching the security of her housecoat around her, and wondered not for the first time just what distinguished marriage from life in a zoo. Could it be that both marriage and zoo offered security? she pondered, one hand fumbling in her dressing gown pocket to confirm the presence of her cigarettes. Regular feeding times, too; though marriage appeared to involve considerable input from the female of the species. Maybe it was simply that the female gibbon couldn't nip out to Tesco whenever she felt like it; though, on the other hand, no-one expected her to clean the cage. Whatever it was, Rebecca concluded dreamily, both zoo and marriage appeared to combine a large degree of boredom with what, she conceded, might be simply the corollary of occasional procreation.

Katy, aloft in her high chair and demanding as a brood of fledglings, rattled her spoon on the plastic tray and stared pointedly at the cupboard withholding her breakfast cereal. Although it was not yet eight, warm sunlight pierced the slats of the half-opened blinds, adding to the sticky summer heat already beginning to build. Rebecca fanned limply at the neck of her once-

aquamarine cotton housecoat, her spare hand fumbling
in the cupboard for a packet of cereal. Shaking a
helping into a bowl of warm milk she gave it a listless
stir and transferred it to Katy's tray. Returning the
cereal to the cupboard, she held the door open for a
moment, her face reflecting in its diamond panes,
crown of dark hair still mussed from sleep, wide-apart
hazel eyes still sleepily half-closed. Gently, she shut the
cupboard and turned to gaze unseeingly at a window
ledge where barely-surviving plants jostled for space
with an empty bottle of washing-up liquid and a scallop
shell ashtray. Behind her a trail of toast crumbs traced
the path the boys had taken to the living room.

* * *

Upstairs, Simon Beresford rested his razor on the wire
bath tidy and ran a satisfied hand over the fresh pink
smoothness of his chin. Taking a deep breath, he
grasped his nose and sank beneath the cooling suds,
provoking a surge of water that slalomed off the end of
the bath then surged back over the taps and splashed
on to the bare floorboards. The dislodged razor slid
beneath the surface, its metallic echo becoming a
depthcharge striking the hull of a lurking submarine, a
fantasy Simon sustained until his breath ran out and he
was forced to the surface. Grabbing the loofah, he used
it to cushion his head as he leaned back and stared
through bent knees at the gently stirring curtains.
Sounds from the kitchen wafted through the open
window as Rebecca emptied last night's ashtray into
the pedal-bin. As he reclined in the rapidly chilling
water Simon's mind filled with pictures of bathtubs
edged with gleaming white sealant instead of the
scabrous grey substance that appeared to have
developed a life of its own and was now progressively
detaching itself from where some previous owner had

nudged the rolled lip of the bath against a wall whose dark green tiles lent the bathroom the air of a Victorian public lavatory.

The bath itself was long and deep and stained with rivulets of rust where generations of users had worn and scarred the enamel to expose its iron soul. It took an age to fill through sclerotic pipes; yet it had been the bath with its lion's feet, just as much as the marble fireplaces downstairs, that had first persuaded them to make an offer for the house. It was an offer which, short of divine intervention, they could not afford, but they had stuck audaciously through confrontations with rival bidders until, with support from both sets of parents, the house had eventually become theirs.

Their wish to keep the bath rather than replace it with something in aubergine or avocado had encouraged Simon to paint it with a substance from a tin proclaiming unparalleled powers of adhesion. It was one of the few assurances they received as they embarked on married life which had, at least in some respects, held good. Now, where rust had once shown through white enamel, it showed through white enamel showing through *eau-de-nil* as, little by little, speck by speck, the paint migrated to the bodies of bathers from where it could apparently be removed only through the elapse of time.

For Simon, the bath exercised a voluptuary fascination in what otherwise remained a jobless and straitened world. Smiling contentedly, he roused himself from the water to fumble for one of the children's red plastic buckets by the side of the bath which he filled from the cold tap then winced as he used it to rinse his hair. Downstairs, the morning's drama continued to unfold as Rebecca attempted to shuffle through the ritual of feeding the children without disturbing the coma that would shroud her until it was her turn to use the bathroom.

"Katy's thrown her cereal on the floor." The voice of Martin, six-years-old and eldest of the three Beresford children, drifted in through the bathroom window as he wandered into the kitchen in search of more toast.

"It was probably an accident," he heard Rebecca say, her voice balancing propitiation with resignation.

A confusion of sounds followed in which Simon identified a startled yelp from Rebecca followed by a muted curse as she stepped in the fallen cereal and executed a glissade that carried her halfway across the kitchen.

"Daddy says you're not to say shit."

An exchange developing between Martin and his mother mingled with the noise of Katy's spoon beating approvingly on the sticky plastic tray of her high chair.

* * *

Almost all Rebecca's friends swore, Simon had observed.

Rebecca's friend Hazel, the children's book illustrator who lived in the matching yellow brick house next door, not only swore but rolled her own cigarettes in what Simon saw as a surreal synthesis of Beatrix Potter and John Wayne. But where Rebecca's swearing was concerned, and where once he might have claimed a tenuous influence, he had long since abandoned attempts at reform. Even the trauma of the school pantomime had produced no more than a fleeting improvement...

Stepping easily out of the bath on to the cork mat, Simon rubbed warmth into his head of fair hair as an equally warm flush of recollection helped counter the permanent chill of the bathroom.

* * *

Only later did he gather that Martin had originally been assigned to the third row of the chorus of varlets where all were destined to be more or less anonymous, save to doting parents, in costumes of russet and Lincoln green. There, however, the raucous power of his Lavender's Blue Dilly-Dilly had so unnerved the more timid choristers that Miss Evans had been compelled to re-cast him as the dragon on the tardily recognised but eminently sane basis that it was the production's only non-vocal part.

The first night came. The pantomime tottered towards the tea interval. The trepidation that for weeks had afflicted Miss Evans like an ague began to melt into the first gentle waves of satisfaction. Parents' nervous giggles had long since subsided into rapt attention and, glancing covertly around, Miss Evans permitted herself a modest smile of congratulation. It was at this point that a misfortune occurred that she could never afterwards recall without collapsing on to the nearest piece of furniture.

St. George, shimmering in cooking foil armour, was sneaking up behind the dragon precisely as the script demanded. Then, in a sadly extempore development, he flourished his sword with such ebullience that he tripped over his own feet and landed squarely on the scarlet felt arrowhead of the dragon's tail. There was a ripping noise followed by a response from the dragon that left nothing implied.

"Shit!" yelled the dragon.

"Wah!" wailed St. George.

"Ooh!" said the audience.

"Good gracious me!" clucked Mr. Pownall, headmaster of Rosehill Infants' School later that evening as he confronted Simon and Rebecca across the arid surface of his desk. Outside, a wan Miss Evans stumbled past the study window as a sympathetic colleague assisted her towards home and a stiff drink.

A frowning Mr. Pownall, eyebrows gathered in studied incomprehension, stared unblinkingly at Simon. "Where on earth," he asked faintly, "do you suppose he picked up an expression like that?"

Simon pursed his lips, frowning at an ancient drip of cream emulsion on the coving in what he hoped represented agonised parental reflection. Having spent most of the interval hiding in the washroom, balancing on a lavatory that appeared ludicrously small even in terms of its usual clientele, he had returned to the hall just before curtain-up to find that Rebecca and her friends had dismissed the incident as a bit of a giggle and were snarfing tea and biscuits as though nothing had happened. The invitation to join Mr. Pownall in his study had come as Simon had been about to rush Rebecca round to the library-cum-changing room with a view to grabbing Martin and heading for home and the baby-sitter via the nearest pub. Instead, he now found himself listening longingly to the revving engines and slamming doors of departing cars as the audience of parents drifted off into the growing dusk. Silence settled like chalk dust and Simon felt his eyes turning traitorously towards a Rebecca shaking her head in gentle puzzlement.

"From the workmen who came to repair the roof, I'm afraid," she said, her smooth brow furrowing beneath its fringe of silky dark hair. "Of course, Simon wanted to dismiss them immediately. . ." Her voice tailed off as she stared artlessly at the headmaster. Simon's face, incapable of dissimulation, registered astonishment battling admiration.

"Falling twenty feet off a ladder is undoubtedly upsetting, but swearing. . ." Rebecca was saying.

"Twenty feet! Twenty feet!" Simon repeated to himself, thankful that Rebecca, unblushingly innumerate, had stopped short of a hundred.

"As you heard this evening, Mr. Pownall, the damage. . ."

The unfinished sentence hovered between them as Rebecca's candid hazel eyes engaged the washed out grey of the headmaster's. Fighting an urge to clap, Simon watched hopefully as Mr. Pownall, having adopted and then savoured an expression of wounded affront, sucked in his cheeks and stared at the Beresfords with what he hoped was a judicial frown. Then, with much pursing of lips and a head-shaking that made his dewlaps quiver, he allowed his expression to melt into one of sympathetic understanding. Though he knew from bitter experience that Martin Beresford was incapable of absorbing any word in the English language, scatological or otherwise, without constant reiteration and the regrettably sterile threat of punishment, he was content to appear mollified. His reputation for benign discipline had been upheld by the manner in which he had courteously yet publicly invited the Beresfords to accompany him to his study at the pantomime's conclusion; and now, propitiated by what he took to be Simon's wordless remorse and Rebecca's hollow but beautifully simulated contrition, he was content to accept the diaphanous untruth - *twenty feet, for heaven's sake!* - so ensuring that the remaining Beresford children would in due course trip up the holly-fringed drive of Rosehill Infants' School.

To Simon's relief the meeting had concluded with expressions of regret from the Beresfords and of exculpation from Pownall. The conclusion was timely as it allowed them to reach the dressing room just in time to frustrate a flanking movement by Martin aimed at smiting an ashen St. George from the arms of parents struggling to insert him into his red plastic wellingtons.

Afterwards, over the wheeze of the car's labouring engine, Rebecca had railed against Mr. Pownall as a pompous little prick, though for several days afterwards she had made a conscious and occasionally successful effort not to swear in front of the children.

* * *

Simon descended from the bathroom in a puce towelling robe that had transmuted from an unwanted Christmas gift for father-in-law into a birthday gift for son-in-law. In the kitchen, her housecoat now recklessly agape, Rebecca was regarding the last traces of cereal on the linoleum from a slumped position seemingly sustained solely by her grip on the mop. Her passion for housework, lukewarm at its most fervent, was at its lowest ebb around breakfast time and, if that was a character defect, it was one about which she was forthright and unconcerned.

"It's not that I'm a slattern," she had once explained to Hazel and the rest of their coterie over the first of several glasses of wine, "but I shall doubtless pass through that stage as I improve."

Simon chucked a rosy-cheeked Katy under the chin, covertly wiped his hands on a tea-towel, gave Rebecca an enthusiastic kiss on the forehead then followed the trail of crumbs along the passage to the living room where, he noted unhappily, each step produced a muted crunching noise that had nothing to do with the crumbs.

It had been Spring when Rebecca had decided the sitting room floorboards should be sanded and, with a zeal Simon found excessive, she had hired the appropriate machine from Hobsons in the high street. Then, after two days in which he had emerged from behind a fog of floury wood dust solely to eat and sleep, Rebecca had replaced the sitting room's faded carpet with what to Simon seemed to be the equally faded scatter rugs she had discovered at a house clearance. Together, scatter rugs and the lingering grit from the sanding machine produced an environment reminiscent of a Bedouin tent. Now, surveying the sitting room's dishevelled rugs, its scattering of hand-me-down furniture, neglected toys and forlorn supper dishes, Simon was forced to admit that the overall effect was of a room only recently abandoned under bombardment.

Martin was kneeling at a glass-topped table, scribbling intently on the morning's unopened paper.

"Crayons," Simon said mildly, "are for the playroom."

The American President smiled up from the newspaper from behind magenta spectacles.

"Only if I'm making a mess," Martin said unctuously and began to furnish the President with a feathered headband.

Simon sighed. A steady thumping noise at the far end of the room led him to where a florid sofa of faded grandeur, a hand-me-down from Rebecca's parents, stood with its back at an angle to the French windows. Beyond the windows stretched a tussocky strip of neglected lawn, turned into an obstacle course by derelict furniture awaiting the restoration it was scheduled to receive once Simon had mastered the technology. On the triangle of bare boards between the sofa and the window stood Nicholas, beetle-browed at three, indulging what Rebecca excused as his middle-child syndrome by gripping the sofa's back and kicking its drooping upholstery.

"I'm practising kicking," he said, forestalling the question and holding up his face for the anticipated kiss.

Simon looked up as Rebecca wandered in with Katy and guided her daughter through a couple of tentative steps before depositing her and an assortment of kitchen utensils on the floor. Drifting towards the door she stopped, studying the expression of puzzled helplessness that proximity to his children often seemed to produce on her husband's face. She raised a single eyebrow, an effect for which Simon had often striven and failed.

"I sometimes think the children are too hard on you," she said, and drifted off in search of a languorous bath.

Anxious to have his case fully understood, Nicholas was saying, "Martin says boys at school kick and you've got to get your. . ." He paused, frowning.

"Retaliation," Martin prompted without looking up.

". . . your retaliation in first."

Conscious that his attempt to hone his child's social skills might appear wheedling, Simon said, "People don't kick. It's. . ."

"Ostriches do." Martin had wandered across, trailing the newspaper which Simon was beginning to recognise as that morning's. "What you need to do," Martin proffered, "is do it without hurting your toes."

"Ostriches don't hurt their toes."

Katy started to beat a colander with a wooden spoon as the boys began an argument about the finer points of mayhem. Simon, redundant, retreated to the kitchen. Rebecca, her own bath time temporarily deferred, was perched at the breakfast bar on one of the boys' high stools, cold toast in one hand, Katy's unfinished beaker of milk in the other. Her cigarette smouldered next to a jar of drooping wildflowers on the window ledge's terracotta tiles. Stooping, Simon slipped his arms round her waist and rested his head on her shoulder. Rebecca placed a buttery hand on his cheek, pressing his large fair head against her small dark one.

"You know," she said wistfully, "you could take me away from all this if only you'd get a bloody job."

~Chapter 2~

Mrs. Benson's ginger marmalade had the bouquet of spiced oranges and the bite of a serpent. For years it had crowned Rowland Mowbray's breakfast with its cleansing fire, yet this morning it seemed to lie on his tongue like ashes. His jaw, gently rotating moments before, now rested in mid-chew as he gazed at the copy of *The Times* he had worried into a shape capable of supporting itself against the silver coffee pot. Sunlight probing past the tied back drapes of the nearest of the tall windows struck the crystal bowl of marmalade, shooting topaz lights across the newspaper's business section; but Mowbray, his expression that of a man who has passed through a familiar door only to find himself in a strange and hostile world, saw nothing.

He remained motionless for several moments then, as though waking from a trance, he stirred in his seat, sighed, removed his half-glasses, used them to rub the side of his nose and, having polished them absently on his napkin, hooked them once more behind the silver wings of hair. Head tipped back, he re-read the line of print and found it had lost none of its bewildering menace.

WbfcOB, the entry began. In itself that was merely the comfortingly familiar Wilberforce Original

Brassworks reduced to the shorthand used in *The Times*'s listing of company share prices. What was perturbing the Wilberforce chairman, however, and would undoubtedly blight what would otherwise have been a morning spent in his beloved garden, were the implications behind what the neighbouring column showed to have been a marked rise in the company's share price.

Later, when Mrs. Benson came in to clear the dishes, she found Mowbray still in that position. "It was like he'd been turned to stone," she explained later to anyone who would listen.

But that was when the pattern of events had become much clearer.

* * *

Grasping the history of Wilberforce Original Brassworks would hardly have taxed the most retarded student of economic history: Albert founded it, Richard expanded it, Henry nearly ruined it and John managed to rescue it. As for Jane. . .

* * *

In Queen Victoria's time, the grey stone Yorkshire village of Bradburn had been a close-knit, barely post-feudal farming community. And, had it not been for the genteel greed of its councillors when the prospect of its first factory appeared, it would probably have continued to turn its back on the smoke and grime of industry for many years to come.

Even in those days, visitors noted, Bradburn's character differed from that of its neighbours. But where one side of that character was inward-looking and resistant to change, another was a Yorkshire willingness to suppress those characteristics when there was a chance of profit. In most respects, however, Bradburn conformed to those neighbours. When

Victoria reigned it had two rows of cottages facing each other across a village green, although it surpassed its neighbours in having the region's sole Corn Exchange, backing on to the canal and built in local stone, complete with Corinthian facade. And at the top of the green, facing the Corn Exchange, was Bradburn's other claim to distinction, a stone bandstand whose roof of faded green copper was a dales landmark. Behind the Corn Exchange, tucked into its rump by the canal, were a chandlers, a smithy and a seed and potato merchant whose goods spilled across the wharf that provided a vital link between local farmers and their markets.

Bounded on the north by the canal and surrounded in every direction by farmland and pockets of woodland, Bradburn had preserved its tranquil rusticity for centuries.

Until, that is, it was discovered by Albert Wilberforce.

Albert was the youngest son of a Sheffield iron founder. As such it was his misfortune to have been born with a weak chest around which the dusty brown air from the family's factories strapped iron bands. And, as his health denied him any active part in the family business, Albert had been following his physician's advice to look for a property that would allow him and his family to enjoy the sweeter air of the dales when his coachman had halted his carriage to give the horses a breather. Albert, stepping out to stretch his legs, found himself staring across undulating greenery in the direction of Bradburn House. An immediate investigation revealed that Bradburn House almost magically answered the strict specifications he had devised, not the least being that it was for sale and more or less immediately available. It also had the extensive grounds to which he was accustomed, as well as adequate stabling and numerous guest rooms of sufficiently Spartan proportions to allow hospitality while discouraging protracted visits. Within a month of setting eyes on the property he had moved his family in alongside the workmen now engaged in the house's restoration. In later years the result came to be much sketched by architectural students to be filed, locals suspected, under 'Mistakes to be avoided.'

Having rapidly regained his health in Bradburn's mild and gentle breezes, it was not long before Albert concluded that what the village needed was a little light industry, though not sufficient to cause the problems that had forced his family's exodus from Sheffield. The question of what that industry should be was decided partly by what was possibly a genetic predisposition towards hot metal and partly by the fact that a brass manufacturer elsewhere in the county went abruptly out of business. Almost before the metal could cool Albert had snapped up the business to the last nut and bolt and transferred the whole shooting match to Bradburn.

Wilberforce Original Brassworks was born.

When he had sought to buy land on the northern side of the canal on which to locate his factory, the local council, landowners to a man, had been graciously accommodating, and their complaisant attitude continued into the dying years of the 19th century when Wilberforces' glowing furnaces disappeared within a substantial stone building that provided Bradburn with its first industrial chimney. Although the plans pored over by the council had volunteered that the chimney would be built in local stone, the prospect of a chimney of any kind had caused brows to furrow. However, once assured that not only would the chimney be built to resemble the campanile of St. Mark's in Venice, but that prevailing winds would waft its sulphurous plume in the general direction of neighbouring Lancashire, they had happily consented.

Albert's business prospered and, once his son, Richard, proved capable of running the business equally profitably, Albert had died a happy, prosperous and contented man.

One of Richard's first achievements as chairman was to persuade the railway company to run a spur line into the factory in return for the modest strip of his canal-side land they needed in order to connect Bradburn with neighbouring Broadbridge and the industrial West Riding. Local fears that the bleating of sheep and lowing of cattle might be drowned by the clang and clatter of shunted wagons proved groundless; improved communications brought booming sales, and the company was in as good a shape as it had ever been when the First World War came along and the government demanded Wilberforces divert their modest resources to the manufacture of munitions.

Although the war brought an unparalleled burst of prosperity, the return to peace proved too stiff a test for Richard and, with the Armistice celebrations hardly ended, he collapsed from exhaustion. Richard's incapacity threatened to overload those ageing family members whom the war had roused from lives of unreflecting idleness to help run the business; and, when doctors hinted that Richard's illness might be protracted, they resigned almost *en bloc*. The sudden loss not only of Richard but of most of the family, each of whom had occupied a position of some importance, found Wilberforces entering the post-war depression at a canter. Next, in what the rugby playing circles of Bradburn perceived as a classic hospital pass, Richard passed the but-limply-grasped reins to his son. Those relatives who had put themselves outside the business, but who wished to continue to rely on its rewards, now found themselves watching with considerable misgivings as Henry succeeded his father; for, they told themselves, the flame that had guided Albert, and which in recent years had flickered somewhat fitfully in Richard, appeared to be guttering ominously where Henry was concerned. The reasons for their unease could be deduced from the way in which the *Bradburn Gazette* eventually recorded his retirement.

'Henry Wilberforce did not have an easy task', the editor had written, somewhat cagily considering that Wilberforces did not even advertise with his newspaper.

'His forebears, to whom Bradburn owes so much, had set standards that are beyond the reach of most men; indeed, they are beyond the grasp of all but that honourable few who contrive to combine intellect with an assiduous dedication to careers which, for some, were not chosen but foreordained by reason of birth. 'Mr. Henry,' as he was known to all, found decisions difficult to take; for, if a decision were to be taken so as to bring advantage to the company, might it not conversely be to the detriment of others? And was that not, potentially at least, contrary to the precept he held most dear: Do unto others as you would be done by? (Matthew 7:12)'

There was much more in the same sort of vein. Written by a more robust obituarist, it might have read:

'Henry Wilberforce stepped out of his father's shadow only to reveal himself as innumerate, profligate, and incapable of deciding which spats to

*wear without going into a cold sweat. His
incompetence was such that the remaining directors
had no option other than to turn up regularly in order
to prevent the wholesale disintegration of the
business.'*

Because those directors now found themselves
more or less compelled to up their performance,
something resembling a professional board began to
emerge, though their enthusiasm was constrained
and their attitude to their chairman distinctly chilly.
Hence, when the stream of complaints his
management of the business engendered at last
forced Henry to resign, the board's expressions of
regret were almost as perfunctory as the greeting they
extended to his son.

John, the fourth generation of Bradburn
Wilberforces, hardly had time to draw breath after
coming down from Oxford before being thrust willy-
nilly into his father's mantle. Despite his youth he
quickly proved capable of making what was considered
to be a decent fist of running the business, at the same
time slipping easily into the entailed roles as Justice of
the Peace, Chairman of the Watch Committee and
judge of the small animal classes at Bradburn Show.

As he was in an exempt occupation when the
Second World War erupted, and with Wilberforces
once more diverted to munitions, John took the
opportunity to perform a courteous weeding of those
family members who remained on the board and
created for those that remained a category of non-
executive directorship which relieved them of any
pretence of active involvement. Eventually to become
known to the rest of the board simply as the cousins,
non-executive directors were expected to attend board

meetings every second month and otherwise shut up and leave their full-time colleagues to get on with running the business.

However, when peace brought with it the election of a Labour government, panic ensued and, in an uncommon show of unity, the full-time directors and the cousins pleaded with John to find a way of protecting them before the business and all it represented disappeared into the crimson maw of socialism. There followed days of agonised debate before it was agreed that Wilberforce shares should be offered for sale to the public. Following that it would be up to the ingenuity of individuals and their advisers to do what they could to stick to the proceeds.

Thus Wilberforce Original Brassworks became a public company with its shares quoted on the London and provincial stock exchanges alongside those of its mightier brethren. In the event, trading in Wilberforce shares quickly settled at a level guaranteed not to overburden the resources of Simkiss and Simkiss, the Bradburn solicitors who had landed the plump sinecure of acting as the company's registrar.

Immediately after the launch, as their advisers had called their Stock Exchange debut, and once the directors had recovered from the shock of paying out the fees involved, they found it impossible to shake off the uneasy conviction that it could only be a matter of time before disgruntled shareholders stormed the offices and ejected the lot of them. Even this fear receded eventually and they were uniformly relieved when they realised that the only material changes public status imposed were the obligations to balance the books a couple of times a year and let shareholders know what the exercise revealed, and to hold an annual general meeting at which shareholders who were so minded could ask impertinent questions. It was quickly discovered that by holding the meeting in the Commercial Hotel in neighbouring Broadbridge, accessible from London only by a change of train, the event could be converted into little more than an outing for directors and their wives.

Shortly after their debut as a public company, and to John Wilberforce's suppressed irritation, his proposal that they should appoint a full-time company secretary to relieve him of some of the duties required by their newly-minted public status was resisted by his fellow directors as vexatious.

"Chap'll only want to stick his nose into things that don't concern him," one had huffed, as though Wilberforces concealed a charnel house of skeletons.

"You can manage, old man," the others had more or less chorused in a greater show of unanimity than they generally managed. But John had persisted, recruiting a sallow, grimly nonconformist chief clerk from a West Riding worsted mill renowned for the diligence and probity with which its affairs were conducted. Much the same reaction had been provoked when John had proposed and once more insisted on the appointment of a finance director and found one who was neat, frugal, and as precise as a decimal point.

Disapproval of what some directors considered an explosion in the board's numbers festered for some time. The finance director's interjections at board meetings, lucid and germane though they invariably were, were initially greeted with regular pshaws! of disbelief until, guided by these fresher minds, the directors found the business entering a period of relaxed stability. This lasted just as long as it took John to drop dead on the twelfth tee shortly after his sixtieth birthday. The board's expressions of grief and condolence to the widow and her daughter were profuse and sincere, for the launch John had overseen had made them wealthy men. When within days John's widow followed him to the grave, their grief was necessarily constrained by the urgency of resuming the debate her death had interrupted.

John, it was conceded, had presided over a prolonged period of prosperity for the business and, more specifically, for its directors. Having floated the company on the Stock Exchange he had gone on to deal more or less uncomplainingly with the distractions presented by shareholders, auditors, merchant banks, analysts and the whole confederacy of interests their public status had called down on them.

At the heart of their dilemma, however, was the fact that there was no longer a further generation of Wilberforces from which an heir could be plucked and inserted into the chair so recently vacated by John.

After more than a hundred years of Wilberforces at the helm it appeared that the family aspect of the business must founder and, had they been left to solve the problem themselves, it almost certainly would have done. But the discovery that they were not alone brought not relief but resentment.

Fittingly, the call that revealed the existence of a concerned third party was received by Ben Bartlett, the company secretary, recruited from the textile industry and noted for a precision of thought that could appear as brusqueness.

"Kettering here," the caller had boomed down the line from London. "Thought you'd like to know, one or two of the institutions are asking questions."

Richard Kettering, suave and eminent, was chairman of Palgraves, the leading London merchant

bank which had earlier condescended to launch
Wilberforces on the market. They had since kept in
desultory touch, having contacted John on perhaps
half-a-dozen occasions.

"Questions?" Bartlett had sniffed.

"Now John's gone."

"What, precisely, are they asking?"

"Who's going to run the show, of course. Need to be
convinced it'll be someone with a bit of form, otherwise
harsh winds, rocks ahead and who knows what might
happen? I've assured everyone it won't be one of the
present lot," Kettering continued dismissively, "though
you'd better wrap that up a bit before you tell 'em. Fact
is, you're going to have to get someone in from
outside."

"I'm sure that's on the board's agenda," Bartlett
said somewhat testily, for although he shared
Kettering's opinion where most members of the board
were concerned, the ease with which that opinion
seemed to have been reached, and from a distance, was
nevertheless galling.

"If we can help. . ." Kettering offered, ". . . but we
must stop 'em asking questions. Ruins confidence,
share price through the floor, next thing you know
you'll be remitting half your dividends to some Johnny
in a burnous. Let me know what you propose to do up
there."

Job done, Kettering had hung up and gone off to
shoot things.

Bartlett, on the other hand, had gone off to face his
board. His account of the conversation, though
discreetly rendered, had considerably ruffled their
feelings.

"'Stonishing," Colonel Temple, a Wilberforce first
cousin and nominally the personnel director, declared.

Then "'Strordinary" and, finally, "'Stounding," as Bartlett relayed a sanitised version of Kettering's strictures concerning John's successor. "Chap might as well come and run the damn' place himself."

By the time their discussion finished, however, cooler heads had prevailed, though resentment had now turned to alarm. In their resistance to bringing in a man from outside, however, they were as one.

But the alternative, when it occurred to them, was in many ways even more disturbing.

~Chapter 3~

Jane Wilberforce, the only child of the recently lamented John, had demonstrated the resolution and independence of spirit that had been such fickle constituents of the Wilberforce character by leaving home at the age of eighteen and becoming commissioned into the Wrens. Now in her mid-thirties, it had for some time occurred to Jane that the pleasure she had always derived from that independence was somehow beginning to fray at the edges.

Not, she frequently told herself, that anything had disappeared from her life; it was more that something indefinable seemed not to have arrived. But what life lacked, and how in its anonymity it was to be recognised should it suddenly appear, was a conundrum of such complexity that she was beginning to conclude that, rather than any constituent part, it was conceivably life's whole tenor that was adrift.

It was a conundrum to which Rowland Mowbray, an army colonel working in a different part of the same undistinguished Whitehall building, had long had the answer, and in a friendship that now spanned several years he had on numerous occasions been close to enlightening Jane. What Jane's life lacked, he was unshakeably convinced, was quite simply Mowbray himself. However, he considered the drawback to any proposal of marriage he might manage to utter was that refusal would not only be inevitable but, in view of the superiority of Jane's appearance, talents, character and intellect, would be totally warranted. Despite this humility they continued to share moments of great tenderness and their friendship had flourished. On more than one occasion a proposal of marriage had risen quivering to his lips, only to be translated into an invitation to take tea at The Ritz, visit Chelsea Flower Show or, indeed, undertake any other activity that might avoid the amused incomprehension or, more probably, the refusal, he anticipated; a refusal which Jane's superiority of character would doubtless render so sublimely gentle as simply to underline the depth of his loss.

It was as they were about to leave Jane's flat one evening for one of their frequent visits to the theatre that the telephone rang. The barking tones of Colonel Temple, Jane's uncle, were unmistakable to Jane though indistinct to Mowbray who had remained at the hall door as she turned back to answer the telephone.

After an exchange of greetings, which appeared to Mowbray to be warm on both sides, there was a pause followed by an exclamation from Jane that Mowbray found impossible to interpret. Jane nodded towards the settle that bracketed the telephone table and Mowbray sat and watched as she toyed with her single strand of pearls and frowned at him across the handset.

"But really, Uncle Harry, the entire proposition is preposterous, simply bizarre." Her eyes remained on Mowbray who raised his eyebrows helplessly. Jane somehow managed to shrug without dislodging the telephone held between cheek and shoulder. "No; running a company is not remotely like looking after the welfare of my young gels, as you call them." Jane, looking slightly cross, intimated that Mowbray should join her at the earpiece and moved aside on the settle as he did so.

"Think about it, m'dear, and don't be too hasty," Temple was saying.

Jane looked at her watch and pulled a face at Mowbray as the prospect of an evening at the theatre began to fade.

"You *are* the last one in the direct line from Albert," Temple was saying, "and you *are* used to handling people. Dammit, it's only fair that you should have a chance before we're all pitched out by those rotters in the City. . ."

A chance? What had at first appeared as an earnest if ill-considered attempt to recruit her into the family firm now seemed to Jane to be acquiring a slightly patronising edge.

Suspecting he had put his foot in it, Temple said:"What I mean is, none of us is capable of doing the job, and if we *are* to have a chance we need someone running the place who will make a better fist of it than we could."

There was silence between them for a moment, then Jane, slightly edgily, said, "We'll talk about it again when I've had time to think."

When the next morning brought a call from an apologetic Bartlett explaining that the merchant bankers had let it be known they were only prepared to consider a woman as a caretaker chairman, and then for a strictly limited period, Jane replaced the receiver with an expression that was both fatalistic and determined.

* * *

Jane's visit to Bradburn occupied several days. She spent some of these poring over papers in her father's study and some at his desk in the Wilberforce offices. In between, she spent hours interviewing key members of the workforce and spoke to the directors individually and collectively. She also held two long conversations with Kettering, one by telephone and one, although she omitted to alert Mowbray to her brief return to London, in the ostentatious comfort of Palgraves' offices. In the first of these she coolly outlined the impressive professional qualifications and experience she had gained as a senior Wren officer. After the second, Kettering found himself completely won over and promised his unfailing assistance should she wish to grip the business and give it a touch of naval discipline, including, Jane suspected, any amount of flogging and keelhauling that appeared necessary. Any suggestion that the appointment should be other than permanent had somehow disappeared.

Back at Bradburn, Jane took into her confidence a blushing Miss Varley, her late father's secretary, and dictated a formal response to the board's offer which stated that, subject to the resolution of a personal matter, she would fall in with their wishes.

The personal matter was resolved in an emotional conversation with Mowbray the evening she returned to London. They sent in their papers the next day.

After a simple religious wedding Mowbray stayed in London long enough to wind up their affairs while his wife returned to Bradburn and immediately immersed herself in the complexities of running the company. In snatched respites from her duties she also found time to involve Miss Varley in supervising the redecoration of Bradburn house which, in her absence, had come to resemble one of the stuffier London clubs.

On Jane's advice Mowbray used part of his modest savings to buy a small number of Wilberforce shares.

Then, in response to the final condition set out in Jane's letter to the board, the two of them were elected directors of the company at an extraordinary general meeting, following which Jane was appointed chairman at a board convened for the specific purpose.

For two years after their move to Bradburn life had assumed a freshness and excitement that dispelled any doubts either might have concealed about its wisdom. Mowbray, to his diffident surprise, found the intricacies of business not only manageable but absorbing, while Jane ploughed the literature in search of more satisfactory methods of management. Having discussed her conclusions with Kettering, she would return to Bradburn and spend hours, or days if need be, arguing and cajoling in the face of resistance from workers' representatives whose natural Yorkshire wariness had been converted to paranoid insecurity as the business had appeared to spend the interregnum stumbling along in blind confusion. Gradually, resistance faltered in the face of Jane's gentle advocacy of constructive change. Finally resistance collapsed, negotiating procedures and working practices were overhauled, and Wilberforces began to go about its business with a sense of purpose that had been absent for months. Some said years.

At Bradburn House guests once more whirled and sashayed to the strains of the small dance band section of Bradburn Band Club, Wolf Cubs and Brownies again practised woodcraft and heaven knew what else in the coppiced land on the edge of the estate, and every church organisation from the Bible Class to the Fabrics Committee breathed sighs of relief as the facilities of the Bradburn House outbuildings were once more put at their disposal.

All in all, life appeared not only to have upended its cornucopia over the Mowbrays but to have given it a good shake.

Whether the birth of Julia was therefore a benison or an act of singular carelessness was a debate whose participants tended to divide broadly by gender. To Jane and Rowland Mowbray, however, it was seen as the culminating blessing and Jane set about using the first six months of her pregnancy to make as sure as humanly possible that the changes she had introduced in the company were immutable. She then telephoned Kettering and, over his congratulations, told him of her plans, any need to dissimulate them as proposals having disappeared a long time ago.

Word of her resignation as chairman followed fast on the heels of news of her pregnancy. The wooden cradle produced by factory workers and the layette contributed by office staff were in due course diverted from the chairman's office to Bradburn House. Rowland Mowbray accepted the chairmanship stoically, in the knowledge that Jane would be there to deal with anything knotty, and life assumed a different but equally harmonious tenor as Julia, her beauty immediately manifest, entered the world and proceeded through a sunny and untroubled childhood.

* * *

Mowbray pushed his chair away from the breakfast table, now cleared apart from the rumpled copy of *The Times*, and wandered over to the carved stone fireplace at the far end of the room. He plucked a spill from a recess above the empty grate and put a flame to it with a lighter then used the spill to light his pipe. Puffing clouds of blue smoke that failed to satisfy, he wandered over to stand by one of the deep bay windows. Beyond lay a balustraded terrace with broad steps leading down to gardens dominated by the three huge elms which obscured much of Bradburn House from the town while serving as a useful landmark when directing visitors. Beyond the elms the lawns swept past a walled garden and down to the ha-ha, after which only a band of coppiced woodland separated the house from the fields stretching down to the canal on the edge of town.

Mowbray saw none of it.

Spiritually he was in the same room three years earlier when Jane and he had last breakfasted together. That, too, had been a Saturday. They had taken their coffee to the comfortable chintz chairs in front of the fireplace. Flames were beginning to lick at the logs of a fire lit, Mowbray remembered, despite Jane's protestations that it was almost Spring. Conversation at breakfast had been an unresolved discussion about Julia's birthday.

"I suppose it's far too late to get her a suede coat," Jane had said over the rim of her coffee cup, "though I'm sure she doesn't wear half enough when she's in London."

Mowbray, starting to lose himself in *The Times*, grunted. He had enough trouble choosing a tie without entering into the mysterious world of women's apparel...but yet. . . His eyes flickered to a small advertisement at the bottom of the page. He read it twice, tapped it with the stem of his pipe, then folded the paper and passed it to Jane.

Space-age comfort
Now, underwear that breathes!

Jane Mowbray studied the headline above what appeared to be a line drawing of a Russian shot-putter in boudoir knickers and brassiere. Turning the newspaper over, she found only racing news and returned to the picture of the underwear. Mowbray shifted in his chair as his wife gazed at him with enquiring blue eyes.

"These?" she asked. "For Julia?"

"Keep you warm and allow the body to breathe," Mowbray enlightened her. "Says so in the small print. Doesn't say you have to be built like a . . ."

Jane continued to stare and Mowbray started to regret a contribution that had so quickly found him out of his depth.

"Perhaps for winter," he added lamely.

Jane stood up, smiling. "I have a slight headache," she said. "We can talk about presents later and perhaps go into Broadbridge."

Kissing the top of his head, she briefly rested a hand on his shoulder and left him shuffling the pages of the paper in a search for safer territory.

A little over an hour later Mowbray breezed into their bedroom to find Jane lying on top of the counterpane. There was a half-smile on her face but she was, he discovered, quite dead.

* * *

That had been three years ago, in a world he and Julia now recollected as warm and untroubled simply because that was how it had been.

Still puffing his pipe, Mowbray returned to the breakfast table and peered at the paper's short line of type, now heavily underscored by his thumbnail. Recent movements in the Wilberforce share price had been discussed at the directors' lunch the previous day as they were well above anything the board was accustomed to seeing. Almost, in fact, enough to provoke one of Simkiss's infrequent pep-talks about keeping one's eye on the shareholder register to spot any sinister newcomers. Two of the non-executive directors, routinely invited to share the occasional lunch with their full-time colleagues, had pooh-poohed the change as a technical adjustment, while Temple had scowled at the entry in the newspaper as though expecting it to amend itself like an airport destination board. The move recorded this morning, though smaller, was still enough to cause Mowbray's scalp to prickle.

With even more than his customary reluctance, he resolved to call a board meeting.

~Chapter 4~

Had Rowland Mowbray known it, the events disturbing his breakfast could in fact be traced back several days to an office within a stone's throw of the London Stock Exchange.

The London Stock Exchange could be mistaken for the unloved headquarters of a declining conglomerate. It stands on the site of what was once Daniel Mendoza's Boxing Academy, separated from its lofty neighbour, the Bank of England, by Bartholomew's Lane, a name conjuring rustic stiles and cuckoo song but in reality a gloomy defile of littered asphalt. Big Bang had long since silenced the Stock Exchange, converting its hectic trading floor to an echoing vault as its operations were replaced by electronic systems through which deals were conducted between screens that glowed throughout a never-sleeping City.

But freedom from the City's physical constraints did nothing to loosen the grip the Stock Exchange Board continued to exert on those who dealt in shares.

For Mervyn Pusey, described by the few who liked him as a speculator and by those who didn't as a disgrace, success derived from his ability to operate at the margins of what the Board regarded as acceptable behaviour. Although any principles he may have once possessed had been jettisoned like ballast so that he might rise, and although he had at one time evicted tenants from his properties with a zeal that made the Highland Clearances look like social engineering, Pusey's City operations managed to tiptoe around the rim of acceptability with a skill that threatened to arouse the City's ire but had so far managed to avoid its retribution.

The City, or Square Mile, is London's financial district. You would search for its name on maps in vain, but it exists in grey canyons of concrete and glass served by streams of acolytes who emerge from below ground each morning and disappear back to their burrows at night. Its very title relegates everything from Barnet to Mitcham, from Southall to Woolwich, to vassal status. To Pusey the City was home, a milieu in which he had created a fortune without once having to justify his actions to those set in judgment over him. His relative anonymity in a world of City bigwigs was, to him, a source of pride and he was unimpressed by those who sought to add fame to their fortunes.

"How many noughts in a knighthood?" he had scoffed when Miss Goring had placed the latest honours list in front of him, its City names picked out in yellow highlighter. Miss Goring, who thought that arguably there were two, had wisely remained silent.

The buff envelope addressed in green ball-point had looked thoroughly disreputable among the otherwise pristine mail that morning. Pusey, however, seduced by its abnormality, closed his office door. Now, peering through rimless glasses at the contents, he congratulated himself on his habit of opening the mail himself. The contents were, he saw, both grubby and various. Carefully, and with only the slightest show of distaste, he spread them out on the desk.

First was a letter, hand written on both sides of several sheets of cheap ruled paper clearly torn from a spiral-bound notebook. Then, on equally cheap plain paper, there was a roughly sketched plan, extensively annotated and executed in the same smudged ball-point. And, finally, a ragged newspaper cutting, folded several times to fit into the envelope.

Picking up the letter, Pusey crossed his stripe-trousered legs and, resting his feet on the corner of the desk, began to read.

~Chapter 5~

Rebecca Beresford was not a cruel woman. Though in the early days of their marriage she had occasionally had to point out to Simon that unemployment smote none more sorely than those who failed to seek work, the shadow this cast across a face renowned for its sunniness invariably produced a pang of guilt in her breast. What she meant, she would explain at times of greater accord, was that, though bills were mounting, the prospects of extracting an increased allowance from either set of parents, or of securing what the bank, when it had been prepared to discuss such matters at all, had called a temporary facility, was beyond the realms of the most purblind optimism. And just what, the unspoken question left trembling in the air always asked, do you propose to do about that?

At the time of their marriage, almost before they had finished brushing confetti from their clothes, it had been made clear to both Simon and Rebecca that the parental allowances they were to receive were provided from motives that once inspired remittances to exiled Victorian youth. As her father had put it to Rebecca, though with his eye clearly on Simon, it was to make the separation endurable rather than to facilitate a return. Not that they would not be welcome as occasional visitors. . . Nor, it had been made equally plain, were the amounts negotiable.

As inflation and the arrival of children pushed the Beresfords deeper into financial crisis, Rebecca's rehearsals of their wretchedness became not only increasingly frequent but gradually acquired embellishments.

One day the rider might be that it was unreasonable to assume she was prepared to be kept in a state of more or less permanent pregnancy simply to boost their entitlement to child benefit; the next, that he might at least attempt to generate sufficient income for her to be able to buy the occasional packet of cigarettes without being made to feel she was condemning the children to rickets.

And Simon was powerless to rebut any of the charges thrown at him. There was no disguising the fact that, at twenty-nine, his experience of unemployment, though occasionally disguised as academic activity, was comprehensive.

He and Rebecca had met while reading sociology at a Midlands university. Each came from a family that could be described as comfortable, though each set of parents would have winced at the demotic description; and, as jobs appeared plentiful, neither had felt the need to divert from their courtship in order to acquire a good degree. It had therefore been disconcerting to discover that not even the most expansive left-wing council would consider employing holders of pass degrees in sociology when their corridors teemed with applicants whose bulging foreheads and festoons of qualifications were invariably allied to a shining desire to serve their fellow person. Even their decision to live in Ealing had reflected not merely their original passion for the house, and a concession to the

sensibilities of parents who lived in Windermere and
York, but also an ill-founded belief that the profligacy
of those governing London's boroughs would offer a
better prospect of employment than might the more
sceptical shires.

Having borrowed to buy the house on which they
had set their hearts, the Beresfords had then sat down
to consider life's priorities. First, however, they agreed
to an initial moratorium on job hunting while they
shaped the house around their own requirements.
Rebecca, already pregnant with Martin and tiring
easily, soon abandoned home improvements in favour
of spending most of her time kneeling on the spattered
floor in order to apply handfuls of plaster to wire
armatures, producing a series of spectral sculptures
that threatened to take over the house until the larger
ones were consigned to the garden. Simon, having
painted the bath, decided that most furnishings could
be extemporised, given the right approach, and began
to make complicated arrangements of bookshelves
from deal planks and common bricks until no surface
was free from its fine film of brick dust.

"This place," Rebecca was driven to protest, "smells
like a builder's yard."

"This place," Simon said, tripping over yet another
wraith-like sculpture, "looks like the last trump had
sounded."

Missing what he assumed would be the intellectual
stimulus of work, and anxious not to put on weight
through torpor, Simon had then decided to keep his
six-foot frame in shape by taking up jogging. Naturally
athletic, his ambition almost overreached itself when
he not only applied to join the London Marathon but
was accepted, and he was absurdly pleased when he

managed to complete it only a dozen or so paces behind the pantomime horse.

Motherhood, with token gestures in the direction of home improvement, displaced sculpture for Rebecca; and, although Simon had graduated to putting up fly-speckled second-hand mirrors in rooms with hardly enough light to create a reflection, then moving them to lighter rooms that were never used, his enthusiasm for refurbishment eventually abated. For a time, too, all else was displaced by the need to provide fresh air and stimulus for the infant Martin. Walks on the common were taken with military regularity until deteriorating weather replaced them with bus and tube journeys to so many sites of interest that, before he was two, Martin had slumbered past much of London's heritage.

When Nicholas was born shortly before his brother's second birthday it provided Simon with the motivation to break free from domesticity, at least for three evenings a week. As he explained to a Rebecca once more surrounded by the odour of nappies and sterilising solution, even if his activity fell short of paid employment, studying for a qualification in business studies would represent at least a step on the ladder at a time when it was beginning to dawn on society that what paid for its sociologists and their kin were the manufacturing and service sectors. Less than a year later, having grasped his diploma like a refugee grabbing a passport, he had made a series of forays into the employment market only to find that jobs remained as elusive as ever.

It was around this time that he began to supplement the domestic economy by raising stunted vegetables in the exhausted soil of the back garden and gathering the occasional egg from half-a-dozen hens given to perching despondently on Rebecca's abandoned sculptures. He also began a novel set in the sociology department of a provincial university as well as a plain man's guide to business studies. Within the space of a month he lost the vegetables to the chickens, the chickens to an urban fox and the manuscripts to an onrush of objective self-criticism. Then, setting failure at nought, he did what he did best and made Rebecca pregnant once more. Katy duly arrived, and it was while watching a Katy now almost capable of navigating her way around the living room by holding on to the furniture that Rebecca had reached a painful conclusion.

That evening, once the children were tucked up in bed, she explained to her husband that, for him, life held but two priorities.

* * *

'Dear Mr. Pusey,' the letter began, *'I don't know you and you don't know me but at least I know of you.'*

The handwriting was untidy, crabbed and, he judged, almost certainly male. Having read down the middle of the first couple of pages with increasing interest, and finding little to criticise other than the author's initial obsession with personal pronouns, he returned to the beginning and began to read more carefully.

'What I want to tell you,' his correspondent continued, *'is that I can make you a lot of money if you will keep my name out of things and see that I'm looked after. The fact is there's money to be made in Bradburn by someone with his wits about him who's prepared to speculate to accumulate.*

'I don't suppose you've heard of Wilberforce Original Brassworks, or of Bradburn for that matter, but they're quite big around here. They're sitting on a

fortune but they don't seem to know it. If you look at my plan you'll see that their factory is at the top edge of town, across the canal and railway after which it's farms all the way up the dales. The office is on the right-hand side of the town square as you look at it. They also own the block where their office is as well as the arcade.'

At this point Pusey began to read the letter in conjunction with the map. Despite the crude draughtsmanship, it was evident that Bradburn, wherever it might be, was built around a square with a bandstand at the top and a Corn Exchange, whatever *that* might be, at the bottom. Cross-hatched blocks appeared to represent buildings facing each other across the square. Roads marked *'From Leeds'* and *'To Leeds'* with arrows pointing into and out of the square bracketed bandstand and Corn Exchange.

Though not quite forty, Pusey was bald. Indeed, his baldness, combined with his rather foxy eyes, was the chief characteristic seized on by caricaturists when their drawings occasionally decorated newspaper City Pages. Now, as he read the letter, he began to tap his scalp rhythmically, as though assuring the security of its contents.

Pusey had already established that the letter bore neither signature nor address. The postmark was smudged beyond recognition and the mention of the dales gave him the first inkling as to where Bradburn might lie.

'As I've shown, the railway's not used anymore,' the letter continued, *'which is what gave me my idea.*

'What Wilberforces are sitting on is a piece of land with the canal in front and the dales behind. Knock down the factory, take up the old railway line and you've got a piece of building land worth ten times

what the factory's worth. If you look at the newspaper cutting you'll see someone tried to do that sort of thing at Broadbridge, two miles away, but they were knocked back by Planning. Planning won't be a problem at Bradburn.'

Pusey turned his attention to the ragged newspaper cutting. Stripped to essentials, it appeared that a nationally-known developer had applied to build at Broadbridge what their plans described, rather grandiloquently in view of their canal setting, as a marina village. It promised an extensive development of holiday homes and leisure facilities alongside the canal, with basin moorings for narrow boats and smaller craft. Their plans had been rejected on environmental grounds and then on appeal.

'You'll see about the environment,' the letter went on with flagging syntax, *'but at Bradburn it's already factory, not green fields, and you're sure to get housing if you know the people I do.*

'The clincher is that on my reckoning you would pick up the whole company, including offices and arcade, for what you would call small change - even allowing something for me.

'If you're interested, put an advert in The Yorkshire Post saying 'O. K. You're on' and I'll let you know how to contact me.'

The letter was signed simply *'A Friend.'*

Pusey tossed the last page onto the desk to join its fellows. Mention of *The Yorkshire Post,* together with the reference to the dales, had removed the mystery surrounding where Bradburn might lie. Swinging his chair round, he peered in the general direction of England's largest county some two hundred miles to the north. After a few moments he turned back to his desk, lips pursed, and punched up the Wilberforce share price on his desktop screen. He then spent several minutes tapping the buttons of a pocket calculator and transferring their results to a small black book. Miss Goring, meanwhile, despatched to find a map of Yorkshire, recovered a reasonably presentable one from among those in the glove-box of her car, a memento of a distant walking holiday with her dogs. It was some years out of date but it included Bradburn, which had been her employer's chief injunction, and what was more she could legitimately reclaim its cost from petty cash.

Had Pusey not been experiencing what for him was a relatively quiet spell it is just possible that matters might have rested there. Wilberforce Original Brassworks, secure in its insignificance, would simply have become one more company over which Pusey had run his ruler only to find that the possibility of a pearl was not worth the price of the oyster. Pusey would have waited for a more challenging target, Simon Beresford might never have tried his hand at spin doctoring, and Splasher Shelmerdine's vaunted chimney-cleaning technique might never have found its victim. But Pusey was suffering a quiet spell, and there was something seductively rational about the letter's contents. . .

Picking up the last page, Pusey studied it again. *'A friend,'* it said. But a friend to be circumvented, or a friend to be rewarded? The tone of the letter suggested a guileful rather than a sophisticated mind, but that could easily have been an affectation. In any event, providing his correspondent had not touted the letter to others, and the fact that he had sent the original of the newspaper cutting and not a copy argued marginally against that, Pusey was content that his speed of operation would, should it be necessary, leave *'A friend'* breathless in the slipstream and Wilberforce

Original Brassworks as a footnote in the annals of industry.

* * *

Simon's vasectomy was arranged, performed and accepted, at least on Rebecca's part, with an absence of regret that produced a mild level of resentment in Simon, tractable and unflinching though he had been throughout. But it was in pursuit of the second priority that he found himself one morning leaning against the facade of the City Job Centre. Though calm and unflustered to outward appearances, he was finding it difficult not to groan out loud at the sensation that some unseen hand in an iron gauntlet was applying increasing pressure to his groin. The job search had already occupied the several days it had taken to arrange the vasectomy, with Simon daily sallying eastwards from Ealing, Job Centre by Job Centre. This morning, thirty-six hours after his operation, the search had resumed. Having reached the City by underground he had approached the Job Centre with the doggedness of a merchantman limping into port with an unexploded bomb in its entrails. A pink haze was beginning to affect his vision and he was starting to wonder whether the throbbing in his trousers could conceivably be visible to passers-by when it dawned on him that he was being scrutinised.

At first, hurrying to lunch at the City Club, the aging but spruce Richard Kettering strode straight past the fair-haired young man hunched against the wall of the Job Centre. Then, struck by something vaguely familiar about the face, he turned and retraced his steps. His own face flushed with uncertainty, he paused by Simon and stared at him, frowning.

"Young Beresford, isn't it?" he said tentatively. "Hurt your back?"

Simon, fearful of sudden movement, studied Kettering with the eyes of a seal pup under the bludgeon. Before him, flickering beyond the pink veil, was some old buffer who had once spent a shooting weekend with the family at Windermere.

For his part Kettering was recalling an importuning telephone call from Simon's father some weeks earlier. In a refrain that had graced numerous fruitless conversations Beresford Senior had held with friends and former colleagues over the years, it had borne several references to a son idling away his time in London.

Simon dissembled. "Rugby accident," he said, squeezing the answer out between gritted teeth. "It catches up. . ."

Kettering appeared not to have heard. His eyes moved from Simon to the sign outside the Job Centre. He stared at it with an expression of refined horror.

"Not looking for a job in this place, are we?" He shook his head, tutting disapproval. Burrowing in an inside pocket of his immaculate striped suit he produced a small notepad with gold metal corners. Detaching an accessory pencil, he fiddled with it impatiently until it produced a lead. Pencil poised, he demanded, "Now, what's it you do for a living?"

Simon, struggling not to throw up over the gleaming shoes, fought to recall his most recent brush with employment. His face lit up momentarily. "Public relations," he said, feigning brightness. As his innate honesty was about to compel him to explain its fleeting and unsatisfactory nature, Kettering glanced impatiently at his watch.

"Sort of spin doctor", said Kettering, clearly finding the information reassuring.

In the ears of one who would have had difficulty spinning a coin, the assessment was both surprising and flattering, though Simon managed merely to blush modestly.

Kettering was pressing on. "What's your number? May want to get in touch. Can't stop. Got lunch."

Simon mumbled the number and watched as it was taken down and consigned to the inner pocket of the elegant suit.

"See what we can do," Kettering said. "No promises, mind. Probably be in touch. Meantime, suggest you get some wintergreen rubbed in."

Simon forced a weak smile as the brisk figure raised a finger in salute and merged with the lunchtime crowds. As Kettering passed out of sight Simon began to count up to ten. When he got there, he promised himself, and if he hadn't succumbed to the internal haemorrhage he was convinced was threatening, he would try to stand up straight.

~Chapter 6~

Early Monday morning found Rowland Mowbray leaning against his pillows and sipping tea beneath a pall of unaccustomed gloom. The gloom accompanied him into the bath like a cartoon cloud, then down to breakfast and throughout a foray into his beloved garden. There he had pottered ineffectually, getting in the way of the Phillips boy who masqueraded as under-gardener, and exasperating George who was dividing his time between the greenhouse and the hothouse in an unsuccessful attempt to be wherever his employer was not. Finally, harassed to the point at which he knocked over a tray of pelargoniums, George rounded on young Phillips over some imagined offence and Mowbray, disturbed by the lack of harmony yet unconscious of his contribution, set off dispiritedly along the drive connecting Bradburn House with the road into town. Walking past the lodge and through the drawn-back gates he turned left at the road that would take him down past the factory on his right, across the narrow bridge spanning the disused railway and canal, then up past the Corn Exchange to the company's office on the right-hand side of the square.

The flow of commuter traffic was already thickening as cars rolling into Bradburn from

surrounding villages crossed with those heading up the
hill to where most would turn off for Broadbridge and
the more urban face of the West Riding. Mowbray
weaved his way courteously through the accompanying
stream of pedestrians until he reached the bridge at the
bottom of the hill. There he paused for a moment,
leaning on the cast iron tracery at one of its recessed
refuges. Free to stand and peer down at events on the
canal without impeding traffic he tried to clear his
mind for a board meeting that would undoubtedly be
even more discursive and irresolute than usual until,
eventually, he would manage to guide his colleagues to
the decisions that would come back to haunt him alone
should they prove in time to have been wrong. A
narrowboat glided patiently into view below, cutting a
channel through the opaque green surface of the water,
its slow wake sucking at the reeds near the bank. It
chugged serenely on, a hinged flap on its chimney
making contented pipe smoking noises. Mowbray
watched until it passed out of sight round the broad
sweep of water leading to the five-fall locks that would
lower it gently towards Broadbridge. Then, setting off
once more, he cut briskly past the shadowy bulk of the
Corn Exchange towards the offices.

The Wilberforce offices were beyond the Corn
Exchange where it gave way to the granite setts of a
square that had once been the village green. Occupying
a broad-fronted three-storey Victorian building in the
local grey stone, the offices neighboured a shopping
arcade that funnelled shoppers down to Milk Street and
its open market stalls. It was an arcade that was much
admired. Many of its shops retained original bow
windows, their recessed entrances bracketed by iron
sconces that had once held naphtha flares. Jewellers
mingled with toyshops, fishmongers with sweetshops,

and on a still day the smell of roasting coffee wafted from the Dalesman Café stole into the deepest recesses of the Wilberforce offices.

"That arcade," Harry Temple would tell visitors, "was designed by the Ogden Nash who designed the Regent's Park terraces," and remained impervious to correction.

The entrance to the offices was to the left of the arcade. A flight of shallow stone steps rising between twin caryatids supporting a stone balcony and led into the marbled Victorian grandeur of the ground-floor reception hall. As Mowbray approached, the immaculately uniformed Adams opened one of the double glass doors of the recessed front entrance and waited as his employer mounted the steps. Inside, a broad flight of stairs ascended to a balcony already busy with the passage of office workers. A bronze bust of Albert Wilberforce just inside the door faced an expansive arrangement of flowers in the open fireplace, their scent fighting against the reek of fresh emulsion paint.

Mowbray smiled absently at Adams as he crossed the cool lobby and stepped into the lift Jane had insisted should be installed. The smile faded as he pressed the third-floor button that would take him to the boardroom. Upstairs, he paused at the boardroom's open door and listened to the mumble of conversation within, tugging at his jacket and straightening his tie like a nervous candidate. Assuming a smile he hoped would appear reassuring he strode into the room and moved straight to his place at the head of the great mahogany table where Miss Varley had set out board folders of dark green leather, each embossed with a director's name. Light flooded in through the tall windows overlooking the square and

Mowbray stood for a moment as his eyes adjusted, fidgeting with his cuffs and acknowledging greetings that ranged from the faintly querulous to the downright bored. Most of the directors were already seated, though he was too old a hand to mistake that for enthusiasm. Temple raised his face from *The Daily Telegraph* crossword long enough to give Mowbray a smile that combined encouragement for the task in hand, whatever that might be, with an injunction to get on with it.

Affecting to examine the contents of his folder, Mowbray noted that the cousins were already grouped together in their customary seats at the far end of the table, as though to dissociate themselves as far as possible from the proceedings. One, a bow-tied general practitioner from Broadbridge, caught Mowbray's eye and glanced conspicuously at his watch. Nearer to Mowbray his fellow directors appeared to be engaged in a debate concerning a painting one had seen at a Manchester gallery during the weekend.

"It was called something like 'The expression on Berengaria's face on hearing Ulysses had fallen from a ninth-floor window'", the gallery-goer was saying. Temple raised his eyes from the crossword.

"Wouldn't be Ulysses, old man. Berengaria was married to Richard the Lionheart." He beamed, his pepper and salt eyebrows executing a victory dance as he returned to the crossword. Richard the Lionheart was military history; and that, together with racing form and the intricacies of organising Bradburn Show, were subjects on which he knew himself to be unchallengeable.

"Not *quite* sure they'd have had ninth-floor windows, either," offered Bill Pritchard, to whom the remark had apparently been addressed. His tone was sufficiently hesitant to suggest, however, that should anyone wish to challenge him he would be perfectly happy to concede that, on the contrary, 12th Century Britain had possessed some fairly notable skyscrapers.

Pritchard was a youngster in Wilberforce terms and survived as marketing director for complex family reasons. The customary expression on his round, pink face was one of droop-lidded superiority, while his boardroom face was a model of respectful attention. He was a generation younger than the others and his ambition was sustained by a vision of a Wilberforces controlled by himself and run by directors who knew not only on which side their bread was buttered but who also knew whose hand wielded the butter knife. As usual, he considered it politic to humour his colleagues. "Couldn't have fallen out of a tree, I suppose?"

Stifling his impatience, Mowbray listened to the inconsequential twittering. As usual, there would be no orderly descent through the agenda. He would, he knew, find himself trying to focus directors' attention on the matter in hand while they wandered irresolutely between the agenda's many distractions. Not that there were many distractions on today's agenda. Bartlett, the company secretary, shared Mowbray's impatience and glanced at his chairman expectantly. Miss Varley, sensing business, threw off what Mowbray regarded as her cloak of invisibility and took her place on a high-backed chair a little to his rear, notebook open on her knee, sharpened pencils within reach on the table. Gazing expectantly at Mowbray she smoothed her skirt over legs that were the envy of the typing pool, though she normally managed to conceal them behind skirts that hung with all the allure of a fire-curtain. Mowbray cleared his throat, Miss Varley selected a pencil and the meeting began.

"I had a word with Simkiss at the weekend,"
Mowbray said. "It could be that we shall be needing
him." He suppressed a smile of mild satisfaction as
raised eyebrows and an exchange of glances greeted the
solicitor's name. "I'm not sure what he had to say takes
us very far, but as our registrar I felt he might be in a
position to tell us how we should be approaching
things."

"Things?" Temple queried, allowing the crossword
to slide from his knees to the floor. "Sort of things?"

Bartlett broke in, his voice thoughtful but
untroubled. "No doubt something about this share
price business," he offered.

"You were a bit guarded on the 'phone, Rowland,"
Pritchard chimed in, then sank back into his chair as
Temple glowered at him. Mowbray, however, nodded
in agreement. In his weekend telephone calls he had
simply summoned the board members to meet and
discuss what he had described as a matter that required
their attention. He had been apologetic about his
reticence, but to have revealed his true concerns
outside the confines of the boardroom would, in
Bradburn, have been tantamount to announcing them
from the bandstand in the square below. He
considered, none too hopefully, that discussion within
the formal confines of the boardroom might inspire a
sense of collective responsibility, particularly where the
notoriously loose-tongued cousins were concerned.

That, at least, had been the theory. Mowbray's
hands were resting on the table and he stared at them
for a moment before looking around the room to
establish that he had the board's attention.

"Those of us who were here on Friday commented
on the fairly sharp rise in the share price, a rise
signifying a relatively high level of activity in our

shares," he began. "Saturday's paper showed that we gained almost as much again before markets closed. We know these things don't happen of their own volition and it is clear that someone out there is buying our shares in significant numbers."

The faces around the table began to show expressions of guarded interest.

"I take it none of us has been buying?" Mowbray asked, then disowned the question with a gesture. "We've had no warning signal from Kettering at Palgraves - that's the merchant bank," he added for the benefit of the cousins, for some of whom the name carried no more associations than that of the Akund of Swat, "nor have we heard from Ryan and Gilliatt, the brokers. That in itself is not necessarily significant: they tend to report direct to Kettering."

As stockbrokers for Wilberforces, Ryan and Gilliatt were officially the company's eyes and ears in the City of London. Officially, but not effectively; for Ryans, as they were more generally known, had only accepted the Wilberforce account out of deference to Palgraves and had since rarely found it necessary to trouble their client. Mowbray paused, aware that his remarks were falling not so much on deaf ears as into a void, a void created by his intimation, albeit quickly dismissed, that members of the family might have been buying shares.

"I wonder if Edwin. . . ?" one of the cousins began, then held up his palms in mock surrender as his colleagues stared at him disbelievingly.

For generations it had been instilled into the family from toddling stage that shares were to be held in trust for descendants; that, while those who for the time being held them were entitled to live in comfortable idleness or otherwise on the income the shares produced, the shares themselves were to be handed over to the next generation in neither greater nor lesser number than when acquired. The unwritten agreement had remained in force even after Wilberforces had become a public company. By such means the balance of shareholdings among different branches had been held in equilibrium.

Apart from Pritchard, whose family's shareholding had been sufficient to secure him his reluctantly conceded place on the board, only Edwin Wilberforce, who had been neither seen nor heard from in more than twenty years, had emerged from the process with a significant part of the forty per cent of the company that remained in family hands. The sounds of traffic in the square below disappeared behind murmured conversations as the board recovered from the suggestion that anyone, even Edwin, would breach established etiquette.

Aneurin Williams, the finance director, caught Mowbray's eye and shook his head. "Shouldn't think he'd dream of it. He certainly doesn't need the money."

There were murmurs of relieved acquiescence from the others. The finance director should know: he saw the dividend cheques.

"Then who?" Temple asked. "Surely the blasted register would show. . ."

"Too early for that," Mowbray interrupted. "It will be our job to find out who's behind this, however, and then to establish whether there is anything we can or should be doing about it."

"So, Rowly, what did Simkiss have to say?" prompted one of the cousins.

Simkiss, the third generation of Simkisses in the law firm, had accepted Mowbray's apologetic telephone call during a noisy drinks party at the Simkiss home on the Saturday lunchtime. His practice's role as solicitors and registrar for Wilberforces was one of the major sinecures underpinning his company's fortunes. He had therefore listened with deepening alarm when Mowbray's expressions of concern seemed to lurk in an area of company law with which the solicitor was scarcely even on nodding terms. Having wound up the party as quickly as he decently could, though not without incurring the wrath of the statuesque Mrs. Simkiss, he felt able to relax only slightly when a call to his chief clerk revealed that there had been no untoward movements in the Wilberforce share register.

"Not that that's significant," the clerk had added. "If Mowbray says the buying's only taken place in the last couple of days, it could take a couple of weeks for the transactions to be notified to us. Even then, they could be in the names of nominees and we would have to file a request in order to identify the beneficial holders. It all takes time." Such requests, Simkiss was vaguely aware, were allowed by Stock Exchange regulations so that companies could smoke out potential predators hiding behind nominees.

Feeling he had nevertheless secured a respite, Simkiss had spent much of the Sunday reading everything from Halsbury's Laws of England to the City Code on Take-overs and Mergers as well as the most up-to-date copy of the Companies Act he could lay his hands on. He had then communicated his meagre findings to Mowbray.

"Simkiss thought there might be something in it," Mowbray said, "but I suspect he was a bit out of his depth. He suggested we should talk to our City advisers..."

He was interrupted by a tentative knock-knock and he paused as the boardroom's green baize door opened to reveal the prettily flushed face of Tracy Harrison,

Miss Varley's willing but imperfect assistant. As the daughter of Sam Harrison, landlord of the Fox & Chickens on the other side of the square, Tracy had long since acquired her sex's ability to treat men *en masse* with pert disdain. Though to the outside world she appeared secure in her blue-eyed, fair-haired prettiness, she lived in mortal fear of Miss Varley and her capacity for frosty disapproval. Wordlessly, avoiding the twin reproaches of Miss Varley's raised eyebrows, she scurried to the wall behind Mowbray and plugged the telephone she had been carrying into a socket on the skirting board.

"It's a call for Mr. Mowbray," she explained to Miss Varley in a loud whisper. "It's a Mr. Kettering. He carried on something awful when I said the chairman was in a meeting. Most important, he says it is."

"Don't tell me, you silly girl," Miss Varley hissed, "look straight at the chairman and give him your message clearly."

Saving her the trouble, Mowbray smiled at Tracy and took the telephone from hands imploring him to do so. Tracy, who appeared to be contemplating a curtsy, intercepted a look from Miss Varley which propelled her from the room. As the door whispered shut Mowbray took up the handset and entered into a conversation which, though incomprehensible to the others, was consolingly brief.

Handing the telephone to Miss Varley who placed it on the floor behind her chair, Mowbray surveyed the expectant faces around the table. "That was more or less what we had been anticipating," he said, "an early warning that something might be up, and that Palgraves and Ryans will keep an eye on things. They'd also like me to pop up to London for a general chat. It's a long time since they've acted on our behalf and they're naturally out of touch. There are also a number of housekeeping moves he feels we should be taking in case it comes to putting up a defence."

There was a glum silence, broken by the finance director. "It could still be a piece of perfectly innocent buying by one of the institutions," he suggested, "a pension fund or some such."

Bartlett shook his head. "It would be nice to think so, but it seems more tentative than that..."

"We could be talking about spending a lot of shareholders' money preparing a defence that might never be needed," Pritchard brooded.

Mowbray smiled. "We may be able to put numbers on that once I've been to London. What we have to bear in mind is something Simkiss said, and that is that we shall have to move sooner rather than later. That's because, once the board has reason to believe a *bona fide* offer is imminent, we are prevented by City rules from taking any actions that might frustrate the offer without first receiving the approval of shareholders. It's probably a little early to think about that," Mowbray mused, "but I take the point. Now, if someone would like to propose that I hold exploratory talks with Palgraves. . . ?"

Temple recovered his copy of *The Daily Telegraph* and raised it in affirmation.

"Any against?"

There was a scraping of heavy chairs against the parquet flooring. The lines, Mowbray told himself, had been drawn. The company could be in for something that might prove to be more than a touch unpleasant. And, seeing the ease with which his fellow directors appeared to shed their concern, he offered up a silent prayer.

* * *

Richard Kettering, long past retirement age but still firmly in charge at Palgraves, replaced the receiver. Young Stephen Causton, from Ryan and Gilliatt, remained at the huge horseshoe-shaped table in a silence reflecting his admiration for the City Colossus as Kettering stood at one of the huge windows and stared down at the shadowed canyons of the City and thought about *noblesse oblige*.

~Chapter 7~

Mervyn Pusey had decided to make Wilberforces a priority, but it was not until the Tuesday following receipt of the anonymous letter that he managed to clear the decks sufficiently to allow him to set off on his reconnaissance of Bradburn; and, by the time the train carrying him north crossed with that carrying Rowland Mowbray to London, he found himself wrestling with a problem he had quite failed to anticipate.

* * *

Mowbray was finally satisfied with the list of points he planned to raise with Kettering and the rest of the train journey alternated between glancing at magazines he had picked up at the station and staring out of the window at the sun-baked England speeding past. It was the sort of summer that exists mostly in recollections of childhood, with the sun, as they said in Bradburn, cracking the flags. But, as the train shuddered and swayed its way through the cross-hatching of bridges and flyovers encircling the capital, Mowbray could not have felt more apprehensive had the bridges burned down after him. Seeking a diversion, he picked up the satirical magazine he had abandoned earlier and tried once more to penetrate the code in which it appeared to have been written. Of the content he could understand, much was either allusive or clearly scurrilous, occasionally both; but, he noted approvingly, the editor appeared to reserve a considerable measure of his bile for City speculators. There, though many of the names were shrouded in schoolboy sobriquets, one was excoriated simply as 'the not-so-choosy Mervyn Pusey, whose ambition is as bald as his head.' Mowbray studied the undoubtedly eggy scalp in the smudged photograph and felt a brief twinge of sympathy for the victim. Then, as the train pulled into Kings Cross, he left the magazine on the seat and, following the short procession out of the carriage, set off in search of a taxi.

* * *

The Palgrave office was a slab of black marble and glass towering disdainfully above less stately neighbours. Its lobby soared through expensive empty space to huge chandeliers suspended from a vaulted ceiling. Dapper young men and silky young women glided past as Mowbray explained his business to a clone of Adams who checked against a list on his desk before ushering him impassively into the nearest of a bank of lifts. Following instructions Mowbray stepped out at the thirtieth floor into what might have been a reasonably important art gallery and was immediately met by a girl around his daughter Julia's age. Smiling mechanically, she confirmed his identity and led him to a pair of floor-to-ceiling hardwood doors which opened at a touch from a manicured finger. Silent as an odalisque, she moved aside as Mowbray advanced into a room that stretched away in an ocean of carpet which, had he but known, was precisely the colour for which Simon Beresford had been striving when he had painted the bath. Some considerable distance to the right was a wall constructed entirely from tinted glass below which the city existed in harsh shadows. Gilt-framed paintings of City worthies hung on either side of the door through which he had entered, while the wall directly ahead was an expanse of darkly polished hardwood interrupted only by upward pointing wall lights and an electronic key pad, a single indication that somewhere in the expanse of immolated rainforest might be a further door. The room itself was furnished with a scattering of chubbily upholstered chairs, a discreet cabinet which somehow managed to announce that it held drinks, and a number of low glass tables supporting orderly arrangements of glossy magazines. Murmuring an apology as she overtook Mowbray, the girl's fingers flickered over the key pad. After a brief pause a glowing red light switched to green and she pushed open one of the barely discernible doors.

Mowbray stepped through into the adjoining room and halted for a moment, conscious of the door murmuring closed behind him. Here the surroundings were opulent in a minimalist manner, as though the board had at the last moment recognised the virtues of restraint. The only adornment appeared to be an arrangement of matt black branches in a white porcelain urn as tall as a man, just inside the door. Feeling uncomfortably theatrical Mowbray approached the open end of a horseshoe-shaped table and rounded one of its arms to where three men had risen to their feet at the table's apex. Kettering, with his silver hair, pink complexion and City suiting, appeared as a slightly taller and older version of Mowbray himself. He stood up and moved half-a-dozen paces in Mowbray's direction in order to grasp him by the hand and draw him towards his colleagues.

"You don't know Stephen Causton." Kettering indicated the earnest young man in glasses. "He's with

Ryan and Gilliatt." The proffered pale hand was limp but cool. "And this is Hugo Russell."

Kettering nodded without warmth in the direction of what Mowbray decided was probably the most opulently obese person he had ever seen. Clad in yards of chalk-striped navy suiting, Russell, jowls wobbling, stirred sufficiently to offer a fleeting touch of sausage-like fingers while staring at Mowbray with eyes forced almost closed by rolls of fat. That accomplished he collapsed once more into his chair. Late thirties, Mowbray decided, probably with the life expectancy of a seventy-year-old.

It was acknowledged at all levels in the bank that Russell's appetite for food was in inverse proportion to his enthusiasm for work, and it was only the fact that he had had the good sense to marry the late founder's daughter during a more lissom youth that prevented the senior partners from firing him like a shot. Where Wilberforces were concerned he was unenthused by their business and contemptuous of their size. On the previous Friday, alerted by Kettering to the movement in Wilberforces' share price, he had stared at the screen displaying the figures with a contemptuous smile.

"Even corpses twitch," he had said to a colleague, his chuckle setting his heavy jowls bobbing.

The courtesies disposed of, Mowbray spent the next hour being taken through an analysis of the deficiencies that had apparently brought Wilberforces to its present predicament, a discourse during which Kettering had the good grace to admit that Palgraves, insofar as they could ever be said to err, had perhaps been remiss in failing to spot the fact that the value of Wilberforces' assets had romped ahead of the company's value on the Stock Exchange. The reproof, however, that any half-alert management would have spotted the fact for itself and, what was more, would have done something about it, was not less trenchant for remaining unspoken. Hugo Russell, Mowbray noted, intervened only when addressed directly by Kettering, and then sullenly. Young Causton listened attentively, rarely interjecting.

The most likely possibility now, Kettering explained reassuringly, was that no bid would appear and the whole exercise would result in nothing more dramatic than a revaluation of the business and a concerted effort by Wilberforce management, aided by Palgraves and Ryan and Gilliatt, to promote the shares more assiduously.

"In the meantime," he decreed, "it will be our job to show the world the rosy side of the apple," which left Causton, fired by the metaphor, nodding so vigorously that he almost dislodged his spectacles.

The meeting progressed amicably. Kettering warmed to the undoubtedly intelligent but obviously troubled Mowbray to a point where he confided that there was a school of thought which actually believed the City encouraged take-over battles on the grounds that, whatever their outcome, they were a source of considerable revenue to those who advised from the sidelines. There had grown up, too, he conceded, though in tones that deplored the fact, a City rumour factory whose chief function was to speculate openly about potential predators and victims in the hope of producing the occasional self-fulfilling prophecy. Even if that failed to generate actual bids, he explained, the speculative buying of shares this induced led to more business being conducted. It was a peek behind the scenes that did no more than confirm Mowbray's suspicions, yet he found it profoundly depressing.

"Where Wilberforces are concerned," said Kettering, having reached the end of his exposition, "whether there is a predator lurking or not, we must proceed on the assumption that you are in play."

Mowbray shifted uncomfortably in his chair.

"Being in play simply means that you have been identified as vulnerable, not that you will necessarily be bid for," Kettering told him placatingly.

At that stage, Mowbray learned, a predator could begin to pick up shares. The only indications the company might have that something was happening would be changes in the share price already seen and notifications to the registrar as transactions were noted by the City authorities. There would be no obligation on the part of the purchaser to make any form of announcement, and even the changes in the register might be disguised behind names of nominees.

At Kettering's suggestion Mowbray agreed that Simkiss would provide a copy of the share register which Ryan and Gilliatt would analyse for suspect names.

"I know that you like to use the local solicitor as registrar," Kettering said. "However, if it looks like the balloon's going to go up we shall need a London solicitor experienced in these things. Issuing defence documents means having a law firm equipped to verify them."

"It's called due diligence," Causton interjected, then blushed at his temerity.

It appeared to go without saying that the choice of London solicitor would be left to Palgraves.

Wilberforces would also, it appeared, require advisers to handle City public relations and printing of the defence documents. Again, Palgraves would produce a company they knew to be experienced, if a touch on the expensive side. As Kettering went on to sketch the fee implications of a defence, Mowbray found it hard to conceal his concern as what he was accustomed to regarding as monthly salaries shrank to hourly rates. Palgraves themselves, it appeared, would operate on a fee basis plus a bonus that would depend on a number of factors, not least among which would be whether the take-over battle, if it began, were to be won or lost.

The only question unanswered as the meeting moved towards lunch was what Kettering referred to as the disposition of forces.

"It's customary for the principals of companies involved in bids to be in London more or less for the duration; in most cases, that's where they are anyhow," he told Mowbray. "That's because it's necessary to trek round the institutional shareholders trying to persuade them to stay with the incumbent management. We'll go through the register with Ryans to see what you might need to do in that direction, but with high family holdings and a fair spread among employees and other small shareholders it's possible the big battalions might not have the last word. In any event," he nodded at a blushing Causton, "we and Ryans could get round to any that seem to matter and just trot you out if they want to see who's in charge up there."

Mowbray, who had recoiled at the prospect of having to spend a protracted spell in London, relaxed.

"It may be, however," Kettering continued, "that we shall need to reinforce your team at. . ." He consulted his notes, ". . . at Bradburn. What we need to do before that, however, is to take a look at you on the ground."

The advisability of a visit to Bradburn by someone from Palgraves had been established at the start of the meeting and Mowbray confirmed his agreement with a nod.

"We're giving you Hugo Russell for a few days," Kettering said, "longer, if the balloon does go up. I'll also be sending a youngster to look after communications - spin doctor type. He can handle local press relations, keep the workers chins up, that sort of thing."

The prospect of a trip north was not news to Russell and his foreknowledge, gained at an early morning meeting with Kettering, accounted in some degree for his present savage ill-humour.

"The likelihood is that it'll be for just a few days," Kettering had said. "They'll probably find you a nice country pub to stay at." He had paused, savouring the fat man's stricken expression. "If things warm up while you're there you'll be wanting some help on the public relations front, I shouldn't wonder. I've got just the man. Sound as a bell, expert at this spin business; son of a friend, in fact."

Russell's eyes had rolled behind their plump lids. Not only was he to be stuck up beyond the tree-line, probably for weeks, but he was to be spied on by some frightful oik with a direct line to the chairman.

"Name's Simon Beresford; you'll like him."

It had sounded like an order.

The fact that it was to be Russell who would go to Bradburn was news to Mowbray, but he suppressed an exclamation of disappointment and undertook to see that accommodation would be provided for the visitors.

The meeting continued over a sandwich lunch and into the afternoon. When eventually it broke up Mowbray borrowed a telephone to contact Miss Varley and Mrs. Benson, the flustered housekeeper, and explained the dispositions he wished them to make.

Briefly he thought of going round to the gallery where Julia was a working partner, but the prospect of explaining his last minute visit to the capital without alarming her depressed him, and instead he walked across London to the station where he caught an early evening train.

Back at Palgrave's offices Kettering shooed the others out. Picking up the telephone, he retrieved Simon Beresford's telephone number from the pocket at the back of his notepad and punched it into the telephone.

The possibility that Simon might by now have found alternative employment, or that he might balk at the prospect of a spell in rural Yorkshire, never entered Kettering's mind. Had it done so it would have been dismissed. As it was, the conversation was brief, the outcome satisfactory, and Kettering set off for the club well content with the final chapter of his day's work.

Noblesse, he congratulated himself, had obliged.

~Chapter 8~

Mervyn Pusey was suffering from unaccustomed confusion. He alone welcomed the breathing space as other passengers fumed at a signal fault delaying the train's approach to the station at Leeds. Beyond the embankment washing hung from lines in back gardens with lawns baked brown, no kind of distraction to a Pusey preoccupied with problems of great immediacy.

A practical man at heart, Pusey had already resigned himself to enduring the lesser of the two problems. Indeed, there was absolutely nothing he could do in the short term about the fact that the shorts which were such an integral part of his chosen persona as a hiker had been cut with an economy of material that meant the only position affording any comfort was an arthritic crouch. That, at least, would be remedied once he got off the train and was able to stand once more.

The other problem, however, concerned a more particular aspect of his appearance and, what was more, it required a prompt decision.

Pusey was well aware that he was only moderately well-known to the business community in person, and even less so to the wider public through his rare appearances in newspapers. The chance that he would be recognised in Bradburn was, he had told himself, remote; but the possibility nevertheless existed. And the fact that recognition might somehow alert the shoals of rivals against whom he considered himself constantly pitted had oppressed him. It had been Miss Goring, poring over a guide to the Yorkshire dales, who had observed that any space not actually occupied by cattle and sheep appeared to be populated either by cyclists or by people in shorts carrying rucksacks. That, together with the realisation that appearing in a dales village in a business suit would render him both uncomfortable and conspicuous, had been sufficient to resolve the matter of clothing.

The more particular problem derived from the fact that, despite his relative anonymity, his bald head and rimless glasses combined to produce an appearance that was as distinctive as it was unappealing. A visit to an optical superstore had solved the problem of the spectacles, replacing them with contact lenses which now lay in his rucksack, snug in their plastic container. The wig, however, had been a last minute inspiration. It had been bought some years earlier at the insistence of a fiancée who had subsequently had the good sense to abandon him and, although its associations were painful, his frugal soul had balked at the prospect of throwing it away. It was, in fact, a very fine wig. It had been created with a skilful imprecision to produce a sort of *trompe-l'oeil* wig which, if spotted at all, tended to lead to a debate as to whether indeed it was a wig at all. Resurrected and brushed out it now reposed in the rucksack alongside the contact lenses.

The nub of the problem, however, was that, be he never so nonchalant, if he were to disappear into the carriage's lavatory bald-headed and bespectacled only to emerge gimlet-eyed and nattily barbered, it would inevitably attract the unwelcome attention of his fellow passengers.

He was still pondering the problem as the train finally pulled into the station, at which point the solution stared him in the face. Passing briskly through the ticket barrier, he affected deep interest in a railway timetable until his fellow passengers had dispersed then shot into the station washroom to emerge moments later looking like his own younger brother. Stooping slightly under the unaccustomed burden of his rucksack and with his shorts lowered in the cause of comfort, he peered nervously around the concourse. Spotting a porter leaning against a stack of wicker baskets and fighting the temptation to clamp a securing hand over the wig, Pusey approached him with the measured gait of a man balancing a basket of fruit on his head. Pusey's accent, once described by a City journalist as improved Cockney, earned him a head to toe appraisal as the porter considered his request for directions to Bradburn.

Indicating the main exit with his thumb, and speaking as though to a retarded five-year-old, the porter said slowly, "Bus station. Across the road. Ask there." Muttering thanks, Pusey headed out of the station as the porter resumed murmuring to the pigeons incarcerated in the wicker baskets that supported him.

The sudden effect of sunlight on his unaccustomed contact lenses gave Pusey the sensation that he was now observing the world through a pair of clear mints. Eyes streaming, he dodged nervously between the traffic in the general direction of the bus station. Operating almost as much by touch as by sight, he was crabbing along the pavement, dabbing at his eyes with a handkerchief, when he bumped into something firm yet yielding. His yelp of alarm was rewarded by a polite gasp of surprise as he stumbled backwards, teetering on the edge of the pavement. As he recovered his balance his vision began to clear and he found himself staring at a young woman he had noticed on the train.

"That was my fault," the girl said. She smiled sweetly at him, her grey eyes studying him as though seeking a connection, and Pusey almost whimpered with relief as she failed to match him with her bald-headed fellow passenger. "It's rather disconcerting, but I have a tendency to stop in my tracks when I have a sudden thought. Are you all right?"

While distinctly not a lady's man Pusey was as vulnerable as most where attractive young women were concerned. It now occurred to him that the young lady from the train, viewed from this proximity and with what was mercifully once more becoming twenty-twenty vision, was probably one of the most beautiful creatures he had ever set eyes upon. Red-hot pincers could not have made him admit that their collision had been rather like running into the padded end of a rugby post.

"I'm more substantial than I appear," the girl was saying, still smiling. Pusey drank in hair the colour of bleached straw scraped back from a forehead tanned the colour of honey. "Perhaps it was all that hockey at school." He watched the opening and closing of her mouth like a trout transfixed by a worm. "I half saw you coming, so I was to some extent braced. That is what I mean, isn't it - braced?"

It was beginning to dawn on a Pusey lost in admiration of the contours revealed by a creamy cotton sweater that he was failing to sustain his end of the conversation. Now, words falling over themselves in his fervour, he agreed that it was indeed what she meant, assured her that he was absolutely all right, had never felt better, in fact, and was still burbling reassurance as Julia Mowbray smiled and stepped into a taxi that appeared to have arrived as the result of some invisible signal.

Pusey watched the taxi disappear round a corner then, thumbs hooked under the shoulder straps of his rucksack, set off to where he could now clearly see the bus stands. A lone double-decker was parked at the nearest stand, its driver leaning out of the cab chatting to the conductor. The destination board indicated Bradburn and, accepting that as a good omen, Pusey stepped aboard, stowed his rucksack under the stairs and joined the handful of passengers on the top deck from where he would be able to get a bird's-eye view of the approach to the town.

Despite his largely urban preoccupations Pusey found himself pleasantly lulled by the scenery as the bus, engine throbbing comfortingly, left the town behind and growled through elegant suburbs that gradually yielded to a winding road picking its way through a countryside of dozing stone villages. Fields of stubble gleamed under a sky that was a cliché of flawless blue while fields flecked with sheep stretched away into a purple distance. After an initial incurious glance the other passengers had ignored him and, secure in his anonymity, Pusey followed the bus's progress from beneath eyelids growing heavy in the early afternoon heat. Gradually, he relaxed.

* * *

"This is as far as we go, love." The voice was somewhere above him. "This is where we turn round."

Pusey's shoulder was being prodded gently but insistently.

Opening his eyes he looked up at the beaming black face of the conductor. The top deck had emptied except for a bluebottle buzzing on the window by his shoulder. Outside, a canal stretched away on either side of a black and white latticed bridge. On the far side of the canal were the low-lying buildings of what was unmistakably the Wilberforce factory, the air shimmering with heat above its elegant chimney. A railway line, its tracks rusted, sleepers barely visible for weeds, separated the factory from the canal while beyond the factory cattle grazed in fields that stretched away up the dales until they vanished in a heat haze. Nearby, people picnicked on a tethered narrowboat as small boys dived repeatedly off the bridge where the sun glinted off a towpath made slick with water.

Pusey stood up slowly, taking in the lie of the land. The bus appeared to have stopped at the back of the Corn Exchange on what his correspondent had marked on the map as the Old Wharf. He could see that at ground level the building had been divided into several small businesses, including a restaurant and what appeared to be a chandler catering for the narrowboat community.

Pushing irritably past the conductor, he descended the stairs, grabbed his rucksack and stepped onto the stone setts of the wharf. To an eye honed in such matters the potential of the factory site was so glaringly evident that he almost squirmed with pleasure. But then came the nagging worm of doubt. If the possibilities were so apparent, might others be interested?

'Someone tried to do much the same sort of thing at Broadbridge,' the letter had said; he could recall it word for word. 'They' had failed to obtain planning permission, so what could be more natural than for them to widen their net until they found somewhere with a more complaisant planning authority? Yet *'You're sure to get houses if you know the people I do,'* the letter had gone on, implying an access to those in power that might be denied to others. Resolving to contact his correspondent through the stipulated insertion in *The Yorkshire Post*, Pusey produced a camera from a side pocket of the rucksack and, indistinguishable from the holidaymakers, strolled up and down the bank taking a comprehensive series of photographs of the factory and its surrounds.

Having filled what remained of the memory card he stowed the camera and consulted his mental plan of Bradburn. This told him that the roads on either side of the Corn Exchange led up to the town square, on the right-hand side of which were the Wilberforce offices. Unwilling to hurry in the heat he ducked into the shadowy road on the left where he was forced to press himself against the wall of a dusty antique shop as the bus on which he had arrived nudged patiently through the pedestrians on its way back to Leeds. There was a smell of food from somewhere nearby and he looked at his watch, conscious that he had eaten only sparingly before leaving home that morning. It seemed aeons ago. Following his nose he found himself at the top of steps leading down to the recessed doorway of a public house lurking in the gloom cast by the Corn Exchange. The name 'Fox & Chickens' blazoned on a sign hanging above his head was also brilliant-cut into the frosted glass panel of a door set several stone steps below street level. Pusey stared at it without enthusiasm. Although hardly likely to be the best that Bradburn had to offer it at least possessed a disreputable anonymity. And it was an anonymity which, on reflection, he considered it prudent to share. Without giving himself time to change his mind he followed the steps down to the door and pressed the sneck of the latch. Inside he found himself in a cool, flagstoned passage dimly lit by bulbs behind the blistered shades of wall lamps printed with hardly distinguishable hunting scenes. A closed door on his right was marked Saloon. At the end of the passage, doors marked Bar and Toilets bracketed an unmanned reception desk tucked in beneath part of a flight of stairs. A couple of stairs beside the desk led to a glazed door behind which it was clear that they turned left to continue their ascent. Pusey approached the desk and struck its brass bell.

Moments passed before a young woman appeared from the bar on his left. Copper-coloured hair hung in ringlets on either side of her face, and the green of her eyes was repeated in a pair of remarkable feather earrings that dangled like mackerel lures. There was more green in the silk scarf tied loosely round her neck cowboy-style and tucked into what appeared to be a paint-spotted man's shirt.

Lunch had finished half-an-hour ago, she explained, smiling apologetically as she took station behind the desk. Had it been up to her, Kitty, she would have been happy to make him at least a sandwich, perhaps with pickle if he liked pickle, but Mrs. Harrison - Hetty - was out and Sam Harrison, the landlord, had locked the kitchen, probably absentmindedly rather than deliberately. Now there was nothing she could do about it until he got back. He could, of course, try eating out. There were some who said the Baht 'At Tandoori higher up the street was good; then, for those who preferred something English, there was the Craven Dairy in Wilberforces' Arcade. The information was delivered without a pause, giving Pusey time to peer around and confirm a dawning impression that the Fox & Chickens would indeed make a good base for his operations, if only because it was impossible to imagine anyone else staying there unless shackled to its walls. There was also an overpowering need to get rid of the incubus of the rucksack and to bathe away the perspiration which, despite the welcome coolness of the pub, was not only making his wig itch but threatening to trickle from beneath. Prompted by the *zeitgeist* that had driven him into the pub, he arranged to take a room for the night and signed the dusty register with the first name that came into his head.

Clearly eager to make amends for the catering shortcomings, Kitty produced a key and led the way through the side-door and up stairs that ascended behind the desk. Trying hard not to be diverted by the display of Kitty's legs, Pusey allowed himself to be led a few short paces along an uncarpeted landing that creaked beneath their feet until Kitty halted and threw open a door on the left. "This is the best room," she announced. "That's because the bathroom's just opposite." Pusey poked his head into the room and peered around without enthusiasm. "There's another one along the landing, if you'd like to look," Kitty offered, reluctant to lose a potential guest.

Anxious to be alone, Pusey assured her that the room would be more than suitable. He made a show of producing his sponge bag from the rucksack and arranging its contents on the marble-topped washstand as Kitty took fresh linen from a cupboard on the landing and, earrings swinging, quickly made up the bed. Promising to see him later she cast a last critical look around the room and clattered off down the stairs. Left alone, Pusey looked around for things to disapprove. It was, he was forced to conclude, adequate in a rough-hewn way, though its low wooden beams would have troubled a taller man. Crossing to the single window he peered into the street from which he had entered, any view beyond being blocked by the sooty stone wall of the Corn Exchange. The unnervingly intimate sound of mooing cattle drew him out of the room and across the corridor in the direction of the bathroom. Pushing through a door half-glazed with ancient patterned glass he sidled by the capacious bath and threw the window open. Below him a herd of mixed cattle milled just beyond the pub car park's wall as a boy in leather leggings urged them through a gate and towards a low building that Pusey, towny though he was, recognised as a milking parlour. A plump Ayrshire, back steaming, stared up at him with limpid, incurious eyes. Beyond the milking parlour were the fields from where he deduced the cattle had been fetched and, to the left and in the middle distance, barely visible behind three lordly elms, the twin towers of what was evidently a substantial house stood out against the rising swell of the dales. Despite the rigours of his recent journey Pusey found himself relaxing into the bucolic surroundings. Sighing almost contentedly, he inhaled at the open window, taking in deep draughts of air sweetened by silage and a musky undertone of cow. While he had no Arcadian strings to be plucked, the unaccustomed sights and smells were beginning to seem strangely agreeable. He returned to his bedroom with a lighter step and, had he been able to carry a tune, he would probably have hummed. As it was he tossed his wig towards the bed with a light hearted flick and washed himself, scalp and all, at the hand-basin.

Although a man of legendary energy, the weight of his eyelids told Pusey that his nap on the bus had done little to compensate for a pre-dawn start and, despite the refreshing effects of the wash, he found his eyes drawn in the direction of the freshly made-up bed. He stared at it for a moment undecided until, prompted by a yawn, he gave a sigh of contentment, kicked off his sandals and flung himself on to its neatly turned down covers.

The bed had the resilience of an autopsy slab. Pusey lay stunned on a straw mattress supported on inch thick boards; then, gingerly lowering his head on to the pillow, he stared at the intricate cracks in the ceiling, his face set once more in its customary frown of discontent.

* * *

Pusey wakened to the rattle of glasses from the bar below. His watch showed it to be almost six o'clock in the evening. Immediately alert, he lay quietly for a moment, listening to what appeared to be men's voices arguing. Although the sound was largely muffled by the solid floorboards it was evident from the regular bursts of laughter that he had probably underestimated the popularity of the Fox & Chickens, if not as a residence then at least as a public house. Swinging his legs down from the bed he crossed to the open window and looked down into the street. Cars passed below in ones and twos, tyres thrumming on the stone setts. Off to his left he could just make out part of the square and the backs of a couple sitting on a bench, throwing crumbs to invisible pigeons. Below his feet the argument rumbled on, frustratingly indistinct.

Although Pusey would have been the first to admit that his purpose in coming to Bradburn was ill-defined, he considered that it should at least produce grains of useful intelligence; even, conceivably, the nugget that could help him outwit Wilberforce management and their advisers. Anxious to make amends for what he now saw as a wasted afternoon, he tiptoed across to the washbasin, removed the tooth-glass from its holder then knelt down and applied it to what appeared to be the largest of the profusion of gaps in the floorboards. By spread-eagling himself on the floor and applying his ear to the glass he was rewarded with a marginal improvement in reception. Though the conversations remained muffled, he estimated that there were probably fewer than a dozen people in the bar, including a woman whom he assumed would be the red-headed Kitty. Unfamiliar though he was with Bradburn's social hierarchy, there was something about the gruff tones of the men that placed them at its lower end, diminishing the level of intelligence he might expect to gather but probably rendering them more susceptible to the interrogation, disguised by pleasantries, he intended to conduct.

Stomach rumbling menacingly, he restored the glass to its holder, splashed his face with cold water and insinuated himself once more beneath the wig. Then, on the assumption that the milieu could only improve as the evening progressed, he abandoned his shorts in favour of a pair of tan slacks that matched his sandals and made his way expectantly down to the bar.

* * *

Kitty was attempting to serve while keeping half an ear on the argument between Shelmerdine and Gibson and half on the sly enquiries of old Isherwood who was now leaning across the bar, beady eyes searching her face for signs of dissembling. Isherwood was from Hough End, an isolated hamlet whose inhabitants had all at one time or another peered over the tops of the chapel pews and intoned, "Forgive us our trespasses, miserable 'Ough Enders," until the dawn of literacy brought its absolution.

"They say you've got someone staying, then," Isherwood said, his tone an accusation, "from down south as well..." The implications of down south, though unspoken, were clearly not complimentary.

Kitty knew better than to enquire who 'they' were. Gossip passed through solid walls in Bradburn in an osmotic process that defied analysis.

"He's from London, a gentleman," Kitty said, "not like that lot." This with a disdainful nod towards the group gathered round the far end of the bar. Waving a hand holding a tea-towel and glass, she gestured towards the ceiling. "He's staying in the best room."

Moments earlier she would have been correct. But now Pusey had passed down the stairs only to hesitate by the desk, uncertain how to proceed. The bar from which Kitty had originally appeared was obviously the one below his room. A burst of laughter from that direction confirmed his impression as he balanced going into the bar against first exploring further. The frosted glass on the opposite door was clearly marked Toilet and Pusey found himself being drawn along the corridor towards the street and the one marked Lounge. He peered in and received a cursory nod from a stocky figure who was wiping the polished dark wood of the bar with a damp cloth. The man was bald, a fact for which he had compensated by growing mutton chop whiskers that completely smothered his cheeks. As though that were not enough, more hair erupted from the neck of his stained tee-shirt and yet more from where it failed to meet the top of his trousers by several inches. As he picked up an empty crate in each hand and prepared to disappear behind the plastic streamers draping the opening at the back of the bar, he said, "Lounge opens in half-an-hour. You can get a drink in the bar before then if you like." He disappeared in a swirl of coloured plastic ribbons, leaving Pusey to conclude that he had just met Harrison, the defaulting landlord. He retraced his steps and hovered for a moment at the desk. His mind was made up for him when someone emerged from the bar and disappeared through the door opposite, a move that released a strong smell of disinfectant, allowing Pusey to step into the bar before the door could swing closed. Conversations stopped as though a switch had been thrown. For Kitty, Pusey was a welcome distraction from a debate that had become increasingly unsettling. Abandoning the now silent group in the far corner of the bar she approached him, eyebrows raised in invitation.

"Hello, Mr. Adams, what would you like me to get you?"

Mercifully recalling his *nom-de-guerre*, Pusey smiled nervously, conscious of the silence his arrival had provoked. The bar smelled of stale beer and sawdust. The wall opposite the bar was pierced at pavement level by a grimy window past which flickered the shadowy feet of hurrying pedestrians. Despite the warmth outside, a group of old men squatted on stools around a corner fireplace producing tendrils of tarry black smoke. The men at the bar appeared to be in a variety of work clothes, including one in paint-splashed white overalls.

"That'll be 'im." Isherwood had returned to his companions by the fireplace and stared challengingly at Pusey. An ancient black and white terrier beneath his seat fixed Pusey with red-rimmed eyes, muzzle quivering in a silent snarl.

An argument at the other end of the bar had broken out again and Pusey, his novelty apparently having faded, considered what he should drink. While alcohol normally disagreed with him, it was clearly an environment in which his customary iced water could only diminish his credentials. Dimly recalling that his fiancée had drunk something Italian with soda, he ordered one, then made a play of sipping it as he tried to distinguish the nature of the argument. The northern voices, he noted with relief, were mostly intelligible on the rare occasions when only one person at a time was speaking.

Leaning companionably on the bar, Kitty followed the direction of Pusey's gaze and shook her head disbelievingly. "It's about cleaning chimneys," she said. Her feather earrings had been replaced by what appeared to be brass mint imperials and she had changed into a faded denim boiler-suit over a white blouse. The word pert occurred to Pusey. "Shelmerdine, he's the red-headed one covered in paint, says the easiest way to clean a chimney is to pour a bucket of gravel down it. Gibson and his lot are sticking up for the rods with a brush on."

Gibson was clearly the ferrety one whose cap followed the contours of his scalp as closely as a newborn's caul. The one called Shelmerdine had the floor and was arguing with the stolid truculence of one backed into a corner. Kitty sighed and shook her head at the foolishness of men although, Pusey noted, there was a warmth in her expression when the green eyes rested on Shelmerdine that clearly switched off for Gibson. Happy that he could now study his surroundings without being stared at in return, he rested a haunch on one of the high stools and looked around. So far as he could see there were only two people in the bar who were neither crowding the fireplace nor taking part in the argument. One was standing halfway along the bar with his back to it, elbows resting indolently on the bar top, staring across the room at the shadows passing the frosted window. He was improbably dressed in a velvet-collared black overcoat with a red and white handkerchief poking foppishly out of the breast pocket. A bowler hat set low over his forehead exposed a half-moon of bald scalp at the back. The other customer sat at the bar within listening distance of the raging debate but taking no part. Dressed in jeans and a collar-less flannel shirt, he sat with his head cocked to one side, making an occasional note on a pad half concealed on his lap. He had a wispy beard and the round lenses of his metal-rimmed spectacles magnified watery pale eyes that had registered Pusey's arrival without interest.

Although looks were far from Pusey's strongest suit, he was capable of combining his brown eyes and fleshy mouth in a foxy smile which, in the right light, was not unattractive to some women. He used it now on Kitty who smiled back happily.

"Who. . . ?" asked Pusey, indicating the others with an inclination of his head.

Kitty, hand propping her chin, looked along the bar without enthusiasm. "The one dressed for midwinter is Monkton Gibbs," she said, keeping her voice below the general clamour. "He's a freelance journalist, mostly sport, and he used to work on papers in London, or so he says. The one making notes is Roger Spofforth from the university. He's supposed to be doing a thesis on Yorkshire dialect, but instead of doing it up the dale where they can barely understand each other he does most of it in the pub."

She broke off and Pusey watched from the corner of his eye as Gibbs, having discerned his interest, sidled along the bar in their direction.

"I have much experience of the capital myself," Gibbs said, doffing his bowler in mock greeting and simultaneously thrusting an empty half-pint glass towards Kitty. He peered at Pusey with sardonic eyes. "Not recently, of course, but fondly remembered, fondly remembered."

His voice was theatrically bass. He collected a stool from along the bar and placed it down by Pusey, revealing what appeared to be an almost equally theatrical limp. To Pusey's horror Gibbs intercepted his gaze, but all he said was "Ah, yes, the limp."

Warily, for the man was clearly a crashing bore, Pusey took the proffered hand and shook it.

"Monkton Gibbs, journalist," Gibbs declaimed. "And. . . ?"

"Ben Adams," Pusey said glibly, "walking holiday."

"'And lo! Ben Adhem's name led all the rest.'" Eyebrows raised, Gibbs waited for his witticism to be acknowledged. When Pusey merely stared back blankly he changed tack. "I could not help but observe that you noticed my limp. . ."

Kitty sighed and Pusey began to throw up his hands in shocked denial.

Gibbs was not to be denied. "Improbable as it seems, I was once knocked down by a white rhino and lived to tell the tale." He stared at Pusey, eyes wide, arched eyebrows expressing his own incredulity at his misfortune.

Although Gibbs's reputation in the community was that of an incurable romancer, his claim, long ago discounted by the regulars at the Fox and Chickens as pure fiction, was within a vowel sound of the truth. The fact was that while leaving a bar in Harare many years earlier he had been knocked down by a white Renault which had immediately sped away into the night. The broken hip and clumsy surgery had subsequently been burnished into legend. He brushed Pusey's mumbled condolences aside.

"Just passing through, I take it? Very wise, very wise...little here to detain a man of culture." He shook a number of coins from the tray of a leather purse and pushed them across the bar in return for the beer Kitty was setting down in front of him. Gibbs stared at the glass for a moment, as though willing it to ascend, then picked it up and drained it.

Pusey decided to deploy the first delicate probes of enquiry.

"I suppose it's wholly rural around here, farming and that sort of thing?" he insinuated gently.

"Except for the brass factory," Gibbs said rewardingly. "It's on the other side of the canal. Sticks out like a sore thumb. Office is across the square there: great stone women holding up a balcony. Caryatids, they're called," he informed Kitty condescendingly.

Pusey feigned surprise. "Brass? I thought that sort of thing was left to Sheffield." Or Kathmandu, or Woolloomooloo, he might have said...but Sheffield, he knew, held distinct metallic associations.

Kitty, bored by the direction the conversation was taking, had begun to move away. Pusey caught her eye and indicated that she should refill Gibbs's glass.

"There's brass, then there's the steel industry." Gibbs rubbed his bulbous nose with a palm. "Wilberforces are in a small way, despite their airs. Mostly hardware. Door fittings, hinges, screws. A few ornaments, that sort of thing."

"Family business is it?"

Gibbs sniffed. "There's family in it, though Mowbray, that's the chairman, married into it." Tiring of the subject, he drained his recently refilled glass and replaced it on the bar as though expecting it to replenish itself.

Sensing that to probe further might arouse suspicion, Pusey took a sip of his drink and set the glass down on the bar by Gibbs's empty one. "I think I'll take a stroll round the town while it's still light," he said pleasantly. "Perhaps we'll meet later on."

He slipped down from the stool as Gibbs's glance began to alternate between Pusey and the empty glass. Signalling to Kitty to replenish the glass once more, Pusey handed her what he hoped would be sufficient change and, flashing her his weasel smile, headed for the door.

The argument among the regulars had petered out. Flushed but undefeated, Shelmerdine turned his attention to Kitty. His curly red hair, as well as face and overalls, were flecked with magnolia emulsion. Only his moustache, an as yet immature innovation designed to give gravitas to a face that remained defiantly boyish, appeared either to have escaped or to have been sluiced clean by beer. Pushing past Gibbs, now pulling on stained kid gloves preparatory to leaving, he looked suspiciously at the virtually untouched drink abandoned by Pusey on the bar. He sniffed cautiously at the contents before Kitty snatched it away and emptied it into the sink.

"Wouldn't clean my brushes in it," Shelmerdine said dismissively.

~ Chapter 9~

Pusey paused briefly outside the pub before turning left up the shady street. He strolled past Janet's Woolshop, glanced without interest at the piled display of books in the Silver Library, sniffed longingly outside the shutters of the Bradburn Bakery and carried on towards where the evening sunlight cast part of the square into dark shadow. A few strides brought him into the square itself, its pedestrian status protected by concrete flower tubs deployed like tank traps. Tourists and townspeople, as distinctive as Hottentots and missionaries, strolled across the stone setts or simply sprawled on wooden benches in the warm evening sun. A young couple lounged on the steps of the bandstand, the boy's head in the girl's lap.

Crossing the square as far as the iron pump of a horse-trough, Pusey removed his camera from its case, inserted a new memory card and, steadying himself against the pump, took several photographs of what were clearly the Wilberforce offices and their neighbouring buildings. Then, wandering across to an arcade guarded for the night by gilded iron gates, he pointed the camera between their bars to record the interior in the light from its vaulted glass roof. Satisfied, he pocketed the camera and followed the

square's steady slope down past the looming wall of the
Corn Exchange to where it emerged on the wharf.

Evening had transformed part of the wharf into a
continental terrazzo where patrons were already dining
at tables covered in crisp white cloths. A smell of garlic
and onions wafted from a doorway through which came
the muted tones of a popular Italian tenor. Through an
open window he could see a girl in a red and white
striped apron chopping vegetables. His stomach
groaned and for a moment he considered sitting down
at one of the vacant tables where he could have dined
with a clear view of the factory across the canal.
Instead, he crossed the wharf and headed for the bridge
spanning the canal and the derelict railway line. Across
the bridge, and at the foot of the hill leading, had he
known it, up to Bradburn House, Pusey turned into a
short side road and approached the large double gates
and elevated sign that proclaimed the site to be home
of Wilberforce Original Brassworks. Like the rest of
Bradburn, the factory beyond was built in the local
stone and roofed in dark grey slate. As he peered
through the chain-link fence a forklift truck stacked
with wooden crates emerged from the main building
and deposited its load on a pile of similar crates. A
workman in a grey overall monitored the operation
then made a mark on a clipboard before hitching a lift
back into the factory. It had not occurred to Pusey that
people would be working shifts and he fidgeted
uneasily as a security guard in a navy uniform emerged
from the weighbridge office inside the gate. The guard
sauntered up to Pusey and stared at him enquiringly
through the mesh.

Pusey summoned an ingratiating smile. "I was
wondering whether the factory permitted visits by

members of the public," he extemporised. "I, er, teach children and thought that, perhaps, a project. . ."

His voice tailed off. The pretext, which sounded thin in his own ears, appeared to receive serious thought before the security guard shook his head regretfully.

"We used to have works visits," he said. "Schools, Rotary, the lot." His expression implied good riddance. "It got so's we'd more visitors than workers, so now we just let 'em into the seconds shop." Having decided that Pusey was harmless he lit a cigarette and used it to indicate a low building, conspicuously newer than the rest of the site. "It's where that sign is. Ten 'til four, everything half price. The knobs and hinges are good value if you don't mind the odd scratch." Tipping the peak of his cap in salute he wandered back to his office. The sound of a radio escaped as he opened the door and disappeared inside.

Pusey had set out for the factory with no clear idea of what he hoped to achieve and he retraced his steps across the bridge dissatisfied with the expedition and further disappointed when he saw that the restaurant's empty tables had now been taken. Wistfully, he resigned himself to the prospect of whatever the Fox & Chickens might produce in the way of food.

Pausing to take in the factory itself, now bathed in the evening sun, he noted that it was separated from its waterside frontage by a chain-link fence on the far side of a low stone wall that ran between the rusting railway lines and the factory. The development potential of what to most tourists was simply a venerable but prominent eyesore was breathtaking. Pausing only long enough to ensure that its contours and dimensions were fixed clearly in his mind, he headed back to the inn, mentally ripping up the disused railway, demolishing the factory and building detached stone houses at eight to the acre; then, shocked by his prodigality, erasing them and building a mixed development of tiered flats, town houses and low, waterfront cottages. The permutations were endless. Still pondering the possibilities, he negotiated the steps down to the gloom of the Fox & Chickens with his stomach rumbling like distant thunder. He would, he decided, allow himself just one cooling drink before satisfying what had now become a ravening hunger.

Having returned his camera to his room and checked that his wig remained in place he made his way back down to the bar. Weak lights had been switched on against the shadowy gloom and it was now possible to pick out red pinpricks of embers glowing among the smouldering coals of the fire. Hesitating at the door, he saw that only the red-headed Shelmerdine and the old man with the dog remained from the earlier evening crowd. Unobserved, he took a step back and considered whether the other bar might offer more rewarding company. Someone laughed in a peculiar braying fashion as he approached it and peered through the half-open door. The first impression was of tweed jackets, gleaming brogues and at least one pair of pristine green wellingtons. The now sprucely white-shirted and magnificently hirsute landlord raised a hand in greeting, causing his customers to look round. Conscious of the dusty toes poking from his open sandals, Pusey waved back weakly before retreating to what he now thought of as Kitty's bar. His loyalty was rewarded as Kitty broke off a conversation with Shelmerdine and flashed him a smile of welcome. The dog he had noticed earlier poked its head from under its master's seat and showed yellow teeth in a rumbling growl. Pusey glanced at it anxiously.

"Ignore it," Shelmerdine said conversationally. "It's got only two rules in life: if it moves, bite it; if it doesn't move, pee on it."

Kitty cuffed him lightly on the arm. Isherwood, whose most accommodating expression appeared to be an inimical scowl, rested arthritic hands on the crook of his walking stick and regarded him malevolently.

"Same again, Mr. Adams?" Kitty invited brightly.

Pusey was conscious that the one called Shelmerdine was stirring uneasily. Recalling the affront that Mr. Adams's previous drink had offered to some unwritten drinking code of Shelmerdine's, Kitty placed a restraining hand on the arm Shelmerdine was resting on the bar and fixed him with a glance commanding silence. To Pusey, hesitating between sparkling water and ginger beer, Shelmerdine said, "Have a pint, man."

To Pusey, it sounded more like a challenge than an invitation. His insides rumbled a further warning as he contemplated the risks of drinking any form of alcohol on an empty stomach. On the other hand, the young man with the pugnacious expression, clearly a local, perhaps knew things worth knowing. His musings were further complicated by what appeared to be a protocol problem. Had the remark in fact been simply advisory, meaning have a proper drink, as opposed to the non-drink which was how he suspected Shelmerdine regarded anything in a small glass? In which case should he, Pusey, both order the intended pint and pay for it? Or had it constituted an offer to buy? Kitty was hesitating, a small glass in her hand, half-turned towards the shelf's array of bottles at the back of the bar. Pusey decided to assume an offer had been implicit.

"Done!" he said to Shelmerdine.

It appeared to be the right response. Shelmerdine's face resumed its customary amiable expression and, reaching for a pint glass from a shelf above the bar, Kitty began to fill it with long, smooth strokes from one of the bar's brass-capped wooden handles. The beer, the colour of polished mahogany, had a shallow head of palest cream. At the purely aesthetic level, Pusey conceded, it was undeniably attractive. Grasping the glass with what he hoped demonstrated easy familiarity, he raised it to Shelmerdine in a token gesture then took a sip, staring at his reflection in the smoke-filmed mirror behind the bar. As he lowered the glass he saw the beer had given him a creamy moustache and he wiped it off with the back of his hand. He had almost forgotten the rejuvenating effect of wig and contact lenses, and the gesture added a rugged cast to his reflection which he found pleasing. He took a somewhat larger sip from the glass and repeated the gesture.

Kitty's voice broke into his reverie. "Did you have a nice walk, Mr. Adams?"

Her huge green eyes gazed at him with something nearer to feminine interest than he could recall having evoked since the wound of his curtailed engagement; and, though its object was to chastise Shelmerdine rather than encourage Pusey, he responded with something approaching a leer as he raised the glass again and took a manly draught.

"It's an attractive town," he said, mentally adding *"for a hell-hole"*. He smacked his lips and continued to consult his reflection over Kitty's shoulder. "Seems a bit of an odd place for a metal works. I should have thought perhaps Sheffield. . ."

"Been here for generations," Shelmerdine said.

Kitty tossed her head in a gesture dissociating herself from whatever opinions he might express.

"It still provides a lot of jobs," Shelmerdine went on.

"It's providing him with one now," Kitty interrupted. She wet a finger to wipe a spot of paint off Shelmerdine's face and showed the result to Pusey. "That's the colour of their reception."

Pusey gave a start, but before he could begin to trot out his mental file-index of unanswered questions there was an interruption from the corner by the fire.

"I were there fifty year." Isherwood appeared at first to be talking to the back of his dog's head as it lay with its head on its forepaws, its bilious eyes still locked on Pusey. "Fifty year," he repeated, shaking his head at the wonder of it.

"That's a remarkable record, Mr...?" Pusey faltered.

"Isherwood," Shelmerdine volunteered as its namesake lifted his head long enough to glare at the three of them.

"Fifty year, and never got me picture int' paper."

"The company newspaper," Kitty explained to Pusey. Raising her voice to counter Isherwood's deafness, she said, "That's because you had broken service. You left and went back. You didn't have fifty years altogether, which is when they used to have their photographs in the paper."

Isherwood glowered at her. "It were fifty years altogether," he insisted. "What's thirty-eight and twelve it in't fifty altogether?"

"Not a continuous fifty, she means," Shelmerdine bellowed. To Pusey he said, "He left in a huff over something after nearly forty years. When he couldn't get a job anywhere else because he's such a bad tempered old bugger they took him back. They even made his pension up and he still hasn't got a kind word for them."

All eyes were on Isherwood who glowered back, unmoved. Pusey went to take a sip of his beer and was surprised to find the glass empty. Somehow, too, the gnawing hunger of earlier that evening appeared to have been replaced by a warm glow that was beginning to spread throughout his insides. He glanced enquiringly at Shelmerdine, received an affirming nod and ordered two more pints.

To Isherwood he said, "Perhaps you'd like. . ."

"I'll have a pint." Isherwood poked the dog with his stick in what Pusey took to be the Yorkshire command for *stay!* and shuffled over to the bar. The old man watched anxiously as Kitty filled the glass to the brim. He sipped from it briefly to avoid spilling any before shuffling back to his seat by the fire.

Pusey, presented with a disaffected former employee and a decorator who conceivably had the run of the Wilberforce offices, decided it was time to peer behind the enemy defences. He wiggled a finger between the two pint glasses on the bar as an indication to Kitty to keep an eye on them.

"Wilberforce's Chairman is presumably a pretty significant figure in the town..." he began.

* * *

Pusey never quite succeeded in recalling the journey back to London in its entirety.

The train, yes, though he had been barely conscious until well after Peterborough. Definitely a taxi at some point, too. Then there had been the persistent sick feeling, and something about goldfish that were not goldfish. . . It had certainly been preceded by breakfast, or an attempt at breakfast.

* * *

Had Pusey had his own way, and had he managed to rise before the world and its wife were about, he would have lost no time in slapping enough currency on the desk to cover any likely bill before shaking the dust of Bradburn off his sandals forever; not, however, before mounting the bandstand to shower it and its ghastly inhabitants with a profusion of baleful curses. But the fact that his attempt to escape at seven o'clock the next morning was foiled by the sudden appearance of the pub landlord was no more than he had come to expect of a community where the beer had the disabling effect of curare.

Though Sam Harrison was well aware that he had only one guest staying at the pub, it had taken a considerable leap of imagination to conclude that the bespectacled and defiantly bald figure supporting itself on the desk and mutely signalling for its bill had to be Mr. Adams. "What you want," said Sam Harrison with a misjudgement worthy of an earlier generation of Wilberforces, "is a good Yorkshire breakfast."

Although his stomach churned at the thought of anything more than black coffee, Pusey had been powerless to prevent Harrison taking him by the arm and steering him to a table in the smarter of the two bars which this morning smelled chiefly of lavender air freshener. Having seated him in a good light, Harrison had then spent several moments surveying him as though the type of breakfast required could be assessed from his degree of pallor. A smell of grilling bacon now assailed Pusey as he listlessly pursued tinned grapefruit segments that wriggled away from his spoon like goldfish.

He gasped as the floor appeared to lurch beneath him. Flinging the spoon aside he grabbed the far edge of the table and waited anxiously until the motion subsided. Nauseous and defeated, he scourged himself with the realisation that everything that had happened the previous evening might have been avoided if only he had had the sense to sustain himself with so much as a sandwich. The words of Sam Harrison as he had gestured speechlessly for his bill echoed through the ringing in his ears.

"What some people forget, Mr. Adams," Harrison had said, "is that up here we speak slow, but we drink fast."

* * *

Conversation in the bar had flowed. Kitty's premonition that the evening might possibly end unpredictably increased as the flow of beer had become a torrent; yet Pusey's hospitality had been relentless and his interest in Bradburn had been persistent and sincere if somewhat narrowly focused. For his part, Pusey had relished the way in which even the taciturn Isherwood had begun to thaw under the tide of ale he was funding. Though neither Isherwood nor Shelmerdine's revelations had produced any hostages, he had been content to learn that the Wilberforce board was more admired for its civility than its acumen.

"To Bradburn and to Wilberforces," Pusey had toasted later in the evening, draining his glass yet again and pushing it across the bar for a refill.

At which point a puzzled look had flickered across his face.

The toast, having formed itself quite clearly in his mind, had not emerged as intended. Not remotely. Blinking in concentration, he concluded that the sentiment had unquestionably been slurred, as well as being accompanied by an unaccustomed sibilance.

Pusey tried again. "Worrimennasay. . ." he began. He flapped a hand helplessly, unable to continue.

Carefully tilting his stool forward, he supported himself with both hands on the bar as he studied his reflection for signs of physical impediment. The gilded lettering on the mirror which had earlier advertised a Scotch whisky was now foggily indistinct. Beyond it, a blurred image of his face revealed an upper lip once more streaked with foam. Employing a now practised gesture he attempted to wipe it off, giggling like a schoolboy as he muffed it and caught himself a glancing blow on the chin.

"Blurry chin," he said. This time the giggle was interrupted by a hiccough. He waved a dismissive hand, dissociating himself from the reflection as he began to urge the stool back on to its four legs. For a moment he was successful as, briefly, the stool settled. Then, for reasons Pusey could deduce neither at the time nor later, the stool appeared to gain a life of its own as it pivoted once more towards the bar.

"Blurry stool," he said, and thrust himself off from the bar with a shove more forceful than wise. Then a series of expressions flickered across his face almost too quickly for Kitty to follow. Surprise clearly yielded to panic as the stool first pivoted past the upright position and then simply carried on going. His face then became a study in dawning bewilderment before finally appearing to settle for an expression of resigned composure as the stool completed its topple backwards and Pusey was projected in the general direction of the window. Kitty shrieked as the wig shot off like a bird from a felled tree and, light as ectoplasm, hovered briefly in the air. The challenge was too much for Spot. Springing from his dug-out, he snatched the slowly descending wig between yellow teeth and, growling spitefully but triumphantly, made a skittering landing on the linoleum and shot back to his lair. There, pinioning the wig firmly between his paws, he fixed one mad eye on the hostile world and the other on his prey which he proceeded to chew with angry snatching motions.

There was a moment or two when nothing further seemed to happen.

The noise of the stool crashing to the floor died away.

Pusey lay on his back staring uncomprehendingly at the nicotine-stained ceiling and hiccoughing gently. Kitty remained behind the bar, frozen, arms outstretched in her futile effort to grab him. Shelmerdine, head shaking gently in disappointment, began to rise from his stool. Isherwood, fearful that his benefactor might be snatched from him, waved his stick impotently with one hand while the other fumbled unenthusiastically for the wig.

Events after that were dim. It was Shelmerdine, Pusey suspected, who had been first to his aid, closely followed by Kitty who had had to make her way round the bar, cheeks streaked with anxious tears. He could remember sitting on a bench under which Spot was growling sourly as Isherwood tussled irritably with the dog. Coffee had been produced and Kitty had insisted that he should drink something white and fizzy. After that he had no recollection of being manipulated up to his room, but manipulated he had been for there he had woken less than half-an-hour ago to find his wig, tousled but intact, and smelling distinctly doggy, gracing the knob at the foot of his bed.

* * *

Having steered Pusey safely to bed, Shelmerdine had rejoined Kitty in a bar abandoned by Isherwood and the enraged Spot who were now making their discordant way across the square to await the last bus to Hough End.

"I knew all along that was a wig," Shelmerdine claimed. He picked up Pusey's stool and restored it to its place by the bar. "It stuck out like a sore thumb."

Despite her disillusion with Adams, Kitty was reluctant to abandon him.

"Grass doesn't grow on a busy street," she said crossly.

"No," Shelmerdine conceded, "and you don't need thatch on an empty barn."

* * *

Pusey clutched the table and listened with rising panic to the clatter of crockery from the kitchen. Slowly, his temples thumping resentment, he struggled to his feet. Steading himself for a moment by leaning on the back of the chair, he then began to edge cautiously and uncertainly out of the bar. The bill was on the desk where Sam Harrison had left it. Focusing with difficulty, Pusey slowly counted out precisely the amount shown; then, picking up his rucksack and placing his feet with infinite caution, he crept miserably up the stairs and into the street.

~Chapter 10~

If Julia Mowbray's encounter with Mervyn Pusey outside the railway station had been preordained, it had been by forces whose ambitions were either capricious or obscure. Julia had completed her errands in the city while Pusey had proceeded to catch the bus to Bradburn and the indignities that awaited him. And, although the contours of the flawless blonde with the swept back hair had slipped in and out of his dreams for some time afterwards, their chance meeting had no more impact on Pusey's ambitions concerning her father's company than a neutron passing through a sack of oats would affect the result of the St. Leger.

Nor had the thought that had stopped Julia in her tracks been momentous. It had simply involved a change from her original intention of carrying out her commission for Miss Fitton from the silver Library, then heading home to loaf around Bradburn House, in favour of enticing friends who worked in Leeds to join her for lunch.

Her afternoon had unfolded according to plan and it was a little after five o'clock when she stepped off the bus at the Bradburn terminus and handed her case to George to stow on the back seat of her father's car.

"Your father didn't tell you he was going to London because he was going straight there and back," Miss

Varley had explained when Julia had telephoned from the bus station to ask if someone could get a message to George and ask him to meet her.

"But he hates going to London," Julia had protested. "Why on earth would he go straight there and back? And he always tells me when he's coming so that we can meet."

"Your father will tell you what it's all about, I'm sure," Miss Varley had said soothingly. "No doubt it's a lot of fuss over nothing. He'll be delighted you've come home."

Miss Varley's opinions about most of the Wilberforce board, which would have been instructive, could not have been drawn from her with hot irons. Her pride and trust in Mowbray, however, were as unshakeable as her discretion. Unsatisfactory or not, Julia knew better than to press for business confidences. Now, as she sat in front of the car alongside a George who, as usual, smelled ever so slightly yet comfortingly of compost, she consoled herself with the knowledge that, whatever the mystery alluded to by Miss Varley, her father would explain all.

She put the problem from her mind as George drove slowly up the drive, stopped the car in front of the house's columned portico and leaned across to push open the passenger door. Julia stepped out and stood on the gravelled terrace facing the house. Behind her twin flights of broad steps led down to the gardens. The late afternoon air was warm and still, heavy with the scent of roses and freshly cut grass. She lingered for a moment, savouring the early evening sunshine, then rejoined George where he waited inside the hall with her suitcase. The oak-panelled hall was as always cool and scented by flowers thrusting from vases on the marble-topped tables either side of the door. Beyond the tables, twin flights of stairs led up to a gallery where portraits in heavy frames frowned from the shadows. George handed over the case then left to put the car away, leaving Julia to take it up to her room and put away the few things she had brought with her. Having quickly freshened up she hurried downstairs and through the hall to the door that led to the kitchen and Mrs. Benson's flat.

In the kitchen puffing noises were coming from where Mrs. Benson was leaning perilously over the opened chest freezer. Julia had time to fill the heavy kettle and light the gas under it before the housekeeper emerged holding a frosted package. She gave a gasp of surprise as Julia flung her arms around her and kissed her firmly on the forehead.

"Where on earth. . . ?" The round pink face attempted to look severe as Julia put her finger to her lips.

"I was going to surprise father," Julia said, "but I couldn't have done anyway because apparently he's in London." She looked at Mrs. Benson expectantly.

Mrs. Benson broke off from rearranging hair-grips and began to scoop tea into a teapot. Julia's visits to Bradburn were as frequent as her social life and her partnership in a small gallery within hailing distance of the West End allowed. Although her home visits were usually prompted by a lingering though unsentimental homesickness, her present one had resulted from a development that was no more supportable for having been self-inflicted when soaking undies had blocked the overflow of the hand basin in her London flat. The flood that followed had rendered the flat temporarily uninhabitable and her old room at Bradburn House had beckoned. What she had not anticipated was her father's absence, an absence that now appeared to be shrouded in mystery. Putting her concerns to one side she assured Mrs. Benson that no, she was not losing weight, and no, there was still no special young man in sight, until at last she managed to broach the subject. Seated at the scrubbed wooden table and provided with a cup of impossibly hot tea, and in a voice betraying more anxiety than intended, she said, "Now, tell me what's been happening in Bradburn. Why has Daddy had to go to London at such short notice? Miss Varley wouldn't say what was happening, but something's the matter, isn't it?"

Mrs. Benson stared at the table and played unhappily with the bib of her apron. "All I know is that your father was upset about something on Saturday morning," she said. "He was on the telephone a lot, and yesterday they had a board meeting and it wasn't a normal board day. . ." She raised her eyes and, in a reversal of what Julia had intended, looked appealingly at her for an explanation.

Julia nibbled a biscuit and looked thoughtful. There was nothing particularly unusual about a board meeting called at short notice; nor was it particularly unusual for her father to visit London, although for him to do so without letting her know in advance. . . Mrs. Benson's eyes, she noticed, were darting glances in the direction of the clock on the kitchen wall.

"That's not all, is it?" Julia prompted. "There's something else. . ."

Mrs. Benson hesitated, then said, "Well, I'm not sure what it all means, but your father's telephoned to say there's people coming to Bradburn." She leaned back, making the chair creak, her expression challenging Julia to make what sense she could of events.

"People?" Julia probed, conscious that to Mrs. Benson anyone from further afield that Broadbridge was irredeemably alien.

"From London. The older one's to have Old Taylor's cottage, and I've booked the young one into the pub, like your father said." The housekeeper shook her head. "I shouldn't really be sitting here. They're arriving tomorrow and that cottage hasn't been lived in since Old Taylor passed away."

Julia knew the cottage. It was one of a terrace still partly owned by Wilberforces, a relic of the days when they had provided low rent housing for employees. Most had now been sold to their tenants, but the company occasionally found itself with an empty cottage on its hands as lone tenants died or were carried off to live with relatives.

"Shelmerdine decorated it as soon as it was empty," Julia protested. "All it needs is a good airing. We can do that in the morning..."

Mrs. Benson looked doubtful.

"I'm to have a meal there ready for him, something he can just pop in the oven."

"I'll make a pudding," Julia volunteered, "my crème caramel..."

Julia's crème caramel was notorious for having the appearance and consistency of earwax and Mrs. Benson deflected her. "You might just give me a hand with the cottage," she suggested. "Now, what would you and your father like for supper? Not that there's anything in the place..."

* * *

Still no wiser, Julia was sitting on the stone bench in the shell-shaped opening scalloped into the wall in the arms of the steps that had led her down from the terrace. Freshly mown lawns stretched out in front of her. Beside her, a glass of white wine, barely touched, rested on an unopened magazine. Her feet were tucked beneath her, her eyes closed as she faced a sun made orange by summer dust. She stirred as a taxi crunched up the drive and stopped, its engine throbbing on the terrace above her. Barefoot, she sprang up and ran quickly up the steps and across the pricking gravel to fling open the passenger door. The customary pink of her father's face, subdued by tiredness, returned in a blush of pleasure as Julia almost dragged him out of the cab. He hugged her delightedly before detaching himself long enough to fumble for his wallet to pay the driver. As the taxi rumbled off he allowed himself to be led into the hall, grinning like a schoolboy. They hugged again and Mowbray held her at arms' length. Julia had showered and changed into a loose yellow top and what appeared to be tennis shorts, although he suspected they were something fashionably less prosaic.

"You look beautiful," he said.

Julia pouted. "You always say that."

"Because you always do."

They completed the ritual as Mrs. Benson emerged from the dining room and headed for the kitchen, bearing an empty tray.

"She could do with another few pounds," she scolded. "Dinner's in twenty minutes."

Father and daughter exchanged a smile as Mowbray excused himself. As he disappeared into the cloakroom Julia retrieved her wine from the garden and carried it to the dining room where she poured a scotch for her father from a decanter on the sideboard.

The dining room was long and narrow and darkly wainscoted. It had been the gloomiest room in the house before Jane Mowbray had consigned the family portraits adorning its walls to the landing above the hall and replaced them with English watercolours. When Julia was away Mowbray rarely strayed beyond the study, morning room and gun room, but when she returned it was customary for the dining room to be used in the evening. Julia just had time to note that Mrs. Benson had opened a window and switched on the electric fire to help circulate the air when Mowbray came into the room. Looking refreshed, he picked up his drink and carried it to where Julia was perched on the box seat at one of the tall windows overlooking the rising flanks of the dales. The lamps around the room had been switched on, giving it the cosy lived-in look he liked, even when the evenings were light. Julia stood up. Taking her father's arm she led him to the chair she had placed near her window.

"I could purr," Julia said, returning to her place on the window seat.

Mowbray stood up again and used a spill to light his pipe from the electric fire.

"No pipes in the dining room, your mother always said. Do you mind?"

Julia flourished a bare foot. "No bare feet, either."

She watched contentedly as her father sank back into his chair, wreathed in smoke.

"Well?" he asked. "What have people been saying?"

Delighted that the topic had been broached so promptly, Julia said, "Mrs. Benson says you're going to flood the town with foreigners, and Miss Varley, whose discretion you would have applauded, suggested that there might or might not be something unspecified going on. Perhaps she thinks I'm a spy." She fixed her father with troubled grey eyes. "Why did you go haring off to London without telling me?"

Mowbray grimaced. "It could be something or nothing; one hopes nothing, of course..."

"To do with the firm, obviously."

It was always the firm, never the company or the factory.

"Are you asking as a daughter or a shareholder?" Mowbray teased.

"As me. Just tell me what's happening."

Mowbray took a sip of his scotch. "You know how the Stock Market works, you've been brought up hearing enough about it..."

"Surely we've not done anything to upset the Stock Exchange...?"

Mowbray waved the suggestion away with a gesture. "Nothing like that. It's simply that someone's been buying enough of our shares to push the price up a few pence. Naturally, the prudent thing was to have a word with Palgraves."

"Do they think someone's planning to take us over?" Julia shifted position, arms embracing knees drawn up to her chin, eyes searching her father's face.

They broke off and stood up as Mrs. Benson came in and placed a tureen at the head of a table comfortably capable of seating twenty.

"It's soup, game pie and salad." Her belief that it failed to match the occasion made her sound cross. Closing the door as she left, she said "You'll have to fill up on cheese."

Mowbray moved to his seat at the head of the table as Julia took the chair to his left. Mowbray helped them both to soup then said, "The question really is what should we be doing in case somebody does try to take us over. Do we simply stick out for the best price, or do we man the barricades and try to fight them off at any cost?"

"What did Palgraves say?"

"In law, it's the board's responsibility to secure the best possible result for the shareholders. That means if someone were to offer a price we consider to be better value than we are likely to deliver, we being the board, our duty would be to advise shareholders to accept the bid."

"And what would happen to you and Uncle Harry and the others?"

"Out on our necks, I shouldn't wonder, with the cousins falling over each other to cash their cheques." His eyebrows raised slightly, as though the thought was a new one.

"And the firm?"

Mowbray shook his head as he worried at the question. "If someone is going to have a go at us, and it is still a big 'if', it will all depend on their motives. There's certainly no fortune to be made in brass, as we know. In any event, it would be commercially unfashionable for any of our suppliers or customers to want to take us over. It could be a property speculator, but it would have to be a fairly dim one. We own the offices and arcade, and a lot of land down by the canal, but it's either greenbelt or zoned for light industry, so no-one's going to get permission to build houses there."

He broke off to sip at his cooling soup as Julia reflected on what she had learned. Happy to be able to outline his thoughts to a sympathetic audience, Mowbray put his spoon down and pushed the soup away. "The most likely predator, assuming there is one, would be someone who has spotted the fact that our shareprice no longer reflects what the company is really worth. If they could persuade our shareholders to sell out at a reasonable price they could probably go on to hive off the factory as a going concern. There's already planning permission for light industry alongside the factory, although we have a gentleman's agreement with the Council that we won't push any closer to the canal. Then there's the office, of course, and the arcade which could no doubt be sold off profitably. Mercifully they're listed buildings, so they'd have to stop short of knocking them down and sticking up a bingo hall."

Julia moved the soup plates and served them both with game pie. When they had helped themselves to salad, she said simply, "Poor Daddy."

Mowbray grimaced. "It's our own fault. The board's, that is. We should have revalued years ago and then paid a bit of attention to the shareprice: prompted a few broker's circulars, courted the City press, that sort of thing. Palgraves could have put us in touch with a City public relations firm to steer us along..."

Julia bristled. "Then why didn't they?"

Her father shrugged. "Too small, I suppose; us, not them. Besides, it's we who should have taken the initiative." Brightening, he said, "Cheer up. We've started to grip it all today. Palgraves are lending us a couple of people to help clear the decks in case anything happens." His expression clouded for a moment at the thought of Hugo Russell. "One of them's a bit of a reptile, but clever, I imagine. He's from Palgraves and we're putting him in Old Taylor's cottage. The other's a youngster, one of those spin doctor types. He'll be staying at the Fox. Maybe you'll be able to give him a hand. If you're staying, that is..."

"It'll probably be some ghastly yuppie with squash racquets in the back of his BMW."

"You like squash."

"I don't like yuppies."

Recollecting her encounter with Nigel, even after the elapse of weeks, made her shudder.

* * *

Nigel Crope-Stewart was something in the City, though, as Nigel would happily have conceded, something not terribly senior. His pursuit of Julia had been of longstanding, unremitting yet unrewarded. Dismissed by one of Julia's friends as a bear of little brain who could do with a cold shower, he had long ago acquired for Julia the status of a social prop, amiably vague, invariably affable and available, whose fate it was to be rewarded with affection rather than the ardour for which he pined. One of Nigel's recent initiatives, knowing Julia's fondness for cricket, had been to acquire tickets for a test match at The Oval.

For much of the day the outing had been a success. Nigel had known a number of people there, Australia had been easily contained by England's bowlers, and the after-match entertainment out of picnic baskets had been followed later that evening by a party at a flat in Islington. Events there had gone swimmingly until Nigel, overcome by the combined effects of fresh air, alcohol and a day in proximity to Julia, had slid drunkenly down the refrigerator door and proceeded to snore quietly until being dragged aside so that others could gain access to its contents. Julia, unimpressed, had made her own way home.

The next morning, a Sunday, when what was really called for was an extended nap, Nigel had leapt fawn-like from his bed only to be felled by a headache that felt as though he had been head-butted by a herd of bison. Having taken certain remedial measures that were effective though unwise, he had appeared on Julia's doorstep at what she regarded as the crack of dawn. With a flourish that almost became a lurch, he had produced a bouquet of roses hastily purchased from a garage forecourt, pressed them into her hands, and delivered a kiss which, catching her unawares, trespassed some distance on the far side of brotherly.

"That," he said, exhaling a cloud of alcohol, "is your goodnight kiss from yesterday...or was it this morning?" He beamed at her complacently.

Although Julia enjoyed a kiss as much as the next woman under appropriate circumstances, those circumstances had to include a substantial element of free will. A kiss on the doorstep, and from one who only hours ago had passed out and left her to find her own way home, was to Julia but one small step from a mugging. Suppressing the inclination to smack Nigel's smirking face with the bouquet, she settled instead for a glare of such hostility that, under normal circumstances, Nigel would have turned and bolted like a freshly branded colt. Had he done so, Julia would probably have satisfied herself by tossing the roses after him and closing the door with a melodramatic slam. Instead, her indignation soared past danger level when, as she struggled to disappear into her inadequate nightwear, she was forced to step aside to avoid being bowled over as Nigel thrust his way past her and more or less fell into the flat.

Crope-Stewart was not a bad person. Though somewhat vague - goofy was a favoured adjective among those called on to describe him - he was good looking enough in a somewhat pink and podgy fashion, generous, without malice, and congenitally incapable of intentionally offending the opposite sex. When sober, that is. When he drank, however, which he did infrequently, there was a tendency for his moral clutch to slip. His intention when he had set out for Julia's that morning had been simply to recover some of the ground he correctly believed might have been lost the previous night. He had shaved with hands made tremulous by his thumping head and by the prospect of having to face a Julia whose attitude would undoubtedly be on the Arctic side of frosty. Having further stiffened his resolve with a large restorative, and then another, he had set off for Julia's in little better shape than he had finished the previous evening.

The inside of Julia's flat was silent and evidently deserted as Nigel brushed past her and practically tumbled into her sitting room. Julia followed warily and stared at him. "I don't wish to appear rude, but if I don't hurry I'm going to be late joining friends for a pub lunch."

Pushing a pile of Sunday papers off the sofa on to the floor, Nigel collapsed on to a cushion and patted the one beside him invitingly.

Julia stared at him through narrowed eyes. "You can make yourself a black coffee, if you wish," she said coldly, "then let yourself out."

In the bathroom Julia hesitated. She listened vainly for the sounds of Nigel pottering off to the kitchen or, if he had regained his senses, stumbling back to the street. There were none and, feeling slightly uneasy, she shrugged out of her brief robe and stepped into the shower.

Although she had often considered the need for a lock on the bathroom door, she had never actually done anything about it. That, plus a persisting sense of unease, prompted her to shower hurriedly so that she was already slipping back into her robe when she heard the first fumbling movements on the other side of the door.

In the meantime, it had begun to filter through to Nigel's fuddled brain that Julia's greeting had lacked warmth. There had, he suspected, even been a touch of *froideur*. What was required, he concluded correctly, was a humble apology and a strategic retreat. He therefore approached the bathroom with the sole intention of uttering something abject from the safety of the living room side of the door before skulking back to his own place for a measure or two of black coffee. What he was not expecting as he tapped at the door was for it to swing open at a touch so that he more or less collapsed into the bathroom. It was a collapse aided by a clump behind the ear from a bottle of bleach wielded like an Indian club. That, and his already delicate condition, was enough. Gallantly averting his eyes from the regions of Julia her attack had exposed, and with the ease of the practised fridge slider, he slid slowly down the wall and finished up with his face pressed against the cool white tiles of the bathroom floor.

From there he blinked up at the indistinct image of Julia's face, his own a picture of puzzlement. "I thought..." he mumbled. He stopped, unsure what, if anything, he had thought before the roof caved in.

Julia, almost as surprised as Nigel at the disabling effect of what had been meant merely as a reproving tap, took a deep breath and waited for waves of panic to subside. "It's perfectly clear what you thought," she said weakly as she restored the bleach bottle to its rightful place beside the cistern. "What is not at all clear is why you thought it."

Nigel tried again. "I was only..." He started to push himself away from the floor but slipped back again and settled for a position with one arm in the bowl of the bidet.

Conscious of her lunchtime appointment, Julia grasped his free arm and pulled him slowly back to his feet. Using his arm to guide him, she drew him slowly in the direction of the shower. Nigel, glazed eyes questioning, balked suspiciously at the rim. "You've had a bump on the head," Julia said superfluously. "This will help to prevent any swelling."

Nigel continued to resist the motion that would have carried him over the rim of the shower tray; but, as Julia smiled encouragement, he yielded. Once past the plastic curtain he stood meekly facing the opposite wall. He blinked at it uncomprehendingly as Julia leaned in and redirected the shower head before stepping back and turning the valve to full pressure. Icy jets stung his scalp with the force of a blizzard. Turning to face Julia, he gave her a hesitant smile before the force of the water compelled him to close his eyes. First his jacket then his trousers rapidly darkened with the weight of water. Relenting, Julia turned the shower off. Nigel opened his eyes, shook himself like a spaniel, and stepped out. Water squelched from hand-crafted shoes.

Julia surveyed him for a moment before handing him a towel. "If I were you, Nigel," she advised, "I think I should take a hint."

* * *

Her father was saying something about money.

"You'll be looked after whatever happens, of course. Your mother and I saw to that a long time ago. Not only the shares..."

Julia gave an unladylike snort. "But what about the people? What about the house? What about Bradburn?"

He gave a gentle shrug. "Some things we can't answer, of course. They'll fall out of whatever happens next. If there's a bid and we fight it off there shouldn't be any dramatic changes, though it's clear we shall have to revalue and start building a few bridges with the City if we're to avoid any sort of unpleasantness in the future."

Julia's face showed her relief. She stood up and moved their used dishes to the sideboard. Putting a tray of cheeses in front of her father, she chose an orange for herself and peeled it on her plate.

"Bradburn House will be all right," her father volunteered, his fingers exploring a tray of crackers. "It's a bit of a white elephant these days, but at least we look after it." He watched his daughter as she abstractedly segmented her orange. "Well?"

Julia frowned at him. "It just seems dreadful, somehow. Some complete stranger could take over Wilberforces and hardly anyone outside Bradburn would even care."

He cupped his hand over hers. "Of course people would care..."

Julia shook her head impatiently.

"The fun would really start if a bidder emerged who wasn't remotely interested in the business," her father continued, sober-faced, "someone who saw it simply as an opportunity to try and develop the land alongside the canal and get rid of the offices and shops to the highest bidders. We should thank our lucky stars planning permission down by the canal is restricted to industrial development, otherwise heaven alone knows what sort of bidder might appear out of the woodwork."

Julia brightened. "Perhaps we'll be able to leave it all to the experts they're sending from London."

Dinner finished, they sipped their coffee together, gazing out of the windows at the evening shadows slowly advancing across the undulating dales.

* * *

Back in his London flat, Mervyn Pusey was gripping a pair of scissors. Holding the fateful wig at arm's length he shredded it carefully into the wastepaper basket where the curls lay among discarded papers like foraging caterpillars. Then, lowering himself carefully into the green leather armchair so as not to awaken his bruises, he opened his briefcase and removed a copy of the letter from his Bradburn informant.

'You'll see about environment,' he read for the umpteenth time, *'but at Bradburn it's already factory so you're sure to get houses if you knock the factory down and know the people I do.'*

He allowed his imagination to linger on the prospect of the factory site as he had viewed it from across the canal shortly before the evening had begun to disintegrate. Pressing a button on the dictating apparatus on his desk he cleared his throat and said, "I'd like the following put in the personal columns of *The Yorkshire Post,* Miss Goring. Quote, To a friend, colon. Oh, full stop, Kay, full stop. Capital Y, You're on. Close quotes."

He switched the machine off and stared at his reflection against the darkness outside the window. There was reassurance in the familiar baldness, the steely glint of the spectacles. Slipping the letter back in the briefcase he leaned back in the chair, careful not to bring it into contact with the egg-shaped lump on the back of his head.

"Sitting ducks," he said contentedly. "Absolute sitting ducks." Then, with peevish afterthought, "Pity they don't own that bloody pub."

~Chapter 11~

Rebecca folded the last of Simon's shirts and tossed it in the direction of the suitcase propped open on the bed. Disturbed, Napoleon, the tabby, executed a half-roll which took him into the finger of sunlight close to where Simon still drowsed.

"One or two of these collars are going," Rebecca said.

Foetal beneath a single sheet, Simon grunted.

"You'd better buy a couple of shirts when you get up there. Once you've been paid, that is."

Simon pushed the sheet aside and sat up, combing his fingers through hair tousled by sleep. The house was unaccustomedly quiet and he looked questioningly as his wife up-ended his long disused sponge-bag on to the bed.

"The children are at Hazel's."

Simon grunted again. He liked Hazel, though she smoked even more than Rebecca. She lived in the equally tall and narrow house next door where she illustrated children's books in a pointillist style that reminded him of a colour blindness test. She swore alarmingly, and her top-floor studio, forbidden to her husband, had a barrack-room atmosphere in which the slight, smocked figure appeared louchely at home.

"They'll probably get bronchitis," Simon said.

Rebecca, gathering up rusting cans of shaving foam
and deodorant, tossed her head. She carried the cans
into the bathroom and dropped them in the bin. She
returned as Simon swung his legs out of bed, stood up,
stretched, then made a grab for her. She ducked easily
under his arm and threatened him with a cricket boot
from the far side of the bed.

"Just because it's Yorkshire doesn't mean you have
to take your cricket things." She made jabbing motions
with the boot as Simon stalked her. "Once you had to
be born there before they'd even let you play for the
county. That's because only Yorkshiremen can play well
enough. "

She spoke with the heedless loyalty of one born in
the county.

"A man born in a stable is not a horse," Simon
countered, wondering vaguely what it meant.

* * *

Simon had taken the call from Kettering late the
previous afternoon. While the businessman had been,
well, business-like, Simon had been almost speechless.
Covering the mouthpiece with his hand he had called
for Rebecca, stooping so that she could put an ear to
the instrument, but she waved him away and ran
towards the kitchen as a vicious spitting noise told her
that her latest attempt at soup was boiling over.

"It could lead to something quite big," Simon
enthused as he leaned on the kitchen table and watched
as Rebecca attempted to dismantle the cooker top.
Defeated, she threw the oven gloves into the sink and
lit a cigarette. "They think someone may be going to try
and take over this company in Yorkshire and they want
me up there to give them a hand with public relations.
Not the heavy stuff," he said hurriedly as Rebecca's
eyebrow began its ascent. "They've got some top-

drawer City outfit to do that, Kettering says. He's sending someone from the merchant bank up there, too." He clapped his hands once, signalling resolve. "It'll be good to get to grips with the press again."

Rebecca listened with mixed feelings as she drew on her gloves again and resumed her battle with the cooker top. She had already established that her husband had omitted to ask how much he was to be paid and, as she later explained to Hazel, while living in penury with a husband under one's feet was undoubtedly an affliction, to lose that husband for the duration and then find that one had done so for a pittance would not necessarily be an improvement. Hazel, who was using a minuscule paintbrush to add roundels to a gossamer wing, grimaced without taking the cigarette from her mouth. "Don't knock it," she said, blinking away the smoke, "I'm still trying to work out how you did it."

Rebecca's emotions were further complicated by the fact that it was she who, indirectly, had been responsible for introducing Simon to the wiles of public relations in the first place. It had come about during an exchange of confidences over a bottle of wine shared by Rebecca and a girlfriend who worked for a company at the frothier end of the business.

"He's an absolute sweetheart," Simon would have been surprised to hear Rebecca say, "but he's not actually very good at anything except cricket. If you hear of anything going..."

Her friend, in whom alcohol produced forgetfulness, might never have had cause to remember the conversation had her employer not fortuitously prompted her.

"We could really do with someone to give us a hand for a few weeks," he had said the next morning. "We've this rash of press do's coming up..."

Simon, looking handsome and impeccably groomed, had duly arrived for an interview and after a five minute chat found himself in a job that appeared to consist chiefly in helping to organise meetings at which the press were invited to consume food and drink in return for not protesting too vehemently when events failed to live up to whatever had been promised. Simon's open, friendly manner, untainted by the casuistries of his new profession, quickly won him a core of friends among the regular press attendees, though the fragile nature of some of his arrangements meant that the events occasionally teetered on the brink of catastrophe.

His bubble had burst one day when his employer, seeing him in relaxed conversation with a senior writer from the *Financial Times*, had sidled across unobserved to monitor his technique. He arrived in time to hear the journalist, arm embracing Simon's shoulders, say, "You know, old man, I love coming to your do's. There's always such a delightful air of cock-up."

That, plus the fact that the flurry of press events was almost over and corners could once more be cut, was sufficient to end Simon's flirtation with public relations. Bruised, but not for long, he had apologised to Rebecca for the sudden snatching away of their financial lifeline. "I was really beginning to get the hang of things," he said penitently.

Rebecca concluded her mental inventory of her husband's public relations experience as she leaned on the suitcase lid, snapped the fasteners closed and wondered briefly whether she might have rather over-catered on the clothing front.

Simon, having quickly shaved and showered, was hopping around pulling on freshly pressed trousers. "I'll probably be able to get back most weekends," he assured her. "Old Kettering says that even if there is a bid there could be a phoney war period when nothing happens except a check of the defences." He frowned, then added with customary honesty, "Whatever they're likely to be."

The sound of a taxi pulling up drew him to the bedroom window. Rebecca gave him a clinging kiss and watched wistfully as he grabbed the suitcase off the bed and headed for the stairs.

"You could have caught the tube, you know," she shouted after him, "you're not on bloody expenses yet."

~Chapter 12~

Julia was not quite sure why she had taken it into her head to meet Simon Beresford at the station. It had somehow grown out of Mrs. Benson's decision to free her after a morning spent dusting and airing Old Taylor's cottage and stocking the kitchen with basic provisions. Mrs. Benson had returned to Bradburn House to prepare an evening meal which she would bring back and put in the fridge ready to be heated up by the visiting banker. It was a task, she had assured Julia earnestly, that required only one pair of hands. Julia had told George that in that case she might just as well rescue her own car from the garage and drive into Leeds instead of him, which was why she now found herself wandering up and down the station concourse trying to recall what her father had said about the public relations man. It appeared not to have extended much beyond a vague, "He's to help with press relations and that sort of thing."

A call to Palgraves that morning had elicited Simon's telephone number, and a call to that number had revealed that he was indeed catching the planned train and had in fact already left. Hackles rising with suspicion, Rebecca had only reluctantly agreed to confirm her husband's travel arrangements. Later, her jealousy rationalised, she said to Hazel, "Actually, she sounded very sweet."

"She's probably built like a Shire horse," Rachel had countered.

For Simon, the sound of his name coming over the loudspeakers as he strode along the platform at Leeds was exciting, flattering even, until it occurred to him that it might presage news of some frightful calamity at home. Instead, it had led to an introduction to a quite extraordinarily good looking blonde, only three or four inches shorter than he and marred, if at all, solely by a chin expressing a determination that was uncomfortably reminiscent of Rebecca.

For her part, Julia saw a tall, fair-haired and distinctly English-looking young man carrying an enormous suitcase as though it were weightless. Furtively, she searched his face for the Mephistophelean signs that presumably marked spin doctors until, reassured by a face that reflected only good-natured admiration, she smiled and offered a hand in greeting. Simon switched the suitcase to his other hand and extended the freed one. As their hands met he said uncertainly, "I had been told to expect someone called George..."

"I'm Julia Mowbray, actually," Julia said. "I hadn't really intended to meet you." As she spoke she set off for the exit, Simon in train. "As you arrived I had just about concluded that my motivation was feminine curiosity rather than a desire to be helpful. That and the need to give my car a run. I hope that doesn't sound rude..."

They left the gloom of the station and Julia looked up and down the curve of the street apprehensively. "I've parked on a double yellow line," she confessed. "I told the traffic warden I was picking up an invalid, so if you see her you'd better limp..."

She stopped at an open-topped car and undid a boot which held the suitcase with an inch to spare. Simon settled into the hot leather seat beside her as she pulled smoothly away from the kerb, hands light on the wheel. She had donned a headscarf which dramatised the smooth curve of her forehead and gave her a faintly piratical appearance. Half-turning in his seat, Simon found himself comparing her relaxed treatment of the car with the way in which Rebecca tended to wrench at the controls as though attempting to dismantle them.

"I spoke to your wife this morning," Julia said, breaking the silence, "just to confirm you would be on that train. She sounded charming..."

"She can be," Simon said. "I mean, yes, she is..."

They both laughed. While leaving the town behind and careering through the countryside by the side of a beautiful young woman appeared to Simon to be a perfectly acceptable introduction to whatever lay ahead, mention of Rebecca had produced a tiny pang of homesickness that caught him unawares.

Julia noticed the shadow cross his face and a modest wheedling produced a description of a family life of a felicity that would have made Rebecca blink. In return, Simon was rewarded by a condensed history of Bradburn and a fiercely lyrical description of Wilberforces which, for the first time, suggested that what was to him largely an adventure threatened life's very foundations for those directly involved. Conversation broke off as Julia slowed down to negotiate a stretch of roadworks. Safely past, and the civilities disposed of, she put the question that had been at the front of her mind.

"What precisely is it you've been asked to do for us?" She glanced at his face as his forehead crinkled in thought. Aware the question might have appeared peremptory, she added, "Father says it's all going to be terribly useful..."

As a question, it had a familiarity that Simon recognised with considerable unease. Indeed, as he had so far failed to answer it to his own satisfaction he saw little advantage in explaining to Julia that, so far as he could see, his role was hardly likely to be more than peripheral, even if he could remember half of what it was supposed to be. A couple of hours in the local library the previous evening had put him in touch with *The City Code on Take-overs and Mergers*, after which a flick through *A Handbook on Public Relations* had produced increasing alarm as it revealed the breadth of activities required of a profession he had hitherto regarded as little more than fig leaf-holders for politicians and captains of industry.

"I honestly don't know," he admitted frankly. Recognising that this was probably carrying honesty too far, he added, "It hasn't been made precisely clear. I imagine it will depend on how events develop."

"I suppose," Julia suggested, "you'll be trying to rally the community around us. Employees, local authority, press. . . that sort of thing?"

It appeared a sound prospectus to Simon who flung his arm expansively over the back of Julia's seat and nodded solemnly. "All that kind of thing. Perhaps some advertising, too."

He tried to recall the prescriptive approach to unwelcome bids from his previous evening's reading. Stripped of its verbiage, Julia appeared to have got the community relations bit about right.

"I should be able to help you," Julia volunteered. "If I shan't be in the way, that is. I've decided I'm home for the duration. I know almost everyone in Bradburn, if that's any help."

She pulled out to overtake a tractor and they both glanced back to where a hugely fat man in a crumpled business suit teetered uncertainly on the drawbar, his hands clutching the shoulders of a driver who was whistling something drowned out by the roar of the engine.

"How distinctly odd," Julia said. "What on earth has Ted Ellingham picked up?"

A sign at the roadside indicated that they were now entering Bradburn and Julia slowed down as they approached the square so that she could point out the offices. At the back of the Corn Exchange she paused briefly so that Simon could see the factory before she turned into the next street and dropped him at the Fox & Chickens.

~Chapter 13~

The way Kettering had treated him had been cavalier in the extreme, Hugo Russell considered. It was a point he had made to Constance several times since returning home on the evening following his introduction to Mowbray.

"He treats me as though I were a junior clerk," he blustered, forcing studs into his dress shirt with irritable fingers. "Worse. As though I were the bloody tea lady. If your father could see the way I'm treated at that place he would have something to say about it, mark my words."

If her father had been in a position to say anything, had his ashes not been scattered over the gallops at Lambourn, mused Constance Russell as she daintily attached a corsage to the bosom of her gown, it would probably have been 'Hurrah!'

It had been Constance's idea, not her late father's, that Hugo Russell should be admitted to the firm. His object in agreeing had been not so much to indulge a daughter whom he loved dearly, as to put a son-in-law he mistrusted in a position where he could keep an eye on his antics. For antics, he was convinced, there would be.

It had been inevitable that Constance would finish up with a large man, though Russell, as a bridegroom, had been a long way from the behemoth he had subsequently become. As for Constance, the description of Junoesque had been attached to her with such frequency during adolescence that she had been galvanised into a regimen of diet and exercise that had left her as fleet as Diana yet not a pound lighter. Hugo Russell, encountered at a house party, had been satisfyingly larger in almost every respect. They had been almost immediately attracted: she by his reassuring bulk, he by what he had learned of her prospects.

Their childless marriage, in a household requiring hardly any of her attention, which ran better in fact without it, had provided her with much time for reflection. This had led to the depressing realisation that whatever attraction might once have existed between them had been as nothing beside the fact that Russell had simply introduced a relativity of scale that flattered her. For a time, too, he had exhibited a sardonic humour that had been much appreciated at dinner parties but which, after marriage, had degenerated into a biting sarcasm, usually at the expense of his wife.

Russell was struggling with a bow-tie he could feel but barely see beneath the reflection of his pendulous jowls. "I hope you're not expecting me to stay up till all hours this evening," he complained, his voice strangled by his efforts to fasten the tie.

"I'm sure that if you wish to retire early again, people will understand," Constance said coolly.

His behaviour at a City dinner earlier that month had provided a goad that she was not afraid to use.

"Any remotely sensitive human being would have seen that I was ill and would have got me out of there before I passed out," he snarled. He threw the crumpled bow-tie on the bed and reached in a wardrobe for a fresh one.

"You were drunk," Constance said airily. "Richard Kettering said you were drunk, I say you were drunk, and the taxi driver who had to help you in and out of the cab said you were drunk."

A combative Constance was not a new phenomenon, though after years when she had been remote but quiescent he still found such spirited responses difficult to counter.

"I have to drive up to Yorkshire in the morning, get an early start. That's what I meant," he said gruffly. "No point in sitting up half the night over a brandy glass and then setting off to drive two hundred miles."

Considering she had already had the better of the exchange, Constance sailed gracefully from the room, leaving behind a trail of the expensive perfume she knew he disliked.

* * *

The dinner had been a disaster.

Hugo had stayed sober, the better to insult their hosts, Constance suspected. When they got home he had gone straight to bed, pausing at the top of the stairs only to hurl down a reminder that he would be off first thing in the morning. The following morning he rose without waking Constance, vainly hoping she would find the omission hurtful. He telephoned the office, reminding them to let Wilberforces know he would be arriving by car around lunchtime and would require an office near the chairman. He then got into his car and headed north with Wagner pouring from its multitude of speakers.

For Russell, the north existed other than as an abstraction only to the extent that he knew its food to be inedible and its inhabitants churls. His exile produced not fears but gloom-ridden certainties, chief among which was the conviction that his banishment was taking him to a gastronomic desert.

It was Palgraves' policy to reward its executives generously. Even those of meagre talent merited powerful motor cars so that, despite a protracted stop for coffee and toasted teacakes in mid-morning, the clock on the dashboard showed well short of noon when Russell found himself off the motorway and in the winding country lanes leading in the general direction of Bradburn. His options, he considered irritably, were either to get to the Wilberforce offices ahead of schedule, causing confusion for his hosts and, worse, inconvenience for himself; or to explore the area in the hope of finding an inn where lunch would doubtless be scarcely edible but which would at least allow him to maintain a lifetime's habit of eating not less than three square meals a day.

The first intimation that he was in fact lost was when he became stuck behind a tractor and trailer he had sped past only minutes before.

Seen up close, the tractor was slow, noisy, and emitting clouds of evil-smelling smoke which leaked in through the car's air conditioning. But when Russell got a whiff of its trailer's rustically pungent load he found himself almost pining for the stench of its exhaust. The contents of the trailer were first revealed as clusters of small, iridescent green bomblets that detached themselves each time the cart went over a bump and landed with a dusty splash just short of the car's bonnet. A stink that would have sent Hercules sprinting from the Augean stables had sent his pudgy fingers groping for the buttons that would close the window and restore the air-conditioning. Visually, the load appeared as a fluorescent green sludge, quivering and pulsing and slopping up and down the sides of the cart as though imbued with life. The sight and stench provided all the incentive Russell needed in order to overtake at the first opportunity on a road that was both narrow and winding. If the tractor driver had anticipated a friendly wave of acknowledgment for pulling on to the verge to permit the manoeuvre, he was doomed to disappointment. Frustration boiling over, Russell drew alongside the tractor and lowered the passenger window to hurl his abuse over the roar of the tractor's engine.

If the driver had in fact been emptying septic tanks, as Russell was later forced to conclude, then he had hit a particularly pungent seam. The car immediately filled with a miasma that brought tears to his eyes and he shot past squealing with rage and shaking his fist at the image rapidly dwindling in his rear-view mirror. He groaned when, minutes later, having missed a turning recommended by his satellite navigation device, he found himself behind the tractor for a third time. This time its driver greeted the encounter by raising his battered trilby in a mock salute so that any illusions Russell might have entertained about the overtaking courtesy being extended again died stillborn. Forced to crawl along behind the bubbling slurry, he ground his teeth and slowed the car to a crawl to allow the tractor and its load to disappear round a bend in the road. No longer preoccupied by the need to overtake, it occurred to him that it was now some considerable time since he had relieved himself. Deciding that any delay in resuming his journey would have the additional benefit of increasing the distance between himself and his tormentor, he drew alongside one of the regular wooded areas at the side of the road and, slipping off his seatbelt, twitched the steering wheel and headed for the narrow grassed area in front of it.

Why there was an overgrown ditch at that point and not where the tractor had pulled off earlier was a thought that quickly became academic. Unperturbed at first as the car lurched slightly on reaching the softer ground, Russell found himself gripping the steering wheel with rising panic as the near-side quickly lost traction before slipping sickeningly over the lip of a hidden decline. The car tilted abruptly. Russell emitted a stifled shriek as he found himself thrown across the automatic gear lever and into the handle of the passenger door. Unguided, the car staggered along at an angle for a moment, its engine racing as the off-side wheels spun against dry grass. Then the engine simply gave up. The car, steering now locked, gave a final lurch and finished up canted at almost forty-five degrees.

Russell lay there, stunned. Gradually, shock dissipated and he strove to free himself only to find that he was so trapped by his own weight that he was totally incapable of moving. Brambles and fans of Queen Anne's lace pressed against the glass of the passenger window on which his great jowls now rested, and he was forced to watch helplessly as something with an inordinate number of legs crawled through the gap at the top of the window and disappeared into the upholstery. It was a world restricted to several square inches of flora beneath his left eye and a patch of sky visible to his right eye through the canted windscreen. He watched bemused as thistledown drifted towards the car only to soar out of sight as it met the heat from the stalled engine. Briefly, the car shifted slightly and some of the pressure on Russell's neck eased. He found he could now peer between his feet at the blue sky beckoning beyond the driver's window. Cautiously, fearful of sudden movement, he tried to move his hips only to send a shower of small change from his trousers clattering against the glass beside his face. Fat calves with red suspenders poked from rumpled trousers where less than a minute before his head had peered above the steering wheel. Metal ticked and he sniffed anxiously for the smell of escaping petrol. Immobilised by his bulk, he pondered what to do next.

Thankfully the crisis had somehow relegated the need to relieve himself and he began to wonder almost philosophically whether, if he managed to avoid either a heart attack or suffocation, he might conceivably be rescued in time for lunch.

Minutes passed. Gentle breezes stirred feathery leaves where his shoes framed the trembling branches of a silver birch. Silky plumes of rosebay willow herb brushed the windscreen as a foxglove, broken and bent by the car's impact, wilted slowly in the heat from its bonnet until it collapsed on to the metalwork. Itching and sweaty, Russell waited. Time, it seemed, stood still. The stoicism induced more by shock than by any resolution of character began to yield to panic.

He was uncertain afterwards whether he had passed out or simply slept. Whichever it was, he had somehow lost consciousness only to waken to find that a ruddy and uncomfortably familiar face had appeared between the driver's window and the gently nodding branches of the birch tree. The face mouthed soundless words as powerful hands began to drag the door open against its own weight. Russell inhaled as far as his cramped posture would permit, relishing the sudden sounds of birdsong and the inrush of fresh country air. The upper half of the tractor driver appeared over the sill, head on one side as he considered Russell's predicament.

Satisfied that the driver appeared to be only incommoded and not dead, he glanced approvingly round the car's interior. "Posh!" he said. "Is that real leather?"

Russell was as helpless as if bound by chains. Though his voice was muffled by his welter of chins, his predicament did nothing to moderate his customary snappishness. "Don't just stand there, man. Get me out," he commanded. Unbelievingly, he watched as the tractor driver, lips pursed, shook his head.

Ted Ellingham was not a hasty man; the seasons by which he farmed were not more measured. Had Ted had his way, the scout pack he led in Bradburn would probably have worn a badge that said not *Be Prepared* but *Don't Even Think About It*. It was clear, Russell decided, that Ted's expression of detached contemplation indicated a man who would be unlikely to be stampeded into action.

"It's lucky for you I'm making round trips," Ted said conversationally. "You could've been here all day on this road."

The accent was heavily northern. That, and his own mounting incredulity, meant Russell had to ponder what he heard before he could fully absorb it. When the truth dawned, he would have shaken his head in disbelief had it been possible to move. Even in Yorkshire, he told himself, the sight of one's fellow man in a position of considerable discomfort, not to say peril, had surely to be something more than a topic for philosophical disquisition.

"I said," Russell repeated through gritted teeth, "get me out."

This produced more head shaking.

"If you've broken summat, moving you could make it worse," Ellingham countered reasonably.

A hint of pleading crept into Russell's voice. "Look," he growled, "I can hardly move. You could drag the car from here to Timbuktu and I still wouldn't shift an inch. The only way I'll get out is through this door I'm leaning on."

Ellingham raised his greasy trilby and scratched his head as he considered the matter.

"If you get me out," Russell wheedled, "I'll make it worth your while."

Ellingham's hesitancy had been prompted by a genuine concern for what any sudden movement might do to the trapped man; but, with Russell's assurance that he was securely lodged now allied to the prospect of a reward, concern evaporated. It did nothing, however, to dissuade him from what he considered the safer expedient of first trying to extract the driver via the open door. His strong brown hands grabbed Russell's ankles and tugged experimentally.

"I can't shift you." Ellingham sounded indignant. "You must be built like a brick..."

"I'm sure it would be easier simply to straighten the car," Russell huffed.

"You might just have moved a bit, though," Ellingham said, tugging again at the ankles. Then, "You must weigh better than twenty stone." His voice was tinged with admiration as he released the ankles and leaned on the sill to gaze at Russell, for all the world like Lord Emsworth contemplating the Empress of Blandings. "The trouble is, I'm having to pull at a funny angle. I can't get my weight behind it." He raised his trilby again and scratched his wiry hair. "If you're really sure you'll be all right, I suppose we could try pulling it back on its wheels with the tractor..."

"Why don't you just do that," Russell encouraged.

Ellingham pursed his lips and shook his head resignedly before disappearing from Russell's view. Russell, basting in his own sweat, listened impatiently as the tractor roared into life and Ellingham drove it down the road to unhitch the trailer. There were sounds of the tractor returning and Ellingham appeared again, arms resting on the sill. "I'm going to fix a chain and pull you forward," he advised. "I reckon when we get to the end of this bit of a ditch it'll right itself."

"An admirable idea," Russell said through gritted teeth. He watched, immobile, as Ellingham lowered the driver's door and allowed it to click shut. He disappeared and clinking sounds transmitted themselves through the bodywork as he set about attaching a chain.

There was a roar as the tractor's engine revved. Russell, already as tight as an egg in its shell, attempted to shrink further into the confines of the car as it jerked and began to slither slowly forwards. For a moment it appeared that the car was going to topple completely and Russell let out a screech of alarm. Then, gradually, the car began to right itself. Ellingham peered back over his shoulder as he worked the clutch and accelerator until the car gave a final lurch and resumed its upright position, rocking gently on its springs. The movement had released Russell's limbs and he now found himself trapped by his shoulders in the footwell by the passenger door. As he fumbled at the door handle with stiffened fingers it flew open against his weight and he fell through on to the springy turf. He lay there for a moment, dazed by his sudden freedom. Then an earlier imperative asserted itself and he struggled to his feet and set off for the privacy of the trees, "Like a rat up a pipe," Ellingham said to his audience at the cricket club that evening. When Russell returned his complexion had lost some of its alarming purple tinge in favour of a shade of puce still sufficient to suggest to Ellingham that his new-found acquaintance might be snatched away before he saw his reward.

"You all right?" he asked, glancing up from fingering the nearside's crumpled body panels.

Russell broke off from scratching the parts of his body to which feeling was slowly returning and nodded. Ellingham shrugged but looked unconvinced.

"If I were you, I'd get in and start her up. Take her forward gently because I don't like the look of this nearside front wheel." He kicked its tyre distrustfully. "Just take it slow."

Russell struggled back behind the wheel and did as instructed. There was a grinding noise from the front of the car. He stopped the engine and got out, joining Ellingham who was staring at the afflicted wheel.

"Bearings," Ellingham said.

The sound of an approaching diesel engine became a school bus full of children which slowed then drew up beside them. The driver leaned across to lower the window and shouted something unintelligible to Ellingham who grinned back and waved him on. As he turned to the car he noticed the short aerial sticking up at the back of the roof.

He gestured to it with his thumb. "You got a 'phone in this thing?" he asked.

Russell opened the door and groped for the telephone. "I couldn't use it to get help," he said, reading Ellingham's curious expression. "I was lying on the bloody thing."

"I'll 'phone Dipstick and get him to tow your car in," Ellingham volunteered. The telephone looked toy-sized in his hand. "You can ride into Bradburn with me."

It was later, as he stood on the draw bar and clung on to Ellingham for dear life, that Russell realised the coach driver had probably been offering him a lift.

~Chapter 14~

Simon had spent two weeks in Bradburn and, other than a slightly edgy atmosphere around the Wilberforce offices, the description of phoney war that was on everyone's lips seemed to him to sum up the situation. True, teams of advisers dispatched from London by Palgraves and Ryans came and went but did little to disturb events and most Wilberforce employees went about their business as usual.

Despite the lack of excitement, it seemed to Simon that only the absence of his family prevented the experience so far from being idyllic, particularly because nothing had yet happened that demanded more than he could provide. Perversely, however, the storm clouds absent from Bradburn had loomed leadenly over the weekend at home from which he had returned the previous evening. He was reclining in the bath at the Fox & Chickens, attempting to unravel the weekend's perplexities, when he was disturbed by a rapping on one of the door's patterned glass panels.

"Simon?"

"Kitty?" Simon sat up.

"You're to go to the office as soon as you can. Miss Varley says Mr. Mowbray's had an important call from London."

Simon leapt out of the bath, wrapped himself in one of the pub's only mildly abrasive towels and shot past the retreating Kitty into the bedroom last occupied by Mervyn Pusey.

It was the beginning of his third week in Bradburn and his consultancy, as Julia chose to dignify his role, had achieved a wholly satisfying balance between work and social life, though the distinction between the two could sometimes appear blurred. While he was modest enough to attribute the warmth of his welcome to Julia's enthusiastic sponsorship, others would have pointed to his own good nature and a performance at the cricket nets that left Bradburn's fast bowlers panting with exhaustion. If anything at all could be said to have marred his stay it would have been what he saw as the limited scope for proving his worth in the eyes of the Wilberforce board. Now, if the urgency of Mowbray's message was to be trusted, he was about to attend a council of war. Feeling absurdly pleased with events, the trauma of the weekend temporarily forgotten, he was soon striding across the square to where the windows of the Wilberforce offices flashed in the early morning sun.

It was not quite eight o'clock and the air was still fresh and cool. Traffic was light and the only other pedestrians appeared to be filing in and out of the newsagent and tobacconists at the top of the arcade. There were already signs of movement inside the Silver Library, however, and Miss Bertram gave him a cheerful wave as she looked up from dusting the window display before disappearing to give the parquet floor the regular buffing that added the schoolroom smell of polish to that of the books.

At the office Simon ran up the outside steps and tried to push through the huge doors before Adams could open one for him. He failed, not for the first time, and they exchanged amiable nods as he headed for the stairs, taking them two at a time until he reached the second floor landing. The office he shared with Tracy Harrison, Miss Varley's assistant, was empty. Borrowing a pencil and notebook from her desk, he checked that Russell was not in his office opposite then raced up a further flight of stairs to the boardroom. The boardroom's double doors were wide open. The directors, as was customary, appeared to be milling about aimlessly, except for Mowbray who was already in his chair at the head of the table, deep in conversation with Hugo Russell. Miss Varley was in her customary position slightly to the rear of Mowbray, her pencil making quick pecking motions in her notebook as she listened. A small group of the London advisers, looking alert and elegant despite their late arrival the previous night, were gathered round the screened fireplace at the far end.

Temple stood out among an array of uniformly striped suits in a tweed jacket that matched the sandy shade of his shaggy eyebrows. He intercepted Simon just inside the door. "My dear fellow," he said, grasping Simon warmly by the elbow, "so glad to see you managed breakfast."

Kitty had left the bacon sandwich by Simon's bedside before summoning him from the bath with her message. Taking the colonel's hint, he turned aside and used his handkerchief to wipe crumbs from his mouth.

Temple had taken an immediate liking to Simon, as indeed had his fellow directors, though he understood less of what Simon was supposed to be doing than Simon himself. "The game's afoot, what?" he beamed. "Some ninny in the City's been on to Gerry to say we're all for the high jump. All frightful nonsense, y'know, sheer bravado." Releasing Simon, he drifted back to his place as Mowbray called the meeting to order.

Simon closed the doors and took a chair with his back to them. Someone had drawn the translucent green blinds half-way down the windows, giving papers and faces an underwater pallor. As usual, the people from London waited with exaggerated courtesy to see which seats would be free, then settled self-consciously into the seats they had occupied with an equal show of deference at every preceding meeting.

"Thank you all for an early start," Mowbray began. "If nothing else, it shows that Simon's system works."

Simon shuffled modestly in his seat and stared at the papers in his lap. The Wilberphone had been his principal contribution to events so far. It allowed any director to summon a meeting of what had been designated the Defence Team by making a single call to a fellow director, after which his hands were free to deal with whatever situation had prompted him to make the call. All directors and senior members of staff had each been given the names of two others to call once they themselves were called so that, in theory, messages cascaded quickly. The system combined the advantages of speed with the opportunities for error of Chinese Whispers. But, Simon congratulated himself, it seemed to have passed its first test. He looked up and received a tight smile of approval from Miss Varley. Mowbray's remarks had been greeted by mumbled hear-hears from the directors and Simon found himself blushing.

"You will have gathered that our fears have been justified," Mowbray was continuing. "As most of you will have learned from the telephone call, a buyer for our shares has revealed his hand, having achieved more than three per cent."

He consulted a note in front of him. "He actually claims a little under four per cent. The buyer..." Mowbray paused for a moment, never before having commanded such undivided attention from his board, "...the buyer is someone called Mervyn Pusey. Some of you may have heard of him." He looked around the table. One or two of the London advisers were nodding glumly. "I actually read something or other about him a couple of weeks ago," Mowbray continued, "not that I can recall much of what it said. However, Hugo Russell is going to tell us more about him..."

At the sound of his name the fat man raised his eyes from the table and stared at each of the directors and their visitors in turn. "Mervyn Pusey," he said coldly, "could buy Wilberforces from petty cash." He glanced challengingly round the table, monitoring the effect of his statement. Rewarded only with expressions of polite interest, he resumed. "Pusey is in his late thirties, early forties. He started in property speculation and graduated to asset stripping. Now, for the most part, he looks for special situations: situations where he can use his speed and resources to make money. And, although he is not personally popular with the institutions, if he wishes to gear his activities, that is, if he wishes to fund them partly with debt, most of them will back him all the way."

"What on earth has inspired him to come after us?" a cousin asked petulantly, as though Pusey were guilty of some breach of etiquette. All attempts to exclude the cousins from meetings of the defence team had failed in face of their combined shareholding in the company. Together, these almost matched that of the reclusive Uncle Edwin, and a compromise had been reached which allowed one of them to attend on their behalf. So far he had contributed little more than an occasional carping criticism.

Russell somehow managed to appear to ignore the questioner while answering the question. "We can only guess what might have brought you to his attention, but the fact is that if he can get you at a half decent price he will be able to make a considerable turn on your assets. The simple fact is that he 'phoned your chairman with his intentions at seven o'clock this morning..."

"Good Lord," Pritchard sneered, "taken over by an insomniac..." Though youngest of the executive directors, Pritchard had been the most resentful of the hours the arrangements for the defence were requiring him to put in, and the morning's early start, announced in a grimly sardonic call from Bartlett, had left Pritchard incoherent with indignation and the company secretary wearing a tight-lipped smile.

Russell ignored the interruption. "...and he is now required to declare his holding in writing..."

Simon's face lit up with recognition as the meeting began to edge into the arcane territory of City regulations he had skimmed over in the local library before leaving London. Yet, as Russell droned on, Simon's attention continued to wander to the blot on his happiness that had preoccupied him in the bath that morning. The blot, and it was a big one, suffused his recollections of what had been meant to be a joyous weekend with his family.

It had not got off to a good start.

* * *

From the outset, Rebecca had been prickly and impossible to please.

In his more reflective moments at Bradburn, Simon had missed his family wretchedly, but from his calls home each evening Rebecca had detected a note which, although intended to reassure her that all was well in the best of all possible worlds, seemed to suggest that she and the children had been pushed to the margins of a mind not renowned for its capacity.

"He's up to something," she told Hazel unjustly after Simon had been away for a few days.

When Rebecca met Simon at the station on his return from Bradburn she had been driving an almost-new Vauxhall. They had agreed over the telephone to replace the collapsing Mini once Hugo Russell had condescendingly conveyed to Simon the terms on which Palgraves proposed to retain him. These had been so far in excess of anything Simon had imagined that, having had Russell repeat them, he had immediately telephoned Rebecca with the good news. Now, one look at her fixed expression was sufficient to tell him that, so far as she was concerned, any euphoria brought about by the new car had evaporated.

"What are you doing home, anyhow?" she asked combatively, turning her head at the last moment so that the kiss intended for her lips landed on her ear. She started the car, stalled it by letting the clutch in too quickly, started it again and bullied her way into the line of traffic queuing to leave the station forecourt.

Simon, taken aback, indicated his suitcase which a car boot full of school jumble had relegated to the back seat. "Maybe they wanted to give me a chance to get my laundry done," he said lightly.

Irony was lost on Rebecca. "Great," she said, changing gear with an angry thrust of her wrist, "who should I write to thank?" The gearbox whined as the car skidded round a bollard and on to the main road towards home.

The weekend had gone downhill from there. The children, who had been parked with friends so that their parents could have their first evening together, were quickly retrieved once the suitcase had been dropped off to make room for them. Rebecca had spent most of Saturday making what Simon considered to be an unnecessary as well as uncharacteristic performance of coping with the washing and ironing he had brought home. She had then spent the Sunday morning preparing an early lunch which had been so late they had abandoned it halfway through so that she could drive Simon to catch his train.

At the station Rebecca had clung to Simon, her pale face stricken with remorse. "I'm a jealous cow," she said tearfully, her head buried in his chest. "What on earth must you think of me?"

Simon, not knowing what to think, had patted her head and made shushing noises until it was time to grab his case, dash into the station and wait forlornly for the reluctant Sunday train to pull slowly in.

~Chapter 15~

If Simon's introduction to Bradburn had so far been a bed of roses, Hugo Russell's had fulfilled his worst premonitions.

So far as the enforced separation from his wife was concerned he had adopted an of out-of-sight-out-of-mind philosophy; and if nostalgia for home comforts occasionally prodded his consciousness he found it easy to send it scuttling. Indeed, on the two occasions he had been required to return to the capital for meetings at Palgraves' offices he had opted to stay at his London club. And, if his less than ceremonial entry into Bradburn had failed to traumatise his ego more than temporarily, subsequent events had done little to create a sense of wellbeing. True, Mowbray's attention to the immediate problems of car and food had been prompt and effective. He had personally contacted Ibstock's Garage and underlined Ellingham's message about the urgency of recovering and repairing the car. A clerk from the office had been sent to retrieve the pigskin cases from its boot, while Julia had used her father's aged but immaculate Rover to transport him to Old Taylor's cottage where he had been reunited with his luggage. An hour later, groomed and with his ill-humour restored to its maintenance level of scowling disdain, he had dined copiously if reluctantly in the staff canteen before being shown to an office on the other side of Mowbray's from Miss Varley.

"I'm afraid it's been used as a furniture storeroom," Mowbray apologised. "We've kitted it out as an office, and we've lent you a carpet from Bradburn House to make you feel at home. The place could do with a lick of paint and Shelmerdine's agreed to do it before he goes home this evening. He'll leave the windows open, so it should be all right in the morning."

Shelmerdine, Russell assumed, was the paint-spattered figure he had seen bouncing around on scaffolding in the reception area. Mowbray disappeared to his own office and Russell subjected his surroundings to a protracted examination. The room itself was adequate in terms of space, with two large windows overlooking the village square. The desk was clearly an antique – probably worth thousands, he mused, while the carpet...The carpet, he concluded, having paced its contours several times, was satisfactorily old and undoubtedly valuable. He decided to regard it as propitiatory. During the afternoon a number of the other directors wandered in, welcomed him, made polite small-talk and drifted off.

"Funny sort of shape, Rowly," Colonel Temple observed to Mowbray. "Probably eat us out of house and home before this lot's through."

Mowbray, forearmed by his earlier encounter with Russell, had already disposed his resources to ensure that whatever else the fat man might find to complain about, food would not be a problem, at least so far as frequency and quantity were concerned. Julia, it had been agreed, would help Mrs. Benson to keep Russell supplied with evening meals, Mrs. Benson cooking them and Julia delivering them to the cottage.

Breakfast and lunch would be taken in the works canteen on weekdays, and the cottage would be stocked with basic foodstuffs should Russell decide not to dine out at weekends; although, Mowbray explained solicitously, they would of course understand if he wished to pop back to London occasionally until the situation hotted up.

Russell had greeted news of the arrangements with a non-committal grunt.

He had spent the first afternoon at the office in the company of Bartlett and Aneurin Williams, the long-serving finance director, studying the structure and financing of Wilberforces with a languid indifference that had convinced the pair that whatever his contribution to events might be it would be unlikely to exhaust him. Shortly before five, the production director telephoned and offered to show him round the factory, an offer that was rejected. Only an ingratiating Pritchard had shown any propensity for voluntarily spending time in Russell's company, and he had already begun to despair of eliciting an opinion as to the likelihood of a successful bid before Russell had struggled up from the desk, taken him by the shoulders and more or less propelled him into the corridor before closing the door behind him.

Nor had Tracy Harrison tapped any hidden well of sweetness.

"You will be looking after a Mr. Hugo Russell," Miss Varley, filled with misgivings, had explained. She herself had been introduced by Mowbray after lunch. "He is rather large and you mustn't stare. If he dictates too quickly, or if you don't understand something, ask him to repeat it. He won't bite you."

To Tracy, who normally occupied a corner of Miss Varley's office, any other disposition came as a

deliverance and she had happily supervised the transfer
of her desk to a newly emptied room across the
corridor from Russell. Yet no sooner had Tracy taken
charge of her new domain than Miss Varley arrived
with two workmen and began to alter everything.

"There's a young public relations man arriving
today who will be sharing with you," she explained. She
felt it unnecessary to add that Hugo Russell, on hearing
the original plan, which had called for Simon to share
his office, had threatened to catch the next train back to
London unless his sole occupancy was guaranteed. Two
workmen had appeared, pushing a trolley bearing a
desk dragged up from the basement. With shuffling
steps they eased it past Tracy's desk to where Simon
would work with his back to a window looking down on
the pitched glass roof of the arcade.

"It seems a lot of fuss to me if it's all going to be for
just a few weeks," Tracy said to the workmen when
Miss Varley had disappeared.

"Nobody tells us anything," the older of the two
said without rancour.

"They must know what they're doing," his assistant
added sagely.

"That's not what I said," amended his elder.

Alone in her office, Tracy mused on the unusual
level of activity at Wilberforces. She had already
spotted Russell, now closeted with two of the directors,
and had been impressed not only by his girth but also
by the fact that he merited an office next door to the
chairman. Producing a bright pink lipstick from her
handbag, she began examining her youthful reflection
in the mirror. Her promotion had come as a surprise
and she was prepared to concede that, under normal
circumstances, Mr. Russell would also have merited a
secretary with greater experience. However, thanks to

the fact that one senior secretary was on maternity leave and another on holiday, Miss Varley had been compelled to take the only practical course and, with considerable misgivings, appoint Tracy. Tracy stood up and pouted freshly touched up lips at her reflection. She tugged experimentally at her skirt to see if it could be persuaded further down her thighs to reflect her enhanced seniority, then abandoned the effort and wandered off to fill the kettle in the kitchen. She wondered idly if the young man would be fat, too.

At the end of the afternoon she paused on her way out to look into Russell's office. She had not yet been called on to demonstrate her secretarial skills, he having spent the afternoon in meetings, she having spent it manicuring her nails, but she already felt proprietorially disposed towards him. "Is there anything I can do before I go home, Mr. Russell?" she enquired sweetly.

Russell had his back to her, staring across to the dales that stretched away beyond the shops on the far side of the square. He swung round and looked at her with unengaged eyes. "You could send the painter up on your way out," he commanded, swinging his chair back to the window. "Good night, Miss Harrison."

Tracy's high heels skipped along the tiled corridors and down the stairs. A minute later he heard the hum of the lift and the swoosh of its doors opening. Footsteps approached. There was a cursory tap at the door which was immediately pushed open and Shelmerdine, hand outstretched, advanced towards Russell.

"Shelmerdine," he said, "going to paint your office."

Russell remained in his chair, his nose wrinkling with distaste. He stared at Shelmerdine's paint-streaked hand and thrust his own hands deep into his pockets. Splasher beamed his indifference and sank into the chair facing the desk, his sandy hair standing up in spikes. As he glanced appraisingly around the room he ruffled his hair unconsciously, releasing motes of paint into the still air. "What we need here," he pronounced, "is a touch of the house magnolia..."

"Off-white for the woodwork and a dark green for the walls," Russell said. He folded his arms across his chest and glowered at Shelmerdine.

Splasher shook his head. "Wilberforce jobs are fixed price," he advised solemnly. "If you have anything other than magnolia you'll probably end up paying for it." He stood up and moved towards the door. "It'll be done the minute you leave the building..."

He stopped and watched in amazement as the fat man erupted from his chair. Leaning forward so that the desk groaned under the weight of his stomach, Russell pointed a quivering finger at the carpet imported from Bradburn House. "What..." he began, his face puce as he struggled for words,"...on the carpet...dammit, man, what is it?"

Splasher glanced down and rubbed an exploratory toe at the nearest of the trail of black smears which marked his progress across the carpet before exploding in a chiaroscuro beneath the chair.

Russell exploded in a squeal. "Don't rub the bloody stuff in. What the hell is it?"

Shelmerdine paused at the door. "I can't be certain," he said consideringly, "but it looks as though it might be oil."

Left alone, Russell waddled round the desk and stared savagely at the carpet. His instinct, as usual, was to leave the mess for others to deal with. So, what if the village idiot had ruined some ghastly bloody Wilberforce heirloom? It was hardly his fault. Yet, he brooded, it was unquestionably a valuable carpet, and the fact that it had been ruined in his keeping could hardly be kept from Kettering. Indolence wrestled insecurity as, chest heaving with anger, he stomped across the corridor to the secretary's office. Surely, out here in the boondocks, the girl would have a typewriter and, no doubt, cleaning fluid. His scowl deepened as he flung the door open and saw not a typewriter but the gleaming blank screen of a computer monitor.

It was a tribute to Tracy's urge to serve that, when not involved in manicuring her nails, she had spent part of the idle afternoon buffing every accessible surface until it gleamed. And, if the office gleamed, presumably there must be...

Russell snatched open the top drawer of the desk and rummaged among the contents for dusters. A plastic bottle with a spray top was labelled Screen-Cleaner. Russell squirted it into the air and sniffed at the reassuring smell of solvent. Delving further he came up with a crumpled piece of material. Snorting with distaste he returned to his own office and, clutching at a chair for support, lowered himself to his knees and set to work. Whatever the stains were, they appeared to be less adhesive than he had feared. He had successfully dealt with those under the chair and was attacking the ones leading to the corridor when the communicating door with the Miss Varley's office opened and Mowbray stepped into the room.

"Everything all right? Has Shelmerdine...?" Concluding that the office was empty he stepped further into the room and gave a surprised "Ah!" as Russell heaved himself to his knees and gestured at the stains.

Mowbray regarded them, head on one side. "Shelmerdine?" he suggested.

"Damned man should be locked up," Russell spluttered.

There was a strong smell of solvent and Russell watched as Mowbray sniffed his way towards the source. No longer screwed into a ball, the cleaning cloth now hung from Russell's hand in the unmistakable shape of a pair of panties.

Russell dropped them as though they had become electrified. "I thought..." he began.

"Took 'em for a duster, obviously," Mowbray said, happy to throw the perspiring fat man a lifeline.

"In the girl's drawer..." Russell stuttered.

Mowbray nodded.

"...with this." Russell proffered the bottle of solvent.

Mowbray raised his eyebrows in mimed comprehension.

"I thought..."

"Perfectly natural mistake," Mowbray consoled. "Doing a good job, anyhow..." He retreated in the direction of Miss Varley's office. "Shouldn't really bother, though. Shelmerdine invariably cleans up after himself. Place would have sparkled like a new pin in the morning. Did he suggest magnolia, by the way? Go well with the carpet, I shouldn't wonder." He disappeared towards his own office, mouth twitching.

Crumpling the offending underwear back into a comfortingly unrecognisable shape, Russell lowered himself clumsily on to the knuckles of his free hand and stubbornly renewed his assault on the stains.

* * *

On that first afternoon, after Julia had given him a lift from the station, Simon had dropped his case off at the Fox & Chickens and, following instructions, crossed the bridge and walked up the hill to Bradburn House. After he had been introduced to Mrs. Benson, he and Julia shared a sandwich lunch on the lawn after which they spent the remainder of the afternoon in the sweltering factory where a delighted production director had explained the manufacturing processes to a rewardingly interested Simon. Shortly after five o'clock Julia disappeared to Bradburn House, having promised to call Simon at the pub that evening. Simon, watching her car turn out of the factory car park and on to the main road, decided to wander up to the offices in the hope that he might meet the Hugo Russell that Julia had somewhat guardedly described to him.

Having breasted the tide of office workers leaving the building, he described his mission to Adams who directed him to the office on the second floor. "He's still up there," Adams confirmed gloomily. There had already been intimations that events were afoot that would call for unusual hours and it was not a trend Adams felt should be encouraged. Choosing the stairs rather than the lift, Simon reached the second floor and found himself being drawn towards a powerful smell of solvent. He halted as he approached the door from which the smell appeared to be emanating and was confronted by a globe-shaped backside clad in navy pinstripe which appeared to be performing a slow rumba as it reversed towards the corridor.

"Hello?" Simon said uncertainly.

The motion stopped. A moonlike face, crimson with exertion, turned slowly towards him from a little above carpet level.

"Whatever you do," the fat man snarled, "do not strike a bloody match."

* * *

Simon's mind drifted back to the Defence Team meeting and he glanced round surreptitiously to see whether his abstraction had been noticed. Russell was leaning back in his chair, wheezing after his speech and regarding the meeting from under lowering eyelids. Mowbray had already thanked him and was saying, "We have the opportunity to make our attitude known through the press release Hugo Russell and I drafted a little earlier. If the board agrees, we shall pass it to Palgraves who will cast an eye over it and issue it through their City public relations people." He turned to Miss Varley. "Would you read it to the meeting, please."

Miss Varley consulted her notes, then read, "The board of Wilberforce Original Brassworks has been advised by Pusey Associates, a property company, that Pusey Associates has bought over three per cent of Wilberforce's issued shares. The board of Wilberforce Original Brassworks sees no industrial, financial or commercial logic in any form of association between the two companies. The board strongly recommends Wilberforce shareholders not to sell their shares pending clarification of Pusey Associates' intentions."

Mowbray glanced enquiringly round the table. "Any questions or comments?"

There was a general shaking of heads. Only Pritchard spoke. "Why should Pusey do anything to make his intentions clearer? Why shouldn't he just sit on the shareholding and watch us sweat?"

Russell shrugged. "There's nothing to stop Pusey doing that, but why should he? The longer he delays once his activities become public, the more likely it is that someone else will start running the ruler over you and the next thing he knows he's in a bidding battle."

"I don't understand why the fellow had to 'phone Gerry at all," Temple complained. "Why didn't he just keep on buying until he had a stronger hand?" His expression defied those present to make sense of it.

After a week in the company of Wilberforces and its directors, Russell was still unsure how to respond to Temple's occasional interjections. His first impression had been that Temple was either barking mad or three sheets to the wind half the time, but that had turned out to be no more than his natural airy vagueness. His comments, when they occurred, came as minor eruptions and Russell suspected that they were often as much Temple's way of relieving boredom as a search for enlightenment. Besides which, there was also something menacingly reminiscent of Russell's late father-in-law about the old boy which had a tempering effect on his own ill-nature. As usual, he decided to give a question from the Colonel a measured answer.

"The telephone call was either a courtesy, which I take leave to doubt, or a deliberate piece of effrontery. Tipping a chap out of bed at seven o'clock in the morning to tell him you now own part of his company is a fairly effective way of putting him on the back foot."

Temple's out-thrust lower lip suggested he found Russell's explanation less than satisfactory.

Russell sighed impatiently before launching into a summary of the rules designed to bring an element of diplomacy into takeover battles. Simon followed the thread for a minute or two; then, bored by the blizzard of percentages, dates and formalities this seemed to involve, doodled abstractedly until he gathered the fat man was reaching his peroration. As his attention returned, Russell was saying, "Once they bid, both predator and target must operate within a specific timetable after the bidder has issued what is called the offer document."

Mowbray let the board ponder Russell's summary for a moment, then said, "All we have to do this morning is to agree the statement. That will be issued once we receive formal notification from Pusey of his intentions. Hugo Russell suspects he will have it delivered to Palgraves today. We could probably insist on it being delivered here, to our registered office, but we consider there wouldn't be much point in doing so. Agreed?"

There were nods, raised pencils and indistinct mutterings of support.

Mowbray stood up. "Gentlemen, some of us have a business to run..."

~Chapter 16~

"We are infested with City types. Bradburn looks like Cannon Street at rush hour." Julia was sitting on the edge of Simon's desk where she had waited impatiently for the meeting to finish. Simon squeezed past tanned bare legs and dropped his notepad on the otherwise barren desk.

"It's not surprising," he said. "There are people here from Palgraves, from Ryan & Gilliat and now from the auditors."

Julia nodded. She wandered over to where Simon was standing by the window, saw only the wired glass roof of the arcade below and sank into his chair.

Tracy Harrison entered from the corridor, thrusting the door open with a hip that sent the hem of her short skirt swinging provocatively. She handed Julia a cup of coffee and put down her own mug, pink with white rabbits, next to her computer. Seeing Simon, she blushed prettily and Julia raised a quizzical eyebrow at him.

"I thought you were still in the boardroom." Tracy, young enough to simper without seeming foolish, did so. "I could go and get you a coffee..."

"He can share mine," Julia offered. She handed Simon the cup then cast him a covert glance of alarm.

Tracy had sighed audibly. Her downcast eyes, Julia feared, would be dewy. She took the cup back from Simon and set it down on his desk before ushering him out of the office. "Tracy is smitten," she said as she followed Simon down the stairs. "What is more, I suspect she has me written in as principal rival. Perhaps you should call Rebecca and ask her to come and rescue you."

A stricken look flickered across Simon's face at the mention of his wife's name which Julia affected not to notice. Outside, Buckley, Bradburn's solitary traffic warden, was standing by Julia's car. It was parked unapologetically on a double yellow line in front of the office entrance.

"One of these days it'll get hit by a bus, and then where will you be?" Buckley chastised. Simon climbed into the passenger side while Buckley held the driver's door open for Julia who climbed in with a display of legs considerably longer than Mrs. Buckley's. Buckley hung on to the open door as long as he decently could before closing it with a mournful shake of his head. Julia thanked him with a radiant smile and set off with a jerk that threw Simon back in his seat. The exhaust was making an ugly rasping noise and Julia pulled a face.

"Don't look so smug," she shouted across the crackle of the failing exhaust, "Buckley is merely lecherous, Tracy is probably in love."

Since Julia had appointed herself his official chauffeuse, Simon had found it unnecessary to accept her father's offer of a car. "I shall be your amanuensis, whatever that is," she had volunteered during their first evening together, "Watson to your Holmes."

* * *

That had been the evening Julia had led him not into the smarter of the two bars he had discovered at the Fox & Chickens, but into the smoky, low-beamed taproom where Kitty had added ice to her friend's tonic water with the parsimony of a gourmet dispensing truffle. Isherwood, evidently prepared to absolve Julia of the sins attaching to the rest of the Wilberforce hierarchy, grinned toothlessly while a schizophrenic Spot managed to wag his backside at Julia while fixing Simon with a glare that dared him to move from his stool. Happy and relaxed, Julia had introduced Kitty and Shelmerdine as friends from childhood.

"Simon is helping us with our communications," she had explained to Shelmerdine, a statement that immediately produced a frown. Only when it was explained that he was connected to Hugo Russell only to a slight and unavoidable extent did the frown morph into a welcoming grin.

Although Simon had occasionally shown his face at the office during the following few days, he had spent most of his time with Julia at the reference library in Broadbridge, partly to find out as much as they could about take-overs and mergers ("I suppose one can never know too much," Simon had said artlessly), and partly to avoid Hugo Russell who appeared to believe that Simon had been engaged solely to run his errands. Only when they had exhausted the library staff and established a role for Simon that was clearly independent of Russell had he moved into the office he now shared with Tracy.

To Simon's initial alarm, Mowbray had promptly invited him into his office and given him *carte blanche* on the public relations front. "Just do what has to be done, young man," Mowbray encouraged, beaming at Simon over his glasses, "We'll find you the money."

Which, though profligate, and almost sacrilegious in the mouth of a Yorkshireman ('Scotsmen with the generosity squeezed out,' according to Dr. Price, Bradburn's acerbic Welsh GP), was not quite as profligate as it appeared to Simon.

"The only philosophy to adopt towards the money side of things," Kettering had advised Mowbray at their initial meeting, "is that if you lose a bid, it will be just one more thing to lament, and if you win you will probably reckon that whatever it cost was worth it. Not," he had added disarmingly, "that your shareholders will necessarily agree."

The problem for Simon had been where to start. Though his latest researches had provided him with a positive pharmacopoeia of nostrums, it had been left to Julia to prescribe a stepping off point. It was perfectly clear, she argued, that people were thoroughly confused by the arrival of a multitude of strangers in their midst. "We really must let them know what's happening," she urged, "before rumour takes over completely."

To Simon, in whose mind the results of his researches had lodged as a series of simple maxims, the advice chimed perfectly with that which said, *'Never allow your employees to find out for themselves something you should have told them.'*

"What we want," Julia reasoned, "is a bulletins system...wouldn't you say?"

The first bulletin, signed by Mowbray himself, had a lightning flash piercing the Wilberforce name at its head and asked, *'What's going on?'* It explained in simple terms that, in the current business climate, no company could consider itself entirely safe from predators. Wilberforces, in the interests of its shareholders and employees, had asked its professional advisers to conduct a review of its strengths and weaknesses, and personnel from those advisers would be either based at the offices or visiting them until the exercise was completed. Staff were encouraged to do everything possible to help them. It had concluded with an apology for any inconvenience.

When Simon, recalling that *'Communication is the responsibility of management, not unions – but forget the unions at your peril,'* had proposed briefing the union organisers in the office and factory ahead of the bulletin's general release, Harry Temple had not only acclaimed it as a capital idea but had personally undertaken to conduct the briefings. Informal soundings subsequently conducted in the bar of the Fox & Chickens revealed warm approval of the management's efforts to improve communications and an unvarying vagueness about the content of Temple's message.

* * *

The rasp of Julia's exhaust was converting the car's customary purr into a bad-tempered snarl, rendering conversation almost impossible. To Julia, however, Simon's silence clearly stemmed from other causes. No doubt, she thought, it was prompted by whatever had caused his earlier grimace at the mention of Rebecca. And, although she felt no desire to interfere, her concern gave a slightly brittle edge to her cheeriness as they reached their destination and waited in the printer's dusty office.

Percy Worrall had disappeared into the inky interior of the building to retrieve the work so far done on the layout of *The Works*.

The Works, Simon had explained to Julia, would be the main prong in the print assault on employees' emotions, while bulletins would be reserved for matters of urgency. They had agreed on a four-page tabloid format that would include social news, normally promulgated in the firm's quarterly magazine, alongside business developments. Simon had been particularly proud of the title.

"*The Works* refers to the factory, of course, but it also implies nothing is being held back - we are giving them the works."

"Mmm. . ." Julia had said

As they sipped machine tea from plastic cups, Simon broke his silence and said, "The weekend was a bit of a disaster, I'm afraid..."

Taken unawares, Julia could only manage "Oh?" and hoped the question mark was not too manifest.

"Probably my fault, getting on the 'phone every evening full of beans and twittering on about things that can't mean a thing to Rebecca. I think she's probably finding the children a bit of a handful, too..."

"It must be very difficult for you both," Julia said tactfully.

Simon appeared not to have heard. "I was thinking in the car that there must be something I could do next time I'm home, a surprise of some kind..."

Impetuously, Julia grabbed his hands in hers. "What a lovely idea. You could whisk her off to the theatre, a champagne supper, lots of flowers..."

Simon looked startled. "I was rather thinking of a conjuror..." He broke off as Worrall came in clutching a large rectangle of cardboard to his brown smock.

He set it down on the cluttered desk in what passed as the reception area and stared at it proudly. "This is what we call a paste-up," he explained. "The type is set photographically, then cut out and attached to a layout grid with wax." The fact that the technology was at least a generation old was lost on his customers who watched respectfully as he folded back a protective cover which, to Simon, was indistinguishable from the paper Rebecca had once used in a vain effort to prevent cakes sticking to their tins ("I'd've been as well off with a page from the *Radio Times*," she'd said, as cake tins joined their contents in the pedal-bin). Simon's chest swelled as Worrall revealed the top of what would be the front page of the newspaper.

The masthead, as Simon had learned to call it, said **The Works!** in a bold modern type. Centred underneath, more modest type proclaimed 'News for *all* Wilberforce employees - and that means you!' To the left of the masthead, unearthed from an old sales catalogue by Julia, was a line drawing of one of Wilberforces' early furnaces, complete with graphic swirls of smoke. Below stretched six empty columns whose slim black borders stood ready to guide the editorial layout.

"Now," Percy encouraged, "all we need is something to put in it."

Simon frowned and bit his lower lip. Not prepared to see her colleague put under pressure, Julia intervened. "There's no hurry. At this stage it's simply a matter of being prepared."

Worrall grunted as Simon stared at his handiwork. "I think that strapline is a bit long," Simon pondered, relishing the editorial jargon.

"'...and that means you?'" Julia queried.

Simon nodded.

"A touch Lord Kitchener?"

Simon nodded again. Worrall produced a scalpel from his overall pocket, trimmed off the offending words and stuck them outside the area that would be reproduced; then, lifting the remaining type he centred it beneath the masthead and pressed it securely into place. Julia and Simon exchanged smiles of satisfaction as Worrall replaced the cover and placed the paste-up on top of a plan chest with a litter of similar material.

"You could help by approving Mr. Russell's revised letterhead while you're here," he invited. Rummaging among the clutter, he produced a letter-sized paste-up.

* * *

Hugo Russell suspected that, despite its veneer of utility, his fact-finding mission was no more than a thinly-disguised ploy by Kettering to get him out of the office for the duration. The farce surrounding his arrival in Bradburn had added to the sulphurous discontent seething beneath the pinstripe, and any balm that might have been provided by Mowbray's evident willingness to indulge him in practical matters such as the carpet had done nothing to propitiate him. Even the innocent stacks of Wilberforce stationery provided by Tracy had fuelled his discontent.

"You'd better get me something better than this," he said to Simon when they eventually met in Russell's office.

He was holding a Wilberforce letterhead between finger and thumb as though it concealed an obscene message. "I've indicated on it what I want."

Ignoring the tone of command, Simon mentally rehearsed the maxim concerning house-style. *'House-style,'* it ran, *'is part of corporate identity and represents the uniform of an organisation. It must at all times present a pleasing and coherent picture to its publics, and must be consonant with the reality your organisation represents.'* Simon embraced the philosophy unquestioningly and was quite prepared to do battle with the fat man if his requirements transgressed. Happily, Russell's instructions amounted to not much more than using a higher quality paper;

that, and adding in the left-hand margin, 'From the desk of Hugo Russell.' Simon had taken the design to Worrall, the jobbing printer, and twenty-four hours later Russell had used his new notepaper to pen an abusive letter to Shelmerdine.

Shelmerdine had accepted the letter of complaint philosophically. Mechanics skinned their knuckles, long-distance drivers were afflicted with piles, and painters and decorators received complaints; at least, in his experience they did. Only weeks out of his apprenticeship he had shown himself sympathetic but unmoved when a misdirected scaffolding pole had transformed one of the stained glass windows in Broadbridge's Masonic Lodge into a thousand jewel-like fragments; and, only months before his contretemps with Russell, he had been unflinching in the face of the hysteria provoked when he had spilled a half gallon of magnolia emulsion over the crushed red velvet of Bradburn's council chamber.

Inured as he was to friction, he had kept the tone of his reply to Russell a model of reasonableness: when he had returned to attend to the marks on the carpet they had already been removed; had they not been, he would, of course, have been happy to remove them without charge. Yours, etc...

Tracy had greeted the letter with a shriek that brought colleagues running.

Shelmerdine's letter began, 'Dear Desk'.

* * *

Simon checked the amended paste-up, noting that 'the desk of' had been excised, and handed it to Julia with a straight face.

"Poor desk," Julia said.

A telephone rang. Worrall fumbled for it under a jumble of papers, spoke briefly, then handed it to Simon.

Simon listened for a moment then thanked someone before hanging up.

"That was Tracy. I've got to get back to the office."

"If you feel the urge to say 'Hold the front page,'" Julia advised, "suppress it."

~Chapter 17~

"You can tell me what it's all about later," Julia said as she dropped Simon at the office. "If I don't have this exhaust repaired I shall be arrested."

With the echo of the exhaust racketing in his ears, Simon was up the steps and through the office doors before Adams had a chance to approach them. Tracy was outwardly apologetic, though secretly convinced that she had managed to interrupt a tryst.

"You didn't need to rush. It's just that they've pinched Minnie Emmett's tea trolley to move documents around on. Mr. Mowbray said that, perhaps, if you'd a moment, you could get her a new one from Hargreaves, the ironmonger."

Simon stared out of the window and tried to ignore her staring reflection as she telephoned Hargreaves. As she replaced the receiver Tracy said, "He's got one, but you'll have to go and sign the paperwork." The 'phone rang again. After a brief conversation Tracy hung up, her expression clouded by a pout as she said, "Miss Julia's car's gone into Ibstock's for a new exhaust. She says would you hire a car and pick her up at Bradburn House. Ibstock's giving her a lift back home. I suppose you'd like me to arrange the car?" Taking Simon's assent for granted, she nodded in the direction of

Russell's office across the corridor. "Then I've got a notebook full of stuff to do for him, you know."

Simon nodded understandingly, though gravely doubting what might constitute a full notebook since Russell had been almost permanently welded to the telephone following his early experiences with Tracy's shorthand.

"That girl is dyslexic," he had said spitefully, throwing an unsigned fax message on to Simon's desk.

Simon had read it through carefully, finding little to fault other than what just might have been a trace of lipstick in one corner.

"There man, there," Russell had shouted, stabbing a fat finger at the opening paragraph. "I said 'all most.'"

Simon looked again. The fax was clearly acknowledging one Russell had received from a city contact and began, 'Thank you for the information about the opposition. It was almost useful.'

That, and having put milk in his Lapsong Souchong tea, had reduced Tracy in Russell's eyes to the status of messenger.

"If you'd tell me how to go about it..." Simon began.

"You go and get your trolley," Tracy said, forcing a weak smile. "I'll see what I can do."

Outside, Simon strolled through the mingled smells of the arcade to the ironmongers in the street below. Hargreaves, whose usual mien was that of an undertaker with acute depression, led him into the cramped storeroom at the back of the shop. There he produced a trolley so similar to Minnie Emmett's original that, although Hargreaves claimed to discern numerous superior features, it might have been designed specifically to replace it. Having signed for it and arranged to have it delivered to the office that afternoon, Simon was about to leave when Hargreaves summoned him back for the complex clerical process that accompanied the release of even the smallest item from his inventory.

It had never been Hargreaves' intention to cast a pall over the rest of Simon's day. All he said, though somewhat lugubriously, was, "The arrangements for Sunday are all in hand, I take it?" after which he had carried on, peering over his glasses occasionally as he pencilled delivery instructions on to a tie-on label destined for the handle of the trolley.

At first Simon simply looked blank; then, as he recalled what Sunday would bring, his face fell.

The Great Chimney Cleaning Debate, as it deserved to be called, had rumbled along ever since Kitty had explained its niceties to Pusey; though why he, Simon, had finished up as Shelmerdine's lieutenant he, Simon, was at a loss to understand. After all, many of those aligned behind Shelmerdine's bucket of gravel theory were supporters of much longer standing.

Julia had enlightened him. "It's one thing to support Shelmerdine's views at what might flatteringly be called the philosophical level," she had explained, "but quite another to become directly involved with someone who has been disaster-prone since birth. The others were familiar with Shelmerdine's record, you were not. *Ergo*, you are it."

Simon stared blankly at the window display of hardware and gardening tools, mentally ticking off the preparations he had so far made on behalf of his champion. The date had been agreed, as Hargreaves had heedlessly reminded him, as had the time. The place had been practically self-selecting insofar as it was the only currently vacant cottage in Bradburn with open fireplaces, and there had been no dispute about the permissible equipment as that had been the origin of the whole debate. To Shelmerdine's disgust, his supporters had conceded to the Gibson camp that the brush and rods method of chimney cleaning, whose superiority they vaunted, had nothing to prove. All that was necessary was for their champion to demonstrate that, in the eyes of a reasonable man, an equally effective job could be performed by a bucket of gravel tipped down the appropriate chimney.

The reasonable man had been as self-selecting as the cottage. Hargreaves, it was agreed, was not merely reasonable but a veritable stickler. Indeed, at heart Hargreaves was not an ironmonger at all. Until he had retired in order to take over the shop from his late father-in-law, Hargreaves had been a railwayman. As such his reputation for impartiality had been forged at the elemental level, a point that had been well made at his retirement dinner. Who, the regional director had enquired rhetorically, could favour Summer over Winter, when one buckled his lines and the other froze his points; or Spring over Autumn, when one washed away his ballast and the other shrouded his lines in leaves? There had been much along the same lines, and Hargreaves had nodded serene agreement throughout, his attention diverting only occasionally to consult a watch he kept producing from his waistcoat pocket, a habit of long standing. Although this had the accidentally benign effect of curtailing the regional directors' speech by several minutes, to those who knew Hargreaves it was no more than a nervous tic, a consequence of years devoted to the demands of railway timetables.

Hargreaves' impartiality, Simon noted, even extended to the man's appearance. His clothes were neither brown nor blue nor striped nor checked, but something indefinably subfusc. Even his parting refused to take sides, being an undeviating cleft down the middle of his scalp in a style unknown elsewhere in Bradburn outside the sepia prints of family albums.

"We're meeting on Friday night to run over the details," Simon said, his heart sinking further at the thought. Considerable sums of money had been wagered on the outcome, and the meeting had been called by a Gibson contingent which, detecting an increasing glumness in Shelmerdine as the event approached, had begun to fear an apostasy.

Arrangements for despatch of the trolley completed, Simon returned to the office to find that Tracy, having drawn a blank with the car hire companies, had excelled herself by telephoning Ibstock's garage and arranging to borrow the battered Volkswagen Dipstick liked to call his courtesy car.

"I don't suppose Miss Julia would have thought of that," she said huffily.

* * *

"Are you absolutely sure it will be alright for Julia?" Ibstock inquired doubtfully. He and Simon were staring at a battered blue Beetle that had unquestionably seen better days.

Hugo Russell's Jaguar, its side taped with newspaper as one wing awaited a re-spray, stood forlornly at the back of the garage.

"Waiting for wheel bearings," Dipstick had explained. Dipstick was not simply tall, a fitting attribute in one of Bradburn's opening bowlers, but etiolated and with a pallor reputed to result from having grown up in the acetylene glare of his father's garage. Without stretching, he lifted a cardboard box off a shelf even Simon would have strained to reach and drew out a plastic bag. "Maybe you could give Russell this. It's his cigars and a handful of coins that were knocking about inside. And this..." He brought out a magazine and handed it so Simon who threw it in the rear of the Volkswagen together with the plastic bag.

Offering Ibstock guarded thanks for the loan of the car, Simon set off through the town, head hunched into his shoulders to avoid banging against the headlining.

* * *

"It is quite the most stupid thing I have ever heard of, even for Shelmerdine."

Kitty and Julia shared a low settee in the morning room of Bradburn House as they waited for Simon to arrive with the car. Julia reached for the coffee pot and china clinked as she used it to top up their cups.

"It would be tempting to say boys will be boys, if they weren't all grown men," Julia agreed. "Still," she said comfortingly, "it will all be over by Sunday."

Kitty munched a biscuit and refused to be comforted. "I find myself wanting to say, 'No good will come of it, you mark my words', like some dreadful old crone."

The ring of the doorbell was followed by the slip-slap of slippers as Mrs. Benson crossed the hall. The two gathered their things together and went into the hall where Simon was dangling car keys on the end of a piece of oily string.

"Dipstick's courtesy car," he announced. "There were no hire cars, so Tracy extemporised."

Julia stared past him at the battered blue car at the foot of the steps. "It will smell of sheep," she declared. "I know it; it belonged to a farmer at the head of the dale."

The women wrinkled their noses theatrically as Simon handed Julia the keys and they clambered in, Kitty in the back, Simon in the front where he struggled to find room for his legs. Finding herself sitting on a magazine, Kitty withdrew it and flicked idly through it as Julia started the car. Almost immediately Kitty found herself staring at the 'not-so-choosy Mervyn Pusey' Mowbray had encountered on the train. She leaned over the back of Simon's seat, holding the magazine so that he could see it.

"What do you know," she said. "It looks as though my Mr. Adams is your Mr. Pusey."

* * *

The misfortunes of Pusey-as-Adams at the Fox & Chickens were now as much a part of Bradburn gossip as Russell's less than triumphal entry on the back of Ellingham's tractor, so Simon's assertion that Adams and Pusey were one and the same required no elaboration when he produced the magazine at a meeting with Mowbray and Russell in the chairman's office.

Russell, reunited with his favourite cigars, lit one and stared at the picture through clouds of blue smoke then pushed the magazine across to Mowbray who nodded in recognition. It was the magazine he had discarded on the train to London.

"I suppose this puts a slightly different complexion on things," Russell said grudgingly. "That's assuming this Kitty woman is right and that Pusey has already been here."

"Kitty was certain," Simon assured them.

Russell ignored him. "If Pusey's taken the trouble to come and look at your assets on the ground, we can be more or less certain that, whatever he might say publicly, he's going to bid."

Mowbray looked suitably glum. Russell stared out of the window and wrestled with his waistcoat where it had ridden up over the mound of his stomach. It was his habit, when required to think deeply, to distend his cheeks as though to blow out and then leave them inflated. He did so now, then turned back into to the room and exhaled a vast cloud of smoke to envelop Simon. "The implication for us is that we must now act as though an offer is likely," he said. "Under the City Code that means we mustn't dispose of assets or issue shares without shareholder approval. The rules are broader than that," he added dismissively, "but that's the gist."

"Perhaps we'd better wait and see what he says in his letter," Mowbray said, consulting his watch. "It's a little past noon and he said the letter would be at your London office this morning."

"They'll fax it up the minute it arrives," Russell said. He heaved himself out of his chair as Tracy entered. He snatched the paper she was carrying and glanced at it quickly before handing it to Mowbray.

"This is it. Usual stuff. No hostile intent...happy to meet for talks...hopes to be able to bring something to the party. . . all the usual tripe."

Mowbray accepted the facsimile letter with distaste. He read it slowly through his half-glasses then passed it to Simon. "Copies to all directors and advisers, I think Simon. If you wouldn't mind asking Miss Varley..."

Simon went through the connecting door and spoke to Miss Varley. As he returned Russell was saying, "We'll have our London PR outfit put out the response we agreed this morning." He sniffed.

Brightlings, it was widely acknowledged, were aristocrats among City public relations consultancies and it pleased Russell to belittle them. Simon's contact with them had so far been confined to a telephone conversation in which they, having been informed of his existence by Kettering, had politely outlined their credentials and reeled off a list of Blue Chip clients that appeared to comprise most of the FTSE 100. If they were simply a PR outfit, Simon told himself, then the Imperial State Crown was a hat. The fact that they employed double-barrelled young men and exquisite young women whose lethal poise commanded City editors and company chairmen alike inevitably made Russell feel bumbling and incompetent, hence his bile.

"What now, then?" Mowbray prompted.

"Pusey will almost certainly be buying quietly until he reaches the point where he's required to inform the Stock Exchange," Russell responded. "Our press notice will let the market know something's happening, but he won't be anxious to confirm his intentions until he's absolutely got to."

"Why is that?" Simon had long ago demonstrated such complete indifference to Russell's snubs that his interruption produced no more than an impatient sigh.

"People will be watching to see what he's up to. He won't want anyone else piling in and pushing the share price up. In the meantime," Russell said to Mowbray, as though he, and not Simon, had asked the question, "it would help if we could get your share price up a point or two. Pusey is not renowned for paying over the odds."

He picked up a copy of *The Yorkshire Post* from Mowbray's desk and scowled at a Wilberforce share price that had returned to stubborn immobility.

* * *

Elsewhere in Bradburn, other eyes gleamed as they scoured a copy of the paper until they located an entry in the personal column.

* * *

In the City, Pusey's brokers concentrated on picking up Wilberforce shares, finding them in tens of thousands and in penny numbers. Conscious that, should their client decide to bid, he would be required to do so at the highest price he had paid in the run-up, they backed off occasionally. But slowly, day by painstaking day, they brought the Pusey holding to within a whisker of the point at which the City's inflexible rules would compel them to call a halt for a week.

~Chapter 18~

Roger Spofforth slumped on his customary stool in the crowded taproom bar as The Great Chimney Cleaning Debate eddied around him. Externally he was his customary bespectacled if somewhat dishevelled self; internally, his thoughts swirled in a mind unbuttoned by a burden imposed on him by the Reverend Norman Butterworth only that afternoon. Having spent a week's beer allowance in an hour and a half in an attempt to drown his depression, it was beginning to appear to him that the regulars were being deliberately unintelligible. That, or he had been afflicted with a sudden hearing impairment. To those observing him, the diagnosis was less charitable.

"Spofforth's as drunk as a rat," Dipstick observed to Simon.

Shelmerdine, to whom Spofforth's study of dialect and comparative phonetics was but a pale disguise for sociology, said simply, "It's probably a cry for help."

"Sorroffancleanyerchimbles," Spofforth advised, then disappeared from view as Simon stood in front of him and called for silence.

Keeping an eye on the ferrety Gibson, Simon said, "Gibson and I have now confirmed everything. We meet at half-past-ten on Sunday morning by the Corn Exchange. We will go straight to Percy's cottage, where

Splasher can use one bucket of gravel of any size he can handle without assistance once he's on the roof. Len Hargreaves will judge."

Hargreaves, on the edge of the throng, checked his watch and gave an impartial nod.

Sunday morning had been Shelmerdine's choice. As he had explained to Simon, all right-thinking people would be in church and the number of witnesses to what he was now glumly convinced would be a catastrophe would therefore be reduced. In a flash of candour, he confessed, "My problem is that I sometimes speak without thinking," before concluding in tortured metaphor, "and then my sacred cows come home to roost."

Glancing at Gibson and his seconds, Simon received a smirking nod of confirmation.

Behind the bar, Kitty polished a glass with angry rubbing motions. "You all want your heads looking at," she said disgustedly.

* * *

Sunday morning was balmily cloudless. Those straggling to church under a cerulean sky cast curious glances at the small crowd assembling outside the Corn Exchange. Behind his parishioners, and at the last minute as usual, the Reverend Norman Butterworth gave an even-handed wave as he scanned the faces for defaulters from his morning service.

Simon stood with Joe Bywater whose builders' yard had provided the equipment Gibson was now auditing, probing suspiciously at the contents of the handcart. Shelmerdine, attempting unsuccessfully to look unconcerned, stood with a foot on the bottom rung of a ladder that leaned against the Corn Exchange wall. He looked up fretfully at a powerful whirring of wings as a flock of pigeons swooped out of the sky and dipped low over the crowd, his eyes following them enviously as they disappeared over the Silver Library. When his attention returned to the handcart it was with all the enthusiasm of Louis XVI contemplating the tumbrel. Hargreaves, having consulted his watch, joined the others and poked among the ropes, hooks and pulleys assembled there. Failing in his attempt to penetrate the mass of gravel in the bucket, he eventually pronounced himself satisfied.

The crowd fell silent as he raised a hand.

"The time is almost ten-thirty, gentlemen," he announced, watch in hand. "We leave in precisely twelve-eleven-ten seconds from now." He slipped his watch back into a waistcoat pocket and patted the bulge to confirm its safe arrival.

For Simon, events could not be over quickly enough. At his signal Splasher and Bywater manhandled the ladder on to the handcart and, taking, the T-shaped handle between them, trundled off in the direction of the bandstand. Behind them Gibson and his supporters chattered noisily as the procession straggled past the bandstand and approached the terrace of low stone cottages. Reaching Percy Frobisher's cottage, Shelmerdine lowered the handcart and, hands on hips, stared at it unenthusiastically. It was one of a terrace of eight separated from the road by low stone walls and each with a small patch of garden. Between each pair was a narrow passage, known locally as an entry, leading through to the back gardens. Extending his arms, Shelmerdine pressed his thumb tips together and affected to regard Frobisher's chimneys through a frame made by his elevated forefingers. His supporters chuckled.

"We'll do it from round the back," he pronounced. "Someone give Bywater a lift through with that ladder."

Eager hands took one end of the ladder, propelling
Bywater down the narrow entry and into the back
garden. The cottage gardens were long and narrow,
backing on to fields that sloped up to hills divided into
seemingly careless shapes by low stone walls. Percy's
garden boasted a neat patch of lawn near the house,
then a vegetable patch leading to a hen run whose
inhabitants cocked their heads and clucked their
agitation at the sudden intrusion. A cockerel appeared
from the open door of a wooden shed. Throwing back
its head it issued a cock-a-doodle-doo that elicited a
faint reply from the other end of the village.

Shelmerdine glowered at it and moved to join
Simon nearer the house. "There's people still in bed,"
he said.

"An' tha'd be one on 'em if tha'd any sense,"
Bywater added.

The crowd had begun breaking up into groups
beginning to detach themselves as they sought vantage
points around the garden. Simon and an increasingly
edgy Shelmerdine grasped the ladder and carefully
extended it until it came to rest on the rough stonework
between the cottage's two upstairs windows. When they
were satisfied, Joe Bywater fumbled in a waistcoat
pocket and produced an old-fashioned key which he
used to unlock the back door.

"Everyone else stay outside," he warned. "I'm
responsible for this place while Percy's off. 'Ere."
Grabbing Shelmerdine's sleeve, he nudged him in the
direction of the kitchen before sliding the bolt across
the door behind them. "I 'ope tha knows what the 'eck
tha's doin'," he hissed. "Perce'll 'ave another flamin'
'eart attack if 'e gets word o' this."

It was later accepted that, had Percy not so
conveniently been carted off to hospital, the Great

Chimney Cleaning Debate might never have reached its sorry conclusion. Being of reasonably sound mind, no-one in either faction had been prepared to offer up their own home for the experiment; and Shelmerdine's home, a rented all-electric cottage, lacked the very chimneys around which the issue revolved. Percy's cottage, on the other hand, had coal fires. The topography of the cottage was common to many of those in Bradburn and Splasher followed Bywater straight ahead out of the kitchen, along the narrow hall and through a door on his left into the front parlour. He picked his way through the cluttered furniture and drew the curtains to exclude the grinning children's faces pressed against the window. As Bywater turned on the overhead light, Splasher produced and unfolded the dust sheet he had been carrying.

They worked in silence, clearing the mantelpiece of ornaments and photographs then taping the sheet to the cast iron shelf and its tiled surround with masking tape provided by Dipstick. When the last of the tape had been used to seal the sheet to the stone-flagged hearth, Shelmerdine stepped back and studied the drum-taut screen that now separated the grate from the rest of the room.

Bywater joined him, shaking his head. "Tha' could show films on that," he conceded admiringly.

Splasher, his confidence rising, slapped him on the back. "You stay here and lock the back door after me," he coaxed, "and we'll show that lot what a bucket of gravel can do in the hands of a master."

Outside again, and affecting the aplomb of Blondini, Shelmerdine approached the ladder and bounced up and down a few times on the bottom rung. Once the feet were embedded securely in the lawn, and shielding his eyes against the bright blue of the sky, he peered up to where a rope ran through a pulley secured to the top rung. From there the rope looped back down to ground level where Simon had tied it to the handle of the bucket of gravel. Shelmerdine twitched the free end of the rope so that it rattled the bucket's handle then handed it ceremoniously to Simon, now poised alongside with his free hand supporting the ladder.

"Don't pull until I give the word," Shelmerdine cautioned, "and then bring it up nice and slow to just below the pulley."

Slowly, with the crowd murmuring below, he began to mount the ladder. As his head reached the level of the gutter he was distracted by movement in the neighbouring garden. He glanced across and scowled at the sight of the bloated Hugo Russell peering suspiciously up at him from the garden of Old Taylor's cottage next door. Russell, eyes narrowed, was dabbing at his mouth with a napkin. Having breakfasted handsomely, he had been just about to settle down with the Sunday papers when he had been drawn to investigate the growing hubbub in the garden of the neighbouring cottage. Seeing Shelmerdine, he shook his head wearily and retreated into the house and its mingling aromas of grilled ham and coffee.

Waving derisively at the retreating back, Shelmerdine continued up the ladder and stepped confidently on to the roof.

Pale green patches of lichen which patterned the thin stone slabs of the roof crumbled to dust under his boots as, crouching perilously above the gutter, he signalled to Simon to begin raising the bucket. Simon began to draw slowly on the rope. The crowd grew silent. Splasher, hand hovering, watched the approaching bucket then swiftly grabbed it and set it down on the roof beside him. Slowly, he undid the rope and held it aloft for a moment before releasing it to snake back down to Simon.

Rubbing his hands together like a weightlifter approaching a snatch and grab, he gripped the handle of the bucket in both hands and began a crab-wise ascent up the shallow slope of the roof to where the stack and its array of chimneys beckoned. As his head appeared above the roofline there were cheers from a crowd across the street and Splasher spotted a leering Gibson at the front. Next to him stood Hargreaves, his face a picture of calm impartiality. Kitty, instantly identifiable by her coppery curls, had evidently had second thoughts about boycotting the event and was standing towards the back of the group. Using one hand to balance the bucket on the ridge of the roof, Shelmerdine directed a wave at her which she affected not to notice. Instead, she turned away and began to talk to a neighbour. Splasher sighed. Gripping the bucket with both hands once again he edged along the ridge towards the stack of chimneys. The crowd's murmuring became a communal intake of breath then gave way to snorts of laughter as, momentarily, his foot slipped on a patch of moss and sent him heading for the stack at an undignified canter. The powerful counterweight of the bucket turned his progress into a slow motion dance as he finished up red-faced and panting and hanging on to nearest of the eight chimneys for support. At which stage he paused. His expression, which had been switching between bravura smile and concerned grimace, became one of complete puzzlement.

As he clung on to the chimney, it dawned on him that he had not the faintest idea which of the eight belonged to Percy Frobisher's front parlour.

* * *

It was a peculiarity of many of Bradburn's early nineteenth century cottages that the relationship between the chimneys above and the fireplaces below was either random or so perversely conceived as to defy analysis. That each cottage had four fireplaces, serving kitchen, parlour and two bedrooms, was acknowledged. Yet generations of chimneysweeps had observed that a brush inserted into fireplace A would emerge from a chimney that logic dictated should have belonged to fireplace B. As this had not detracted in the least from the efficiency of chimney sweeping operations, nor remotely concerned the occupants of the affected cottages, it had been filed with that body of knowledge that informs without enlightening.

But, as Shelmerdine was repeatedly to say once the soot had settled, *some*one should have bloody well told *him*; while Gibson, eager to capitalise on Shelmerdine's discomfiture, claimed that he had known all along until, finding it won him no friends, found it wiser to desist.

* * *

Briefly, Splasher considered whispering down each of the eight chimneys until it evoked a response from Joe Bywater, but a discernible increase in the crowd's volume suggested that the time for niceties was past. Besides, come what may, the exercise had to conclude with some degree of aplomb if victory over Gibson was to be achieved with any degree of distinction.

And the crowd's earlier stillness was now beginning to betray a flutter of restlessness.

The chimney on the front corner of the stack, squarely over Percy's parlour, beckoned. Easing himself towards it, Shelmerdine raised the bucket to the crowd and paused for a moment. Then, lifting the bucket until its rim rested against that of the chimney, he uttered a silent prayer, inverted the bucket and shot fifty-six pounds of half-inch gravel down the chimney's sooty throat.

* * *

"Ready when you are."

Joe Bywater's voice floated up from the chimney immediately to its right. The spasm that hit Shelmerdine like an electric shock almost made him lose his footing. Fighting to retain some sort of composure, he lowered his head to the chimney that had given voice and addressed Bywater in a strangled whisper.

"How do you mean, 'Ready when you are'? I've already tipped it." He broke off as soot got into his nostrils, forcing him to withdraw his head in order to sneeze.

The crowd, sensing a richer drama, had become ominously silent.

Bywater's voice drifted stolidly up from the chimney. "There's nowt come down 'ere, I'd've 'eard it."

"Look behind the bloody cloth then," Shelmerdine hissed.

Ripping noises followed as Bywater peeled the tape away.

"Nowt," he confirmed more loudly. "Tha sure tha's done it?"

Splasher, sooty faced streaked with runnels of sweat, became conscious of a wave of sound from the front of the cottage. Screams mingled with great barks of laughter.

Then the noise died.

It was the abrupt change from hilarity to stunned silence that might greet a clown's despairing fall from the highwire.

Led by a grim-faced Kitty, people were streaming
not towards Percy's cottage but to its neighbour.
Sensing the commotion, those in the back garden
fought their way out on to the road to swell the
converging crowd. Shelmerdine took in the sight below
and felt a chill he subsequently found himself quite
incapable of adequately describing. Something like
being wracked with 'flu while marooned on drifting
pack ice was as near as he ever got. But, as he readily
admitted, that hardly began to do it justice.

* * *

There were a number of reasons for the delay that
punctuated the release of the gravel and the stunned
silence of the spectators, though these were connected.

Firstly, Hugo Russell, having breakfasted hugely,
had been once more deeply immersed in the Sunday
papers when the gravel was tipped. Secondly, he had
spent uncomprehending moments rooted to his chair
as a heart-stopping roaring from behind the chimney
breast became an almighty whoomph as the soot hit the
fireplace and shot across the hearth to envelop him in a
reeking black cloud. And, finally, he had found
considerable difficulty in locating the front door
through soot-blackened spectacles he was reluctant to
remove for fear of what that might reveal.

A crowd which had threatened to become
hysterical at his first appearance was now shrouded in
a guilty silence provoked by Russell's blind
helplessness as he stood forlornly outside the cottage.

Momentarily marooned at the back of the
neighbouring house, Shelmerdine knew instinctively
that the sudden silence, whatever its cause, meant that
there was a good chance the tide in his affairs had
taken a distinct turn in the direction of what the Bard,

with whose work he was only dimly acquainted, had niftily identified as life's shallows and miseries.

By the time he had slid down the roof on his backside then shot down the ladder on trembling legs, the silence had achieved an intensity that scourged. His last sight of the street below had shown Kitty, skirts flying, borrowed handkerchief in hand, outpacing the crowd as she dashed towards the neighbouring cottage. He lingered for a moment in the now deserted garden before heading through the entry and into the street with the enthusiasm of a Christian emerging into the Coliseum. An accusing murmur enveloped him as he made his way through the crowd to where a concerned Simon was assisting Kitty as she ministered to the blackened and thoroughly subdued Russell.

Kitty had removed Russell's glasses and was wiping them clean on the borrowed handkerchief. Russell continued to regard his predicament with an air of stunned incomprehension. He gazed around short-sightedly until Kitty handed him the hastily cleaned spectacles; then, calmly slipping them over his ears, he continued to look around him with owl-like indifference. At last, and without a flicker of recognition, his eyes came to rest on a crimson-faced Shelmerdine.

"I'm..." Shelmerdine began, then broke off, aware that nothing he was likely to say would be remotely adequate.

Kitty's eyes were hard as emeralds. "I'll tell you what you'll do," she said, her voice trembling. "You will find your stupid friends and you will clean this cottage until it sparkles. Before that, you will rescue some clean clothes from in there and bring them to the pub where this gentleman will probably spend the next hour under a shower."

Fixing Shelmerdine with a glance that did nothing for nerves already frazzled, she took Russell's sooty arm and led him unresisting along the footpath towards the sanctuary of the Fox & Chickens. Gibson, attended by a handful of gleeful supporters, took a step backwards as Shelmerdine walked menacingly towards him.

"One of your lot find Hargreaves," Splasher said. "He's still got the judging to do."

~Chapter 19~

One of the many frustrating aspects for those compelled to do business on Mervyn Pusey's behalf was his unpredictability. It was, City wags maintained, his only consistent quality. Equally annoying was his impetuosity, which meant that decisions he arrived at on Saturday could not rest until Monday. As a result, his merchant banker, having retired to his home for the weekend with the intention of doing nothing much before getting out his golf clubs and toddling over to Wentworth, found himself instead on the other end of the telephone from a Pusey with a decision to communicate.

"I've decided to go for an immediate bid," Pusey said without preamble. "I don't like having Palgraves against us and this should catch them on the hop."

There was a pause as the banker pursed his lips and considered the implications. His firm had bought wisely and well to bring his client within sniffing distance of the holding that would trigger rules delaying a dawn raid, a possibility that was top of the agenda for a meeting planned for the following Monday. If adopted, it would involve Pusey's team in snapping up parcels of Wilberforce shares before dealers could recognise what was happening and therefor hold out for a higher price. Instead, his client was now proposing to approach the target company direct, thrusting both predator and target into the timetable within which City rules required bids to be concluded.

"Are you sure this is wise?" the banker queried diffidently. "The shares have come in quite nicely without putting 'em up more than a couple of pips."

"I've already decided," Pusey said irritably. "Just get on with whatever you need to do."

* * *

Mowbray had already breakfasted and was beginning his morning wander in the garden when Mrs. Benson answered Pusey's telephone call. By Mowbray's side was Pritchard, the marketing director, who had already cast a gloom over the day by arriving at the house at the crack of dawn to subject Mowbray to what appeared to be a third degree aimed at plumbing his chairman's innermost thoughts concerning a bid. Easily holding his counsel, Mowbray privately dismissed the younger man's anxiety as a sign of his insecurity and abandoned him to the fragrance of the rose arbour as he went back into the house through the French doors and took the call in his study.

Pusey's voice was unpleasantly clear across the two hundred miles. Without preamble he stated his name then said, "I've decided to bid for your whole company. I'm sure we can agree a take-out price that will see you people alright, and I suggest you now leave the details to your advisers."

It was not true that hearts sank, Mowbray discovered. What appeared to happen was that they gave a sort of lurch before apparently trying to fight their way out of the chest, leaving those afflicted with the sensation that they had been smitten behind the ear by a sockful of wet sand. He allowed a second or two to elapse before responding.

"In your letter you denied any hostile intent," he said, wishing he could have thought of something more forceful.

"There will be no hostility...if you accept." Pusey allowed his words to hang between them for a moment, then added, "We'll be making a formal announcement today, unless we hear by noon that the bid will be unopposed. Think about it."

There was an impatient click as the receiver was replaced.

Pritchard had not been prepared to be abandoned and had followed him indoors where he now hovered at Mowbray's elbow, eyebrows raised in enquiry. Ignoring him, Mowbray picked up the handset once more and dialled Kettering. The adviser appeared unperturbed by the development. Agreeing that they would speak later that morning, Mowbray set off to walk to the office, declining Pritchard's offer of a lift.

"Please round up the defence team as quickly as you can," he instructed Miss Varley. "Meeting in the boardroom at nine."

"Mr. Russell will be in already," Miss Varley said, "he's rather an early starter." But when Mowbray looked into Russell's office, it was empty.

At Bradburn House, Pritchard sat in his car and wondered about the future.

* * *

While it is generally acknowledged that medical receptionists vary only in terms of their winsomeness and affection for humanity, it was widely accepted in Bradburn that Dr. Price's receptionist was definitely at the lower end of the scale. But her natural venom paled into insignificance when compared with that of her

employer on a Monday morning. Dr Price's natural
acerbity, having been honed to a fine point after forty-
eight hours in the company of his wife, required an
outlet. The fact was not lost on his regular patients so
that the pole position of Monday's eight-thirty
appointment tended to be shunned other than by those
either at death's door or with a secret longing for
abasement. Price was aware of his reputation and
content with an arrangement that usually allowed a
relatively contemplative introduction to the working
week. When tradition was breached by the arrival of
the fat man on the stroke of eight-thirty, it earned his
receptionist such a peppery response that it was almost
noon before she had worked it off on the rest of the
morning's patients.

Physically, Price was the antithesis of Russell.
Small and neat and with a fiery Welsh intentness, the
eyes with which he now regarded his patient were so
dark as to be almost black. His thinning black hair,
brushed sideways across his scalp, remained plastered
in place as he lowered his eyes to his desk and used a
paper-knife to prod a pill along the scuffed leather.
Russell, lethargic, a metronomic tic affecting his right
eye, watched as the pill rolled over the edge and landed
with a ping in the wastepaper bin.

"So, you've lain awake all night listening to your
heart beat, Mr. Russell..." Thirty years in Yorkshire had
done little to modify the Welsh intonation.

Russell, confused and glum, could only manage a
nod.

"And you find that worrying rather than
reassuring?"

Again, Russell nodded.

"Worried that it might stop, perhaps?"

"I was afraid, at the time..." Russell broke off, his voice listless, his glum expression deepening. The night sweats, the pounding heart, the sensation that life was about to be snatched away, seemed fanciful in the antiseptic atmosphere of the small surgery.

"'The days of our years are threescore years and ten,'" intoned Dr. Price, a Bethesda Chapel man, "'and if by reason of strength they be fourscore years, yet is their strength labour and sorrow, for it is soon cut off, and we fly away.'"

Russell, who had woken red-eyed, mouth rank with the taste of soot and with barely the strength to walk, let alone fly away, stared miserably ahead.

"Full of solace, the Psalms, Mr. Russell. You should read them."

Though Bradburn had long ago ceased to be a village in the quaintly rural sense, it retained many of a village's characteristics. Not least among these was the speed at which news flew among its citizens, and the sheer bulk of Russell would have instantly made his arrival a news item. However, allied to an entry made on Ted Ellingham's tractor, allied to Tracy's unshakeable conviction that the theft of the panties from her drawer revealed a deviant underwear fetish, all allied to the previous day's activities at Percy Frobisher's cottage, meant that Russell's fortunes had achieved a notoriety that had reached the ears even of the aloof Dr. Price. And it was not surprising, Price noted from below lowered lids, that the fat man appeared to be suffering a degree of deflation. There appeared to be a looseness about the clothing, despite the man's remaining girth, that suggested his misfortunes were beginning to take their toll.

Briskly, he took Russell's pulse and blood pressure, shone lights in his eyes and ears, peered down his cavernous throat and then, with practised skill, drew from him a halting recital of his travails since arriving at Bradburn. Finally, Price put his pen down alongside his notes and leaned loweringly across the desk as though to peer into his patient's soul.

"And what, in your opinion, is called for here, Mr. Russell? A holiday, perhaps? A break from whatever you people are getting up to at Wilberforces?"

Russell's spirit flared briefly. "Out of the question, I'm afraid," he blustered, then subsided beneath the hypnotic stare.

"Well?" Price's eyes bored into him.

"I thought, perhaps, pills of some kind..."

Price gave the mildly surprised nod of a teacher pleased by a backward pupil. "A boon to my profession," he enthused. "Perhaps we can start with something to get some of that weight off."

Russell stared miserably over the doctor's shoulder and Price relented. "Your basic problem, Mr. Russell, is anxiety and depression, though not necessarily in that order. In view of your recent history, I can't say that I'm surprised." He pulled a prescription pad towards him and began to write. "There's something here to help you relax, and something to help with the weight. You will, if you want to get within bun-throwing distance of the psalmist's threescore years and ten, start to lose some of that weight. Good morning."

Meekly, Russell took the proffered piece of paper and, avoiding the fierce Welsh eyes, made his ponderous way past the admiring stares of the feebler spirits in the waiting room and out into the sunlit street.

~Chapter 20~

The board and its advisers were assembling and Mowbray was looking even more than usually preoccupied as he approached Simon and took him to one side.

"Hugo Russell's not here," he said quietly. "I gather from Julia that he was involved in some sort of contretemps yesterday - covered in soot, Julia said."

"Good for the onions, soot; got to be weathered, though," Colonel Temple offered as he strolled towards his regular place.

Mowbray kept his eyes on Simon's face. "If you wouldn't mind, I think you should pop across to the cottage and see how he is."

* * *

Prompted by Julia, Simon had already been.

* * *

Having spent most of the Sunday afternoon with the fatigue squad Kitty had pressed into restoring the cottage, and having seen a strangely quiescent Russell reinstalled, Old Taylor's cottage was now firmly at the head of the list of places Simon would have preferred never to have to see again. Julia, however, had returned from a visit to an aunt elsewhere in the county to learn from Kitty what had happened. She had telephoned

Simon that evening and insisted that he call on Russell early the next morning to ensure he hadn't decamped.

"Kitty's told me all about it," she said neutrally. "I know he acts like a wretched fat bully, but he is here to help and we owe it to Wilberforces to see that he isn't driven away."

Dutifully, and reluctantly resigned to being the lightning conductor for what would no doubt be Russell's considerable wrath, Simon had called at the cottage shortly after eight on the Monday morning. It had been deserted. At first, knocking firmly on the front door, his mind had struggled for suitably apologetic phrases. "I'm terribly sorry about what happened yesterday," would be both true and conciliatory, but might imply an excess of complicity. "I can't imagine what people thought they were up to," would be distancing but also traitorous. Still testing expressions of regret, ears pricked for sounds of movement within, he heard nothing. Frowning, he renewed his attack on the door, grasping the cover of the cast iron letter box and rattling it until it echoed in the small hall. Still no Russell. With a growing sense of unease he looked through front and rear windows before kneeling in front of the door to peer through the letter box. He was greeted by a smell of soot and furniture polish and a stillness which, to a conscience sensitised by Julia's fears, spoke of abandonment. As he stood up and dusted the knees of his suit, Joe Bywater emerged from Frobisher's cottage next door.

"I've just fed 'is 'ens," Joe said.

Simon smiled a wan acknowledgment. "I'm looking for Hugo Russell," he explained, striving to appear unhurried. "I don't suppose you've seen him this morning?"

Joe removed his cap and scratched his scalp, a gesture, Simon had noted, that often accompanied thought in Bradburn. To Simon's relief, he said, "Ay, 'e left a few minutes ago. 'E were lockin' t'door as I arrived."

Simon began to relax until, recalling Julia's concern that Russell might decamp, he asked as casually as he could manage, "I don't suppose you happened to notice what he was carrying? Any luggage, for instance?"

"A briefcase," Bywater volunteered. "Ox-blood wi' gold initials. 'E went that way." He gestured towards the square.

"Probably going to the office then," Simon said, exhaling with a relief that was palpable.

"Or t'canal," Joe amended, unsmiling.

Simon stared at him, his relief departing as quickly as it had come. "You don't think...?"

"Pale, 'e looked," Bywater volunteered lugubriously. "Didn't even notice I was 'ere." He studied Simon's face expectantly.

Simon continued to stare. Any question of suicide was clearly out of the question. Yet the canal... But wouldn't a stroll along the quiet banks of the canal be precisely the sort of relaxation that might commend itself to the oppressed Russell's soul? And yet again, might not the sombre, isolated stretches offer precisely the seclusion a desperate man might need to end it all?

Mumbling thanks to Bywater, Simon shot off down the square, darting through the light early morning traffic until he reached the canal at a smart trot. Halting at one of the refuges on the bridge, he looked along the canal to where a number of the moored narrow boats were coming to life. Life in the rest of Bradburn was clearly untroubled by Sunday's events.

On one of the narrow boats a young girl in T-shirt and shorts was idly rubbing gleaming brasswork that had probably originated in the Wilberforce factory opposite. The restaurant was closed but there had been a delivery of vegetables which stood outside in uncovered boxes. A clerk from the chandlers was lowering its green and white blinds, slowly winding the handle of a long pole attached to its mechanism.

But of Russell there was no sign.

The only movement along the canal banks was provided by a boy and girl riding bicycles past a solitary, immobile fisherman shaded by a golf umbrella advertising the beer sold at the Fox & Chickens. Simon dodged across to the refuge on the other side of the bridge and stared along the deserted banks there. Briefly, he considered searching beyond where the canal looped out of sight, but if the fat man had left the house at the time Bywater reported, it was unlikely that he could have travelled so far on foot. Russell, Simon was happy to conclude, had probably not got as far as the canal at all. Most probably, of course, he would now be at the office rather than beneath several feet of water the colour of pea soup.

Mentally crossing his fingers, Simon hurried to the office in the hope of finding him there.

* * *

Unaware that at that moment Russell was plodding to the chemists at the bottom of the arcade to have his prescription filled, Simon had arrived to find the board and its advisers already assembled and he faced Mowbray's anxious enquiry with a sensation of gnawing guilt.

"I've already called at the cottage - Julia asked me to," he said. "He wasn't there, but he's definitely up and about because Joe Bywater saw him leave. He was carrying a briefcase and I half expected to find him here already."

Mowbray harrumphed. "Probably gone for a walk," he suggested. "Get some of that soot out of his lungs." He studied Simon for a moment over the top of his glasses, then turned to Bartlett who was hovering at his shoulder. "We're already late. We'd better start without Hugo Russell."

There was something invigorated, almost brusque about Mowbray as he moved to his place at the head of the table. Conscious that a number of eyes were straying to Hugo Russell's empty chair, Mowbray started the meeting briskly.

"Hugo Russell will be along later, I expect," he began. "In the meantime, you should know that Mervyn Pusey telephoned me at home this morning to say that it is now his intention to bid for us without delay."

There was a momentary commotion as the news was absorbed. The advisers remained either inscrutable or affected only polite interest, forewarned by Mowbray during a conference call with Kettering minutes before the board convened. Wilberforce directors appeared to be glum or - Temple - angry; or, in Pritchard's case, watchful. The cousin, who had been persuaded to appear at short notice, wore an expression that proclaimed all was lost as clearly as though he sported a balloon proclaiming the thought. Miss Varley, having set up the meeting without being aware of its purpose, pressed so hard on her pencil that the point snapped and she blushed as she exchanged it for another from the array in front of her.

The hubbub subsided as Mowbray spoke again. "We have until later today to call him and arrange talks. In other words, to capitulate. Needless to say, we have no intention of doing so, therefore he will bid. His attitude is that we will not survive in the long run, but I believe - and I have already spoken to Richard Kettering - that he is unlikely to bid at a knock-out level, at least in the first instance. We should be able to reject his first bid comfortably."

There were murmurs and nods of agreement from around the table.

"The moves each side will be allowed to take once he makes his bid are closely circumscribed by the City Code," Mowbray continued. "In Hugo Russell's absence, I've asked Ben Bartlett to outline what that involves for those of us to whom all of this is quite new." With a half-apologetic smile in the direction of the professional advisers, he nodded encouragingly to the company secretary.

Already primed by his chairman when the meeting's delayed start had failed to produce Russell, Bartlett took a handwritten note from his file and studied it quietly. Satisfied with what he had prepared, he placed it in front of him and referred to it only occasionally as he explained the next moves.

"Pusey will now have to announce formally that he intends to bid," Bartlett began in his dry, unemphatic tones. There followed several minutes of explanation that set Simon doodling madly until he sat up with a start as the company secretary paused in mid-sentence. The door had opened and Russell edged in. Wearing an uncharacteristically sheepish grin, Russell almost tiptoed to his place on the other side of Mowbray from Miss Varley and listened carefully as Mowbray leaned towards him and began to whisper. The company secretary held his silence until Russell nodded and he and Mowbray turned their attention to him.

Bartlett took up his thread. "The bid timetable will apply once Pusey posts his formal offer document to our shareholders, but he has a couple of weeks from now to do so. You will have a full copy of the bid timetable before you leave the meeting."

On cue, the door opened and Tracy came in. She held the door open long enough for Minnie Emmett to push in her squeaking trolley with its cargo of urns and crockery. Placing a sheaf of duplicated papers in front of Miss Varley, Tracy offered a semi-curtsy before once more holding the door before following Minnie out.

Miss Varley passed up and down the table handing out the papers as Simon and a junior member of the audit team passed round coffee. It fell to Simon to serve Russell. He was rewarded with what could have been a weak smile as the merchant banker declined cream and sugar. For a moment his hand hovered over the biscuits like a falcon over a chicken run before he withdrew it, only to follow their progress around the table with covetous eyes.

Back in his seat, Simon sipped coffee and tried to make sense of the little he had taken in. Whatever the conditions imposed by the City's takeover guidelines, there was clearly a prospect of conflict and drama whose dénouement would affect the lives of hundreds, possibly thousands, and where the scope for catastrophic error would doubtless be boundless. Such drama, he knew, was oxygen and lifeblood to the Palgraves and Brightlings of this world. But where Simon was concerned Mowbray had made it perfectly clear that his role, crucial though Mowbray had made it sound, would be simply to concentrate on the morale of employees and on rallying the populace of Bradburn to Wilberforces' support. It was, he reflected modestly, a role tailored to his abilities.

Bartlett had finished and Mowbray was once more addressing the meeting.

"We have already deployed our resources for a defence," he was saying. "Hugo Russell and representatives from the auditors will aid the defence team at Bradburn. Their job will be to put together a profit forecast, complete the work on our financial position, approve the asset revaluation and provide whatever business information and forecasts the London team might require.

"I shall go to London, more or less for the duration, and work with a team drawn from Palgraves, Ryan & Gilliatt and Brightlings. We shall be trying to get to see the main institutional shareholders to put the case for the defence, drafting defence documents and putting them through the due diligence process with the lawyers..." He glanced at Hugo Russell, who nodded.

"The defence team here," Mowbray continued, "will act as contact for the London lawyers who will be responsible for verifying any information we put forward in our defence documents. Those procedures are particularly tiresome, I'm told, and you will have a full time job here once that process begins.

"Harry Temple and the others remaining will, so far as is possible, continue to run the business as usual. Simon here will look after employee communications, community relations and the local press." He glanced round at the now attentive faces. "Are there any questions?"

The cousin, the Broadbridge GP, said, "What I can't understand is how Pusey intends to write to all our shareholders. How on earth does he know who they are?"

Russell's raised eyebrow invited Mowbray's permission to reply. Noting the unaccustomed courtesy, Mowbray nodded to him to go ahead.

"Under the City Code on Take-overs and Mergers," Russell informed the meeting, "we are given a fixed time in which to provide the bidder with our shareholders' names and addresses."

It was Julia's contention that her Uncle Harry was the only person who ever actually said Pshaw!, and he said it now. Eyebrows bristling, he looked around the board for support. "They'll be wanting 'em on sticky labels next," he said, and subsided into his seat, crimson with indignation.

"That's actually not unheard of, if that's the form in which the target company normally runs them off," Russell said, remaining straight-faced behind what might have been the ghost of a smile.

Silence descended, and members of the meeting began to stir as they sensed it was moving to a close.

"One final thing," Mowbray said. "We shall be holding an informal reception at Bradburn House tomorrow evening. I shall be staying here for it, and those of you who will still be here are invited for seven-thirty. Sorry about the short notice."

* * *

The idea of the reception had been Simon's, egged on by an enthusiastic Julia. Plans for the event were stored under Community Relations in the filing cabinet Tracy had provided, even though the paperwork Simon had so far generated could comfortably have been kept in his jacket pocket. The purpose, he had explained to a quizzical Mowbray, was to counter growing gossip in the town by meeting its leading citizens face-to-face and letting them know what was happening.

*'Do not underestimate the value of good
community relations. Treat the communities in which
you operate as your neighbours. Let them know what
you are doing and why you are doing it. In the words
of André Gide, "Understanding is the beginning of
approval"'*

The exhortation had leapt off the page of a
publication whose name Simon could no longer recall.
It had burrowed into his mind as an eternal verity,
italics and all.

* * *

Pusey was not attracted to the chunky gold watches and
personal number-plates that symbolised notches on the
greasy pole of success for the *parvenu*. Nor, in his
frugal existence, would he have invested in a portable
telephone any more than he would have invested in a
portable wastepaper basket. Instead, when business
took him away from the office, which was often, he
would provide Miss Goring with a list of ports of call at
which he could be contacted. And, in case that should
prove inadequate, he would call her from kiosks in the
street, from hotel lobbies or from the offices he was
visiting. Such calls were usually sterile exchanges that
did little more than confirm to each the whereabouts of
the other. Hence it was out of duty rather than
expectation that he telephoned Miss Goring from a call-
box on the embankment that Monday morning.

When Miss Goring then gave him the message he
had begun to despair of ever hearing, he ensured the
kiosk door was tightly shut and listened with finger-
tapping impatience as Miss Goring placed the handset
in a position that would allow him to hear for himself
the recording she had made on the answering machine.

"I'm calling now you've put that notice in the
paper," the caller said. Pusey rubbed his bruised hip as

the northern tones, whether natural or assumed, recalled the humiliating conclusion to his visit to Bradburn. "It's time we came to some agreement," the voice continued. "They've got consultants running all over the place at Wilberforces, and if you want that planning permission it's time we talked." The line went quiet except for a squeaking and a rattling of crockery as someone pushed a trolley past. When the voice resumed, it spoke more quickly. "It's a bit public here, I can't talk for long. This is what you have to do..."

Pusey listened in puzzled silence until the message finished. Miss Goring had acted with admirable despatch when he had asked her to put his reply in *The Yorkshire Post* but, as days had passed without a response, he had allowed himself to become preoccupied with the bid and not with his correspondent's offer that might transform a merely successful acquisition into a massively profitable one.

Investigating what precisely his correspondent could do to secure the crucial planning consents could be a vital next step, even if it now meant another trip to the wretched Bradburn. And that under the bizarre conditions his caller had stipulated.

~Chapter 21~

The recognition that Wilberforces were now defined in City-speak as a target had had a profoundly depressing effect on directors already cringing beneath the mere prospect of being bid for. Nor was there any salve for their feelings when the letter arrived from Pusey announcing his intentions.

In a conversation with Mowbray, Kettering had appeared apologetic about the fact that the letter went out of its way to be offensive.

"Hoping for a quick kill, by the look of it," Kettering told Mowbray over the telephone. "This sort of stuff would normally be held back for his first circular to the target's shareholders. He'll be feeding this to the press as a shot across your bows."

Forewarned, Mowbray arranged for the directors to study the content of the letter before inviting the external advisers into a quickly reconvened meeting. Although each director had been given his own copy, Mowbray began to read the statement aloud, a process constantly interrupted by Colonel Temple's expressions of incomprehension mingled with outrage. Eventually abandoning the reading as the incensed Temple began to read it out in unison, Mowbray was forced to listen gloomily as the Colonel picked his way through it with the air of a man defusing a bomb.

"'Fusty and Victorian management,'" he read out, consulting the faces of his fellow directors in puzzlement. "'Fusty *and* Victorian,'" he repeated. "I wonder what they're getting at?"

There was a silence as, to a man, the rest of the board developed a sudden fit of introspection. "I rather think it means all of us," Mowbray said. "Kettering explained that this sort of thing might happen. Apparently it's known as slagging off the opposition."

"Hardly the language of diplomacy," Pritchard said, his prim mouth expressing disapproval.

Temple was not to be distracted. "Fusty *and* Victorian, does it say?" he asked, doubting the evidence of his own eyes.

"Fusty," Mowbray confirmed, glancing at his copy.

"Fusty." Temple rolled the word round his tongue, as though, like a childhood sweet, it would dissolve to reveal inner shades. "Funny sort of word to use. Dingy, I suppose he means. Or musty. Probably have settled for musty, myself." He looked up brightly, nodding satisfaction.

Having picked his way through to the end of the letter, Temple pushed it away from him with an expression of distaste.

Russell shook his head in commiseration. "Entirely in character, I'm afraid. Pusey is not a man who minces his words." Conscious that in the current charged atmosphere this might appear to be endorsing Pusey's assessment, he added quickly, "Scurrilous nonsense, of course."

Mowbray looked at him thoughtfully.

Russell was feeling uncommonly at peace with the world. Dr. Price's pills had already begun to cast their

benign spell and the tone of Pusey's letter was now
stirring in him a languid resentment. After all, if
someone elected to make brass trinkets and
doorknockers or whatever it was, and to do so at barely
sub-polar latitudes, then they surely demanded
sympathy and not the sort of abuse that would affront a
Billingsgate porter.

"I imagine he'll have fed the same sort of thing to
the press," someone said. "Whatever we do, we mustn't
be drawn into a slanging match on his terms."

There was a chorus of support from directors.

"I think, chairman, we ought to invite the external
advisers in and see where we should go from here," the
company secretary suggested.

At Mowbray's nod, Pritchard pressed the button
that summoned Miss Varley.

"I suppose we've got to show 'em this claptrap?"
Temple queried, gingerly prodding his copy.

Mowbray gave a tight-lipped smile as Miss Varley
entered. Mowbray asked her to invite the external
advisers to join the meeting and to produce sufficient
copies of Pusey's statement for each to have one.

"Now *musty* I could just about have understood,"
Harry Temple was saying as she left the room.

* * *

News of the impending bid galvanised Simon and, as
Julia was committed to helping Mrs. Benson with
arrangements for the impending reception, he found
himself having to bring out the very first edition of *The
Works* himself.

It was, had he but known it, also destined to be the
last.

* * *

After a brief discussion with Mowbray, Simon dashed
from the reconvened meeting with a copy of Pusey's

statement together with the company's formal statement of opposition. Mowbray had agreed that a summarised version of the bid document and the Wilberforce reply should be issued to employees and had agreed with Simon that it should be the lead item in *The Works*. Back at his office, Simon completed the summary as indicated by Mowbray and began pulling together the remainder of *The Works*' editorial content. From the corner of his eye he was vaguely conscious that Tracy appeared to be studying the official statements he had put down by the side of her word processor. Soon, he noted, tears began to trickle down her porcelain cheeks.

"They'll throw us all out of work, I know they will," she sobbed, pushing the statements away from her as though that would distance her from the threat. "How can Sean and me get married if we've no jobs?" She turned tear-filled eyes to Simon who, far from quailing at the sight, had to fight to control a sudden surge in his spirits the mention of Sean had inspired. Whoever Sean might be he clearly represented a release from whatever place he himself might temporarily have held in Tracy's affections; if, as Julia contended, there had been such a place. No doubt, he pondered, drawing on his shallow well of knowledge of the feminine psyche, there had been some rift in the lute between Tracy and her Sean during which he, Simon, had filled an emotional gap.

Tracy dabbed at her eyes and proffered a hand that sported an engagement ring. "We'd only just got back together again and now this happens." She stared at Simon forlornly.

Fighting to conceal his relief, Simon risked a comforting hand on her shoulder, then snatched it away quickly in case it should be misinterpreted.

"Nobody knows what would happen if the bid were to be successful," he counselled, "and it's certainly far too early to start worrying about that sort of thing."

Tracy stared at him, blue eyes magnified by tears. Simon stared back, his face a model of resolution. "The best chance of keeping jobs is to ensure that the bid fails. All right?"

Tracy nodded weakly as Simon moved back behind his desk and read from the notes he had made of Mowbray's comments during the meeting. "The best defence against a bid is a well-run company," he read aloud. Tracy, brow furrowed and lips pursed, propped her chin in her hand and stared at him admiringly. Slightly unnerved, Simon nevertheless carried on, "We shall best serve the interests of our shareholders and our employees by grasping this opportunity to show that we can run our business better than any predator, even if we have not always done so in the past."

Tracy gave a delighted little clap then foraged in her handbag and began spraying herself with the scent she used. It reminded Simon of fruit pastilles and it appeared to be a sign that the storm had abated. That done, she gazed at him with eyes now as clear and untroubled as a kitten's and holding, he was happy to see, no more affection than a niece might bestow on a favourite uncle.

"Our first job must be to get the bulletin out for employees," Simon explained. "Then I shall go to the printers and use it for the first edition of *The Works*. Rumour will be our biggest enemy in the days to come, and facts, Tracy, squash rumour."

"Well," she said decisively, "let's get on with it."

With an expertise that confounded Simon, she used her word processor to download brief summaries of the Pusey document from wherever in the ether they dwelled and began to edit them into the format Simon had devised under Mowbray's guidance. Simon handed her a handwritten paragraph stating what was known about Pusey Associates. Tracy typed it in and, just beneath the space reserved for Mowbray's signature, she typed: 'For the latest on the bid defence, call Wilberphone Factline on Internal 200. '

If pressed, Simon would have admitted that Wilberphone Factline, which he tended to think of as Son of Wilberphone, filled him with even greater pride than had creation of its parent. It had quickly become clear, following arrival of the bid, that Wilberphone would quickly outrun its usefulness as a rallying system once the hitherto loose coalition of directors and advisers gelled into the Bradburn and London defence teams. As each would then be in more or less continuous conclave, the need to summon them to the sort of hastily convened meetings that had spawned Wilberphone would disappear.

Wilberphone had therefore become Wilberphone Factline.

Wilberphone Factline, Simon had explained in an introductory bulletin, would provide callers on the internal telephone network with a recorded message, also available on their screens to those who had computers. The message, the first of which had yet to be produced, would be updated twice daily to report the latest developments in the company's fight to remain independent. The necessary equipment, little more than an elaborate answering machine, had been installed in a basement room of such stark dimensions that not even the most junior of the visiting auditors had been persuaded to use it as an office. As Tracy disappeared to secure Mowbray's signature and begin running off the bulletin, Simon grabbed a duplicate copy and retreated with it to the basement.

There, secure in the knowledge that *'spoken communication is more readily assimilated than the written word'* (or was it, he wondered, vice versa?) he made assurance double sure and recorded the bulletin. He then collected a package from Irving Bell, Bradburn's sole commercial photographer, and hurried along to the printers to put the first edition of *The Works* to bed.

* * *

Simon sipped at the plastic cup of tea and tried not to spill it as he followed Percy Worrall into a room where what now appeared as a daunting expanse of paper, blank except for the masthead he and Julia had devised, was laid out on a table covered in brown linoleum.

"A four-pager, I think we agreed," Worrall said as Simon visibly shied at the area to be covered.

Apart from the masthead the only other blemish on the four virgin pages was Worrall's own imprint at the foot of the sheet destined to be page four. Mentally inventorying the package he was about to hand over to Worrall, Simon cleared his throat and announced his first editorial decision. "I think," he advised Worrall firmly, "we'll go down to two pages for our first issue." Less certainly, he added, "That should give it a more urgent appearance than something more substantial." Finally, unnerved by Worrall's stolid silence, he sacrificed any attempt at editorial certitude by adding, "Don't you think?"

"Printers aren't paid to think," Worrall said phlegmatically.

With deadlines threatening to close behind him like waterproof doors, Simon experienced the first pangs of editorial indecision. "Er..." he said.

"But if you *want* my opinion," Worrall continued, riffling through the paucity of the package Simon handed him, "I agree. Now, what do you want and where do you want it?"

Heads together, they compared notes. One thing at least was clear: the main content would be versions of the rival statements, plus a photograph of Mowbray provided by Julia.

"It was taken in London," she had explained to Simon, "not by Bell."

"I have also," Simon announced triumphantly, "photographs of all the directors, together with short statements from them aimed at their parts of the organisation. That should give us the back page. The only photograph missing is Colonel Temple's. Irving Bell will be dropping that in shortly."

Worrall spread the material out in front of them and studied it. "It'll be a bit thin. Still..."

With the exception of Mowbray's, the photographs had been the result of a photographic session in a cramped room at Irving Bell's studio more used to the sight of smirking mothers clutching naked babies. The executive directors had suffered the ordeal in resigned silence. Only Pritchard had taken the trouble to have his hair cut specially, and only Harry Temple had shown open resentment at having to submit to instructions from Irving Bell, a sandal-clad Vegan who had recently re-established an ancient right of way through Temple's paddock. The major had glowered throughout and the photograph of Temple that Irving Bell had first included with the proofs had shown that old soldier glaring at the camera with a snarl that would have put the fear of God into a regiment of Uhlans. Simon had insisted that it be replaced with something more pacific and left it to Bell to deliver it to the printers.

Worrall studied the photographs without comment. "I suppose you want it yesterday?" he complained, "they usually do." He held up a hand as Simon began to say something. "You can have 'em about five o'clock this afternoon," he promised.

~Chapter 22~

During his first days at Bradburn, it had been impressed on an un-resentful Simon by Brightlings' Crispin Biggs-Baker that, while the national press were to be held firmly in thrall to the London consultancy's own spin doctors, he, Simon, would have complete freedom to galvanise the local press in Wilberforces' defence.

"Just take 'em to whatever passes for the Savoy Grill up there and feed 'em the party line between drinks," Biggs-Baker had advised airily.

Although any resemblance between the Savoy Grill and the Fox & Chickens was remote to the point of invisibility, the pub's virtues of proximity and familiarity weighed strongly in its favour. Simon's planned lunch with Monkton Gibbs had a high potential for *ennui* and he had hesitated in the shadow of the Corn Exchange before pushing through the door and down the steps into the pub's gloomy interior.

"He's in the saloon bar," Kitty said as he put his head round the tap room door. "He's had Sam putting drinks down to your account for the past half-hour."

Grimacing, Simon retraced his steps to the saloon bar where the tables among which Pusey had once pursued grapefruit segments were now set for lunch.

He exchanged nods and smiles with diners he recognised and made his way to where Gibbs was seated at the bar, water jug in one hand, a tumbler of scotch in the other. Water dribbled into the glass as Simon approached and Gibbs held it aloft in greeting. Despite the heat outside, he wore his tilted bowler and velvet-collared coat as though he alone occupied a freezing micro climate.

Simon flinched as Gibbs boomed out a welcome. "Dear boy!" he said, attracting stares from around the room. He peered at Simon waggishly over the top of grimy spectacles and patted the vacant stool next to his own. "Pray take a seat."

Simon sat obediently and Gibbs released his grip on his glass for a moment to deliver a portentous handshake. Sam Harrison passed by, having delivered a tray of food to a table where two women sat behind a barricade of carrier bags. His glance intercepted the handshake and he gave Simon a theatrical leer before putting the tray on the bar. Taking a soft drink from the glass-fronted fridge, he poured it into a glass and set it in front of Simon. Without asking, he took the now empty glass from Gibbs and added a double measure from the optic.

"The wife recommends the steak and kidney pie," Sam said to Simon, pushing the refilled glass in the direction of Gibbs. He noted the drinks on a slip of paper and put it back by the till.

A sign in the window of the Fox & Chickens, cruelly intersected by a glazing bar, called to the unwary with the eerily prophetic 'Home Cocked Food'. Within, Hetty Harrison catered for her customers with a blithe disregard for the seasons and, some held, for the digestions of her customers. Today, with the temperature again in the high seventies, the chalked menu behind the bar appeared to have been created to meet a cold snap in Tomsk.

Sam picked up the tray. "I'll say you'll have the pie, then," he said, and disappeared through the dangling coloured streamers.

* * *

Gibbs, having picked up on the incursion of strangers at the Wilberforce offices, had failed to glean anything useful from his customary contacts in either office or factory and had been awaiting developments with antennae twitching. Although chiefly a sports reporter, like many journalists he could turn his hand to whatever stories presented themselves, secure in the knowledge that accuracy would pass unremarked and error unreproved. Simon's invitation to lunch had been received with muted relief and he watched pleasurably as his host reached into an inside pocket and handed over a piece of paper.

Adjusting his spectacles, Gibbs held it at arms' length and read through the statement, silent except for an occasional clucking sound as he absorbed its message. Putting it down on the bar, he smoothed it with the flat of his hand.

"Room for a little flair there," he said, mildly reproving. "A touch of colour, a spry adjective or two, perhaps."

Simon's explanation, that its content had largely been dictated by Wilberforces' City advisers, was waved airily away. "I shall do a quick piece for the *Chronicle,* then put it over to local radio and TV," Gibbs said, his manner lordly. Carrying the statement and the scotch, he made his way to his office, which was also the pay 'phone in the passage.

Simon used the reprieve to consult the small notebook that held his checklist of actions, narrowly

avoiding putting it down in the heaped plate Hetty
Harrison almost simultaneously placed in front of him.

Hetty Harrison approved of Simon. He was the
cheerfully uncritical type of resident to which the pub's
hospitality was best suited. Hetty was tall and reduced
the impression of height by scraping her brown hair
until it was flat against the scalp before being captured
in a coil above the nape of her neck. To Simon, who
could detect no beginning or end, it had the fascination
of a Mobius Strip. As she turned to go back into the
kitchen she unshuttered her horsey teeth in a smile
meant to absolve Simon for his part in the chimney
cleaning debacle which had left the Fox's spare
bathroom smelling like the ruins of Carthage. Simon,
unaware, head wreathed in cabbage steam, began to
study his list and tick the actions so far accomplished.

Internal communications merited a particularly
sharp tick. Printed systems were operating smoothly,
Wilberphone Factline had been commissioned, *The
Works* had been safely put to bed, and now it only
remained to establish the War Rooms. The War Rooms
involved setting aside space at factory and offices
where employees would be able to study the latest
statements from the combatants. A browse through
copies of press coverage to see how the battle was being
perceived by the outside world would, Simon was
convinced, fill them with a steely resolve. Each War
Room would have a telephone dedicated to
Wilberphone Factline, the general idea being that,
should steely resolve fail to be stirred, the facility would
at least stifle idle rumour.

Shortage of space at the offices dictated that there,
at least, plans had to be scaled down to a notice board
in the lobby which, as Simon was happy to point out,
would also be seen by visitors. As this meant it also

contributed to external relations, he saw it as
something of a double-whammy in public relations
terms. On a broader front, external relations had taken
yet another step forward in the last few minutes with
the release of information to Monkton Gibbs, copies of
which Mowbray had also personally dispatched to the
leader of Bradburn Council and the Chairman of the
Chamber of Commerce.

Meanwhile, Biggs-Baker had assured Simon, the
Wilberforce case would now be dripped into pertinent
ears in the City at the appropriate time.

"Part of the art," Biggs-Baker had confided, "and
one realises one is probably teaching one's
grandmother to suck eggs, is not to go off at half-cock,
but to keep one's powder dry until one can get in one's
most telling shot."

"I think," Simon said to Judith, "he means they're
not actually going to do anything just yet."

The party planned for Bradburn House the
following evening was categorised by Simon as external
relations with a community relations spin. Invitations,
their black script crisp against round-edged ivory
cards, would shortly be delivered to Bradburn's leading
citizens together with a summary of developments to
date. Despite the short notice, the defence team were
confident in their conviction that the townspeople
would be happy to associate themselves with the battle,
if only to the extent of eating and drinking to the
success of their hosts.

Having disposed of most of his lunch, and having
secured a further large scotch for Gibbs, Simon
returned his notebook to his pocket just as the
journalist settled back on his stool. Gibbs was beaming
complacently.

"Consternation at *The Chronicle,* polite interest from local radio," he reported. "*The Chronicle* will be sending someone to Bradburn this afternoon for a *vox pop* reaction, and both radio stations will be happy to interview your Mr. Mowbray if this thing turns out to be a runner."

Simon thanked Gibbs and watched as the scotch was drained at a gulp. "I'll keep you posted," he promised. "If the other side puts anything out, I'll see you get a copy."

To Simon's relief, Gibbs had waved aside the fact that Wilberforces had produced only a summary of Pusey's letter in the bulletin. Ostensibly, this was because they claimed not yet to have fully checked the arithmetic of Pusey's assertions. In fact, their reluctance stemmed from the board's disquiet at the prospect of some of Pusey's more lurid descriptions of their incompetence awakening sympathetic echoes in the town.

As Simon stood up to go, Gibbs reached for his hand and gave it a languid shake. "While I wish you every success," he said sonorously, his spaniel eyes on Simon's, "*do* try to keep it running just a little while," and, turning back to the bar, ordered another large scotch.

* * *

As any of Simon's lecturers at university could have testified, the manner in which he acquired knowledge was indiscriminate to the point of caprice, facts apparently lodging in his mind in a manner that bore no relation to their likely usefulness.

"Your progress through life will be like that of a man trying to use the underground by following a central heating diagram," he had been told shortly before graduating. Thus, while life had somehow taught him that Loch Ness could be reached by bus from Drumnadrochit, and that *wyjscie* was Polish for exit, he had remained blithely unaware that the seat of editorial power is ringed by coiled serpents.

His intention that afternoon was to call at Worralls to pick up the first edition of *The Works,* after which, having abstracted a copy to show to Julia, he would drop the bulk off at the office and factory for distribution. Before that, he was due to call at another printer, this time in Broadbridge. This one had been entrusted with the task of printing the window decals and posters planned for distribution around Bradburn. Though dramatic in design, they were simple in content as haste had meant that they had had to be commissioned without board approval. And, as Julia conceded, anything with an ounce of imagination would have led to the type of protracted debate they were keen to avoid. They had settled for 'Hands off Wilberforce!' which, Julia assured Simon, made up in salience whatever it might have lacked in originality.

Simon was forced to kick his heels in a waiting room at the Broadbridge printers which a degree of natural light made only slightly more agreeable than that at Worralls. The technicians, he was informed, were wrestling with a minor technical problem, though the fact was that the printer had simply dawdled on the job until Simon had telephoned that morning to confirm the pick-up time. The delay left Simon kicking his heels for an hour, so that by the time the job was finished and the packages had been stowed safely under the bonnet of Ibstock's Beetle, his arrival at Worralls left him with no time at all to study his hot off the press copy of *The Works.* Acknowledging a greeting from a Percy Worrall whose effusiveness was prompted by the knowledge that a job required in haste could be charged for accordingly, Simon grabbed the two packages and placed them on the passenger seat of the car.

* * *

When Simon arrived at Bradburn House he found Julia dressed like a World War II munitions worker in dungarees and headscarf, flicking a feather duster over the heavily rococo plasterwork of the hall's elaborate cornice. Edging carefully down an antique pair of wooden steps, she led the way into the kitchen.

"Mrs. Benson's gone shopping," she explained, pouring coffee from a simmering percolator. "She's got a shipping order for the party, so most of it will have to be collected in the morning."

Before ringing the bell Simon had managed to abstract a single copy of *The Works* from one of the packages. It now resided in an inside pocket from where he produced it with a flourish and handed it to Julia.

"It's *The Works*," she said delightedly. She pounced on it and spread it out on the table. Smoothing it with her hands, she stared at it with wide-eyed approval. "Simon, it looks wonderful." They stood side by side, studying their production avidly. "I'm delighted I chose that picture of Daddy."

Simon beamed, basking in her approval as she traced the columns of type with a dusty finger. She turned the single sheet over. The finger stopped. Her expression clouded and she sank on to Mrs. Benson's chair as though winded.

Simon felt sick. Forcing himself to speak, he asked, "What...what's the matter?"

Feebly, eyes welling with tears, Julia pushed the paper towards him. "Uncle Harry..."

* * *

Worrall predictably pointed the finger elsewhere, and with some justice. It was, he explained, a joke that had gone wrong. A bad joke, needless to say, and the whole thing would, of course, be amended and reprinted at no cost to Wilberforces. As for his son-in-law, the perpetrator, this would provide precisely the excuse Worrall had been seeking in order to chuck him out of the firm. Not that it was solely his fault, of course. His friend the photographer, Irving Bell, was the chief culprit.

It had seemed a good idea to Bell, whose resentment of the land-owning Temple matched Temple's loathing for him. By the time Bell had arrived at the printers with the more acceptable photograph of Temple demanded by Simon, Worrall had left for a Rotary meeting, leaving the last stages of preparation in the hands of a son-in-law injected into the company by Mrs. Worrall who affected to discern qualities in him that would forever be invisible to her husband. When Bell decided to share the manic photograph of Temple with the son-in-law, it was no time at all before they had incorporated it in the almost finished page where, with suitable additions, it soon had them reeling around the room in fits of hysterical giggles. Their mistake, they confessed later, was to have then gone off to their home brew class, during which time the paste-up was gathered up by an impatient printer and prepared for printing.

* * *

The colour drained from Simon's face as he followed Julia's pointing finger to where Major Temple glowered from the page with a baleful intensity that appeared little short of psychopathic. Underneath, in the italics reserved for captions, it said:

Major H. J. C. Temple, shortly before being removed by men in white coats.

Tears coursed down Julia's duty cheeks. "Your lovely publication..." she said.

Simon fought an inclination to scream. "It's a...it's a travesty," he gasped. "Thank heavens they're still in the car."

Julia stared at him. Her eyes widened beneath glistening lashes.

"I was held up at Broadbridge, so I came here before going back to the office."

Leaping out of the chair, Julia threw her arms around Simon and planted a kiss on his cheek that brought the colour back to his face faster than it had disappeared.

Minutes later the sun beaming down on the gardens of Bradburn House illuminated ashes dancing in a sooty spiral of smoke which, had he cared to look out of the window, Temple could have seen from his office.

~Chapter23~

*M*y *dear Mowbray,*

What news of the winsome Russell? I gather from your Miss Varley that all is not well and trust it is nothing too dire. She appeared to say, too, that he is on some sort of medically imposed diet; can that be true? If so, your northern medics are made of sterner stuff than ours.

Now, as to yesterday. It seemed to me Safe & Wise were on the friendly side of neutral...

Emails from Kettering appeared regularly on Miss Varley's computer when Mowbray was in Bradburn. Almost two weeks had passed since the Pusey bid, and it occurred to Mowbray that he was being required to spend more time in London than actually appeared to be useful. The letters from Kettering in the meantime were, he suspected, an emanation of the banker's goodwill, morale sinew-stiffeners in a battle whose rumbustiousness Kettering knew to be painful to his client, not least because of the glee with which some sections of the press had taken up Pusey's colourfully offensive attack on the Wilberforce board. In the process they had managed to make it sound like an amalgam of the Drones Club and a provincial retirement home.

The relationship between the two men had warmed considerably since they had begun jointly presenting the Wilberforce case to those insurance companies and pension funds which, as Wilberforce's most powerful non-family shareholders, would have a critical say in whether Pusey's bid would be successful. Usually, Mowbray was convinced, they agreed to see him simply out of courtesy to Kettering, one of the City's most senior figures. The case for Wilberforce's defence which they toted around the City, a confection by Palgraves with top-spin from Brightlings, appeared so far to be leaving its audiences interested but non-committal. Despite these efforts, Richard Causton, his ear close to the ground for Ryan & Gilliatt, had reported gloomily that one or two of the institutions were threatening to sell out as the Wilberforce share price had first risen then, when no rival bidder emerged, was now threatening to flatten.

Mowbray pushed the email aside and turned his thoughts to Hugo Russell's recent indisposition. The first symptoms, if that is what they could be called, had appeared at the meeting following Russell's ordeal by soot. The unwonted politeness, allied to an abstemiousness in the face of refreshments, had persisted. In fact it had, if anything, increased. When Russell had subsequently telephoned to say that he was rather less than well and would be taking a couple of days off, alarm bells had rung. The ringing became a clangour when Julia reported rumblings on the Mrs. Benson front that had caused Mowbray to stare in disbelief. A contented Mrs. Benson, essential to the wellbeing of those who lived or were entertained at Bradburn House, was taken as one of life's constants.

"He's not eating the meals Mrs. Benson prepares for him," Julia reported. "He says he's on a diet, but

Mrs. Benson's got it into her head that her cooking's no longer good enough for him." As an afterthought, she added tartly, "I think you should point out that the alternative is the Fox & Chickens."

Mowbray had promptly dropped his takeover concerns to hurry to Old Taylor's cottage where he had found an abashed Russell fervent in his praise of Mrs. Benson. "Nothing to do with the wonderful cooking," Russell had effused. "Can't get enough of it; under normal circumstances, that is." He kissed his fingers and sent the kiss aloft with a podgy flick.

Mowbray was nonplussed. "But Mrs. Benson says you're not eating anything," he persisted.

Russell stared from his overstuffed armchair. To Mowbray, there appeared to have been a diminution in the man's bulk that was quite remarkable. With an ease he could not have managed mere days earlier, Russell inserted a couple of fingers into a waistcoat pocket and drew out a small brown bottle with a white cap. "Doctor's orders," he said, his voice slurring slightly. "Pills to stop me worrying, pills to get the weight off."

Further than that he refused to be drawn, and although he returned to his duties at the office the following morning, Mowbray found himself interfering to the extent of consulting Dr. Price. The catalogue of symptoms he related to Dr. Price sounded remarkably like an encomium.

"He's being remarkably civil and accommodating to everyone," Mowbray had explained worriedly, "and he's being positively gallant to young Tracy Harrison. Then, of course, weight seems simply to be falling off him."

Following a house-call at Russell's cottage that evening, Price had reassuring news for Mowbray. "He's been popping pills like sweeties," Price explained.

Patient confidentiality being unknown in Bradburn, he added, "I'd given him something for his nerves and something to help shed a few stone. He'd got them out of balance but is now conscious of the error of his ways." His black eyes gleamed at Mowbray. "His problems didn't start in Bradburn; he probably brought most of them with him. Fortunately, he started off with the girth of a cooling tower and hasn't come to any harm." He gave a tight smile that put a full stop to the diagnosis. Then, in an uncharacteristic show of interest, asked, "How's this bid business of yours going?"

Taken aback, Mowbray muttered platitudes about early days, straight bat, bit early to say, and tailed off weakly as Price continued to stare at him.

"When it goeth well with the righteous, the city rejoiceth; and when the wicked perish, there is shouting," Price proclaimed, his sonorous Welsh voice giving the statement an air of loony prophecy.

Russell, his pill regimen adjusted, continued to spread sunshine wherever he walked, and he was soon not so much wearing his suits as inhabiting them. Impressed despite herself, Julia forecast that he would soon be able to execute quite complex manoeuvres without disturbing the expensive suiting any more than the progress of a turtle disturbed its shell.

* * *

Simon had been flattered to be invited to a council of war at Brightlings ("Sounds a solid chap on the 'phone," Biggs-Baker had reported to his superiors, "but we ought to have him in for a decko.") and had fitted in a brief visit home where he had found Rebecca melting and conciliatory. The fact that he had entered into an arrangement with Hetty Harrison to have his laundry done by the company that handled the pub's linen had something to do with the change; but by far the most important contribution had been made by Julia's occasional telephone calls to Rebecca. These had had the magical effect of snuffing his wife's suspicions so effectively that not even Hazel could rekindle them.

"Bloody brazen, if you ask me," Hazel said scathingly. Then, archly, "How brave of you not to mind."

"She sounds amusing and thoughtful," Rebecca retorted.

Hazel snorted derisively. "Keep perfectly still or you'll ruin it." She dabbed expertly at the portrait that was to be a present for Simon. Carefully, subtly, she adjusted the light reflected in one of Rebecca's eyes to give it a divergent squint.

When Rebecca showed adequate contrition she would correct it.

* * *

Simon's lunch with Monkton Gibbs had produced a torrent of lurid prose in the *Chronicle* in defence of what was inevitably described as the 'beleaguered brass fittings manufacturer'. The two local radio stations, further prompted by a call from Simon, had conducted their promised interviews with a reluctant but courteous Mowbray. Thus stirred, Bradburn's reaction to the takeover bid had been predictably supportive.

The only sour note was struck by Elton Jarvis. Jarvis, a local councillor and leader of a youthful splinter group on the Trades Council, had fired off a statement, completely ignored by the media, that savaged the cavorting of the capitalist hyenas in a welter of dialectical profundity that had left its author sated and its recipients uncomprehending

Julia and Simon, having cremated *The Works* in its entirety, arranged for the quickly amended edition to be distributed, while Worrall, counting the costs he would have to bear in view of his company's culpability, prepared the ground for sacking his son-in-law; but, contemplating the domestic ructions the move would involve, went out and got drunk instead.

Following their bonfire, Julia had showered and insisted on preparing an early supper for herself and Simon, Mowbray having taken a number of consultants to a restaurant out in the country. Mrs. Benson, resting ahead of the following day's exertions, had decided to visit her daughter.

In the kitchen Julia produced a chilled bottle of wine, half-filled two glasses, and began vigorously chopping and mixing ingredients on the kitchen counter.

"We are practically ready for tomorrow night," she said, the chopping action giving her voice a fetching *vibrato*. "Other than the shopping in the morning, we're just about there."

Tipping the ingredients into the pan, she added a generous splash of wine and placed it on the huge range. Simon wandered over and peered in diffidently.

"What are we having?" he asked, conscious of Julia's reputation in the kitchen.

Julia poked the contents with a spoon. "It's called clean-up kitchen," she said. "This time it's mushrooms, cream, red peppers..." She removed the spoon, bearing a grey lump that looked like an excised tumour. Lips puckering in disapproval, Julia dropped it in the waste disposer.

"Sounds delicious," Simon said cravenly.

"You put it on toast, sprinkle it with cheese, then put it under the grill. It has the advantage that the ingredients are infinitely variable. "

Julia completed the recipe with a concentration that excluded conversation. Given its provenance it had, Simon discovered, an amorphous piquancy.

"What we have got to decide now," Julia said once they had dined and toasted confusion to Pusey, "is exactly who should be in tomorrow's reception line."

~Chapter 24~

Elton Jarvis had not expected to represent the Trades Council at the Bradburn House reception. Here he was, however, in what he believed to be a Chairman Mao suit but which looked more like something from the props basket for *The Mikado*. His additional role as a member of the District Council had secured him a position mid-way along the reception line, cheek-by-jowl with the most opulent members of the class enemy that Bradburn could muster. A covert glance at his watch between handshakes told him that he had now been there for three or four minutes, grasping and shaking the hands of people whose contempt for him and his politics was as plain as if it had been tattooed on their faces. Jarvis remained stolidly aloof, even when the Silver Library's Miss Fitton, wondering in her distracted way why she was being greeted by Pooh-Bah, had recognised the owner of the hand and thrust it away in a reaction that had practically dislocated both their wrists.

The procession of guests was showing no signs of diminishing and Jarvis's attempted air of aloofness was slowly yielding to ill-concealed concern as it dawned on him that having called in at the Fox & Chickens on the way to Bradburn House probably fell short of the wisest decision he had ever made. As the recognised advocate of an apocalyptic form of communism, Jarvis was inured to the derision that had greeted his appearance in the bar and only the fact that he had a hide like an armadillo had enabled him to withstand the company for the short time it took him to consume three pints.

The predictable result was that he was now afflicted by a sensation that was eating away at his composure like the Bard's worm i' the bud. At first it had appeared as little more than a nether tickle. Only after he had shaken hands and mumbled greetings to another dozen or so guests had the tickle begun an impertinent ascent during which, he was alarmed to discover, it managed to increase considerably in intensity. Mercifully the volume of conversation now appeared to be shifting from the hall, where guests were being received, to the bar and buffet in the library. The end, Jarvis concluded, was in sight, and he continued the mechanical business of offering a hand now filmed with moisture. Glancing past the remaining guests he could just see the foot of one of the curving flights of stairs that bracketed the hall and ascended to the first floor. As he watched, two dinner-suited men, arms round each other's shoulders, descended the last few stairs of the nearer flight. They stood in conversation for a moment before being joined by two women drifting into view from the other side of the hall. One of the men, Jarvis noted, had furtively patted the front of his trousers. It was sufficient to convince Jarvis that they must have descended from the men's cloakroom.

Yet any reassurance he might have felt yielded to panic as the diminishing flow of guests ground to a halt. Peering along the line he saw that it was being held up by a guest grasping the hand of Councillor Vera

Whitaker, Conservative Mayor of Bradburn and, so far
as Jarvis was concerned, unrivalled exemplar of the
class enemy. As the line began to move again Jarvis
noted that a safety pin securing the mayoral chain to
one shoulder of the mayor's dress had sprung open,
allowing the chain to droop unevenly. His smirk fled as
a twinge from his bladder snapped him upright.

Seconds passed. What minutes ago had been
merely discomfort was now becoming a pressing
affliction. Perspiration began to break out on his
forehead. The array of black suits and bright dresses
seemed to shimmer, at one stage appearing to advance
and recede so that he overshot one hand altogether and
almost karate chopped the turbaned owner of the Baht
'At Tandoori.

Jarvis's greetings were now being accompanied by
the staccato tattoo of his left foot against the polished
wood floor. He also, he found, had started to shiver
slightly. Having resigned himself to a humiliation in
which he would either wet himself or faint, in which
case he would probably do both, Jarvis's time frame
appeared to slip. A surge of people glided past, hands
thrusting at him from the far side of a veil until at last,
wonderfully, he was alone. Miraculously his vision
cleared and he found himself staring after the receding
backs of the reception line as they trailed after the last
of the guests in search of refreshments.

Emitting a stifled mew of anguish, he scooted
across the hall and, taking the stairs two at a time,
raced to the top only to stop as though he had run into
a forcefield. The men he had seen had undoubtedly
come from this direction, but from precisely where?
Humid with indecision, he peered down the corridor in
front of him. Immediately to his right the gallery
crossing above the hall appeared to lead to a matching

corridor on the far side. He hesitated. Panic led him half-a-dozen faltering steps straight ahead to where light spilled from beneath a door. Eyes watering with anticipation, he sprang forward and thrust it open. Men's coats littered two huge and ancient beds. Flinging himself to the floor he scrabbled beneath them only to emerge empty-handed. Thumping the carpet with frustration, he propelled himself out of the door on his knees and collapsed against the door opposite. A man's voice shouted something gruff and discouraging.

Jarvis began to whimper.

Scrambling to his feet and bending almost double, he retreated to the head of the stairs and glared across the gallery to where logic suggested the corresponding ladies' cloakroom should be. Unconscious of curious stares from the hall below, he managed a mincing trot past the wall of ornately-framed pictures and fell sideways into the corridor. Wiser now and desperate, he flung himself against the door corresponding to that of the men's room.

Inside, a woman's voice protested mildly.

Pop-eyed with disbelief, Jarvis stumbled back from the door only to come up abruptly against something hard at calf level. Peering through the gloom he could make out an arrangement of spray chrysanthemums glowing from a cast iron plant trough. Head swimming at the prospect of relief, he barely troubled to look before tugging one of the plants from the stand. The base was open ironwork.

It was the final straw.

Then, just as he was about to hurtle back down the stairs and out into the twilit gardens, it dawned on him that he was not alone. Half hidden in the gloom stood a rocking horse.

At this point his bladder prompted him with a cramp so fierce that he groaned aloud. Ahead, the tail of the rocking horse beckoned.

Hands betraying him with their slowness, Jarvis grasped the tail and, giving it a single frenzied tug, flung it down triumphantly at his feet. Smiling idiotically he began to relieve himself into the uncomplaining toy. So deeply was he engaged, so blissful the sensation, he failed to hear the lock snap back as the bathroom door slowly opened.

Councillor Whitaker had been adjusting the pin that secured the mayoral chain. The way in which she now materialised at his elbow gave Jarvis a shock that almost consigned him to the urology department of the cottage hospital. He stared at her, dizzy with embarrassment and disbelief. Councillor Whitaker's expression of wide-eyed incredulity slowly melted into one of dawning admiration.

"Tell me," Mr. Jarvis, she asked confidingly, "did you smell the smoke or see the flames?"

Her words broke the spell. With a glare full of Siberian ice, Jarvis shot upright and headed off down the stairs in a racing crouch, hands fumbling for his zipper as he galloped through the hall and disappeared into the balmy anonymity of the night.

Smiling beatifically, Councillor Whitaker descended the stairs and joined her fellow guests.

~Chapter 25~

Unaware of the drama being played out above their heads, the Bradburn House guests continued to browse among the delicacies provided by Mrs. Benson as others drifted back through the hall and out into the evening sunshine. For those lingering on the terrace, the strains of Beethoven played by a string trio from the Broadbridge Conservatoire mingled with the muted thunder of Bradburn Brass Band, tactfully located in the walled garden beyond the lawns. Ant-like processions of cub scouts in carefully pressed uniforms traipsed in and out of the house in opposing files, bearing trays of canapés under the watchful eye of Miss Varley, her luscious legs almost discernible behind soft drapes of pale lilac. The Reverend Norman Butterworth, a deft hand with a corkscrew, supervised from inside the house as Tracy Harrison and two of her father's part-time barmaids moved among guests with trays of drinks.

After much parading in front of Kitty, Julia had chosen an ankle-length gown of white cotton which set off her golden shoulders as she drifted across the lawns accompanied by a Kitty restricted to hobbling geisha steps by a shiny green sheath. Arms linked, they joined other guests as they drifted towards the sound of the band, visible through an arched opening that led to the walled garden's geometrically patterned lawns and flower beds. Chairs for the band had been set out on portable wooden staging beyond which guests with glasses in their hands lounged against the bars of a gate leading to the wooded fringe of the grounds. The band, elegant in scarlet uniforms dripping with gold frogging, were playing something subdued and mournful behind a muted cornet, their instruments sparkling in the late sun.

A glass and timber structure jutting into the garden from the nearby wall housed a long-disused plunge pool whose green tiles and iron pipes had witnessed Julia's earliest swimming lessons. Julia guided Kitty into its shady porch from where they could watch a crimson-faced Shelmerdine blowing solemnly into a euphonium.

"He looks almost sensible when he's playing," Kitty said wistfully.

Shelmerdine, still struggling for rehabilitation in Kitty's eyes, had not helped his case after the great chimney cleaning debacle by insisting that, once the soot-shrouded Russell had been escorted away, Hargreaves should fulfil his undertaking to adjudicate. His delight when the chimney had been judged immaculately clean lasted only as long as it took Hargreaves to disqualify him for cleaning the wrong chimney.

As Kitty spoke the music ended. The band stood up, variously scratching, lighting cigarettes, sipping from glasses placed discreetly under their seats, or simply turning their faces to the declining sun and fingering the scores on their music stands. Shelmerdine, spying the girls, stood his instrument on its bell and made his way across. As he pecked them impartially on the cheek the faint sound of the dinner gong floated across the wall.

"That will be for father's speech," Julia said. "I promised we would give moral support."

Hurrying, the three joined the flow back across the lawns to the foot of the terrace steps. Those who had been nearby when the gong sounded were already perching on the stone balustrade where a relaxed Hugo Russell stood by the gong, its soft mallet hanging from his wrist by a leather thong.

Mowbray, pink but unflustered, smiled and waved occasionally as he waited for the chatter to subside. He had arranged for a chair to be placed by his side for the Mayor. Monkton Gibbs stood strategically close to the speaker, his notebook on a plinth that supported one of George's giant urns of flowers, pen in one hand, glass of scotch in the other.

Kitty whispered, "Doesn't your father look handsome." Someone behind made a shushing noise.

Raising his voice slightly to reach the back of the crowd, Mowbray welcomed his guests then, assured of their attention, he paused. With a half-smile he approached the subject.

"It has been said that Bradburn owes Wilberforces a debt," he began, "and perhaps at one time that was true. We happened to come along when traditional jobs in farming were threatened by early mechanisation.

"But it is also self-evidently true that Wilberforces owes Bradburn a debt..."

The crowd stirred contentedly.

"We have since built our business on the willingness of Bradburn people to work hard for long hours which were not always as fairly rewarded as they are today," Mowbray continued, smiling as good-natured catcalls rose from a small group of employees.

"Madam Mayor..." A slight turn and a nod of the head acknowledged Councillor Whitaker, concealed from him beneath her cerise hat.

Unseen in the shadows, Miss Varley wrung her hands. "The correct form of address for a lady mayor," she had informed her employer that afternoon, "is either Your Worship or Mr. Mayor."

"Damn' nonsense," Harry Temple had huffed. "Woman's either a chap or she isn't."

"But talk of who owes what to whom is irrelevant," Mowbray was saying, then dismissed the subject with a wave of his hand. "Bradburn and Wilberforces work well together because, Madam Mayor, you and your Council colleagues have recognised that industry cannot exist without having at least some impact on its environment. For our part, we have tried not only to limit that impact but to compensate for it."

There were whispered conversations and nodding heads as his audience fleshed out the allusion: saving the office side of the square, landscaping the factory, subsidising Bradburn show...

"We have, I believe, a partnership that finds itself under threat, and under threat from people to whom Bradburn means nothing, to whom Wilberforces means nothing, and to whom the future of our community means nothing." He coughed gently, unaccustomed to speaking in raised tones. Simon, self-effacing behind one of the balcony's stone pillars, disappeared then re-appeared at his elbow with a glass of water. Mowbray took a sip and handed it back to Simon who handed it back to Norman Butterworth who passed it to someone out of sight inside the house. For all the world, someone whispered, like a human chain putting out a very small fire.

Mowbray prepared to pick up his thread. He could see Pritchard near the front, the light as he drew on his cigarette revealing an expression of bored irritation.

"We know little of Pusey and his friends," Mowbray began, and proceeded to draw a picture of what would happen to Bradburn and its inhabitants should a takeover lead to the closure of factory and offices. His audience listened, their faces growing sombre at the picture he painted. "But we will beat Pusey in the only way open to us," Mowbray continued, aiming to finish on a note that would send his guests away uplifted rather than downcast. "We shall convince our shareholders, including many of you here, I have no doubt, that they - you - will benefit by staying with the existing management, dedicated as we are to improving the rewards of investing in Wilberforces."

Someone began to clap as Mowbray took half a step backwards then held his hand up for silence. "Before we begin to disperse, ladies and gentlemen, Colonel Temple has asked me to remind you that Bradburn Show is nearly upon us. Show schedules for those who haven't already got theirs are available from the Silver Library. Madam Mayor, ladies and gentlemen..."

As Mowbray thanked his guests, Kitty passed a tissue to Julia who had been furtively wiping away a tear.

"I know how you feel," Kitty said, "just look at them all."

Male chins jutted in an expression not uncommon among Yorkshiremen who perceive their wallets to be threatened. Women clutched their evening bags and looked at husbands for reassurance. Mowbray's speech, though he had had to be persuaded by Julia and Simon to make it, had touched an audience who, as intended, would return home reinforced in their belief that

Wilberforce's fate was not an abstraction but a threat to their own prosperity.

"Let 'em see it'll hit 'em in the pocket," Temple had counselled, adding his voice to those of Simon and Julia.

Mowbray stepped back a pace to indicate that he had indeed now finished. Cameras continued to flash and the dying rays of the sun were extinguished as garden lights sprang into life at the press of a switch somewhere inside the house. Leaving Kitty in the applauding crowd, Julia hurried up the steps and pushed her way through the well-wishers surrounding her father. Mowbray spotted her and opened his arms as she ran forward and embraced him.

Councillor Whitaker, whose eyes had calmly surveyed the crowd during Mowbray's speech, gesticulated to a Russell who was still clutching his mallet. Russell struck a single booming note and the crowd hushed again as the Mayor approached the top of the steps where Mowbray had stood.

"Nobody has come here this evening to hear local politicians," she said, nodding to acknowledge the chorus of hear-hears from the back of the crowd, "but I should be failing in my duty if I failed to tell you that Bradburn Council stands firmly behind the management of Wilberforces in its fight for independence. I unreservedly pledge that support."

Cameras flashed anew as Mowbray grasped her outstretched hand. The crowd, beaming its goodwill, applauded contentedly before beginning to move towards cars parked along the drive and in the stable-yard where cub scouts were thrusting posters and stickers through windows left open to catch the hoped for breeze. The brass band, having quietly reassembled on the lawn, played a rousing if *prestissimo* chorus of

On Ilkla' Moor Baht 'At before stowing their instruments and heading for the marquee where their supper had been laid out.

Having watched the bulk of the crowd depart, Mowbray headed for the dining room where drinks had been set out for the board. Tail-lights flickered in the drive as car engines fired. Julia waved to Kitty, teetering in the direction of the marquee on her high heels, then turned to find Simon grinning at her from inside the hall. He stepped out into the growing dusk and handed her a glass of wine. Julia took a sip then placed her glass on the balustrade. Moths battered against the light above them as, without speaking, she took Simon's arm and led him down the steps to the seat in the scalloped opening beneath the terrace. The air was lush with summer garden scents. Somewhere out in the darkness there was a gentle plopping sound as a fish leapt out of the small lake. Bushes stirred ahead of them and Tracy Harrison appeared out of the shadows, dragging her cornettist boyfriend by the hand and looking happily flushed. She exchanged a wave with Simon and Julia before disappearing into the marquee. Having sat in silence for a few moments, Julia stood up and, arm linked with Simon's, drew him back towards the steps.

"What did you think of what father had to say?" she asked, "you haven't said."

"Spot on", Simon said enthusiastically, though privately convinced that it could have been a little more forceful had more of his own ideas been incorporated.

At the top of the stairs, the Mayoral car, summoned from the stableyard, purred to a standstill, its rear screen already displaying its 'Hands Off Wilberforces!' sticker. Mowbray appeared from the house deep in conversation with Councillor Whitaker. He motioned to

the driver to remain in the car and opened the rear
door so that the Mayor could step in to the deep pile
interior. The window slid smoothly open as he closed
the door with a soft clunk. The Mayor extended a hand
which Mowbray took lightly between his fingers.

"Remember what I said," she said cryptically.
Placing a finger against her lips, she subsided into the
soft upholstery as the car pulled away, its tyres making
a discreet crunching sound against the gravel.

* * *

"That's what comes of having communists in the
house," George grunted.

It was the following morning and he and young
Philips were hosing out the rocking horse in the
stableyard.

The previous evening George had been putting the
finishing touches to the two huge urns at the head of
the garden steps when Elton Jarvis had erupted from
the house like a berserker. Having followed at a more
leisurely pace, Councillor Whitaker approached
George, explained the problem, and charged him with
finding a solution that would conceal events from the
rest of the household.

Later that evening, the guests having departed,
George and young Philips had entered the house from
the staff door and, with muffled curses from George
and youthful forbearance from his assistant, smuggled
the horse, tail and all, down the backstairs and into an
empty stable where it had spent the night.

Philips, from whose incurious mind the name of
the transgressor had been withheld, absorbed George's
comment and gave an uncomprehending nod.

"There's know so queer as folk, Mr. Potter," he
volunteered.

For once, George bestowed on him an expression that verged on approval.

~Chapter 26~

The following morning, Mervyn Pusey picked up a tabloid newspaper from the pile on his desk and almost dropped it again. The headline, dauntingly terse, said, *'"Hands Off," says Brass Boss'*. A photograph identified as that of the Chairman of Wilberforce Original Brassworks stared back at him. The photograph had been taken from below. It showed Mowbray looking suave, untroubled and very much in charge of events. Sufficiently startled to have slopped coffee on to his desk, Pusey put down the cup, adjusted his spectacles and approached Monkton Gibbs's report with deep misgivings.

Very much like Dickens's *Eatanswill Gazette,* which wrote on Chinese metaphysics by combining the encyclopaedia's information on China with what it knew of metaphysics, Gibbs, who knew little about brass manufacture and less about take-overs, had combined the little he knew about each.

'Besieged brass fittings manufacturer Gerald Mowbray rapped out a stern warning to the city's wiliest predator last night,' Pusey read, *'and before you could say Ee bah gum, the quaint Yorkshire town of Bradburn had rallied round its doughty champion as a man.'*

Although by the end of the previous evening Gibbs had little recollection of what he had heard and even less of what he had drunk, and although he was usually far more at home on the sports page than elsewhere in a newspaper's columns, he had sufficient mastery of his profession's clichés to have done Wilberforces proud. Pusey, having shied at *wiliest*, read stolidly on.

'Gerald Mowbray heads a venerable business in the Yorkshire Dales,' Gibbs had written. *'It makes brassware ranging from,'* and here Gibbs had taken a misjudged leap into the dark, *'collar studs to coffin handles. And his company, Wilberforces, owns a large part of England's green and pleasant land. Now, take-over whiz Mervyn Pusey has set his sights on grabbing the lot.*

'Lines have been drawn for a take-over battle that will pitch the Goliath of the City and his billions against this David of industry.'

There was more, much too much more it seemed to Pusey, and it was with considerable apprehension that he followed the newspaper's injunction at the end of the piece and turned to what passed for the leader page.

There, under the heading *'Rus v Urbs'*, he read, *'Might is not right. The City must not get its way regardless of the merits or morality of its ambitions. The Meteor will ensure that the battle for Wilberforces is played out before the bar of public opinion.'*

Pusey pushed the paper away from him, his forehead leaking beads of perspiration.

A similar sensation had afflicted the editor of *The Meteor* when he had scanned the first edition of his paper late the previous evening. It had been sent round to him at what he liked to refer to in the office as his club.

* * *

"Who in hell told you to lead on some tin-pot outfit no-one's ever heard of?"

His voice exploded down the 'phone into the ear of the night news editor. The editor was still in what he casuistically referred to as his club, in fact a night club of a type he had delighted in exposing before own his marriage had broken up.

"You did." The night news editor snarled back. Feet on desk, handset tucked under his chin, he was simultaneously casting an eye over his computer screen and stretching out to depress the button on the telephone that would relay the conversation to the rest of the news room.

The editor smiled weakly at his mini-skirted companion. The rolled up copy of *The Meteor's* first edition he had been brandishing slipped to the floor of the sour smelling kiosk as he fumbled to recollect events. Dimly, he recalled being about to leave the office as the story had come in from some northern stringer. By-passing the night news editor who had recently handed in his notice and was therefore not to be trusted, he had handed it to a lanky young sub-editor whose name he could not recall with the instruction, "You're from up there. See what you can make of that."

McKinnon, the sub-editor, who was from Wick, had taken umbrage at the topographical slight. With the connivance of the night news editor he had then made Wilberforces front page news in a national newspaper, though one of little reputation, for the first time in the company's history.

As swallowing his rage was a more attractive proposition than abandoning his companion, the editor contented himself with glowering at the telephone and hissing, "Well change it for the second edition." He was about to smash the telephone back into its rest when a further exhortation surfaced from his massive reservoir of bile. "And you can stuff that 'bar of public opinion' drivel. They'll have forgotten it in the morning, anyway."

"Don't they always," said the night news editor, staring at the reassuringly banal 'WOTTASCORCHER' he had already called for from the splash sub.

* * *

Simon had been mildly miffed to discover that the board seemed to have regarded the party as an agreeable diversion rather than as the telling public relations coup he had anticipated, and the fact that it had succeeded in achieving media coverage provided welcome balm. It was evident that Gibbs had made the most of his opportunity by selling the 'colour' story to *The Meteor* while sending a factual piece to the rest of the press. As the clutch of press cuttings testified, most of the rest had made short, objective references to the battle, though only *The Meteor* had seen fit to use a photograph. Even *The Meteor*, Biggs-Baker had apologetically informed Simon, had relegated the story to an inside page in its later editions, with neither photograph nor leader.

"This is the first time we have had so many mentions in one day," Simon confided to Julia proudly, "and the first time it hasn't been assumed we shall lose."

* * *

Monkton Gibbs pushed the rest of the morning's papers to one side and rubbed his hands as he stared at *The Meteor's* front page. Wreathed in smoke, he drew his typewriter towards him and began to prepare a follow-up for the local press.

'The power of Britain's national press today began to line up behind the Wilberforce board,' he typed.

For him, the Pusey bid was a story that could run and run.

* * *

Harry Temple stared disbelievingly at his copy of the press cuttings and marched into Mowbray's office waving the sheets of paper. He cast a hurt look at a baffled Simon who was just about to leave and slapped them down in front of the chairman.

"Not a single damn' mention of the Show!" he snorted, and stalked out, eyebrows quivering with indignation.

* * *

Pusey's immediate reaction on recovering his composure had been to telephone his merchant bank. It was imperative to move quickly, he instructed them, before there was a swell of public opinion that prompted second thoughts among the institutions.

His advisers tried to appear reassuring.

"Wilberforces have provided their share register ahead of time," the chairman told a sceptical Pusey. "Presumably they want to get the whole business over as quickly as possible."

"More likely Palgraves being cocky," Pusey said, with an uncanny eye to the truth.

"We'll whiz 'em a copy of the share register right away," Kettering had advised Mowbray. "Make 'em think we don't give a damn. We've got as far as we can go on the defence document until we see what Pusey actually comes up with. If we can keep a bit of pressure on, we'll have them playing off the back foot instead of us."

"What about our offer document," Pusey pressed his advisers.

"Posting it today, as planned," they assured him. "We'll also use the Friday night drop to the Sundays so they can have a go at it before Wilberforces can come up with a measured response. The idea is to keep them on the hop."

"I know what the idea is," Pusey growled. "It was my idea."

* * *

Once the offending newspaper had been removed and his choler had subsided, Pusey struggled to achieve a reflective mood. The problem in dealing with his mysterious Bradburn informant, he mused, was in deciding just how well placed he might be to deliver the all-important planning permission for the canal-side development. Without it, of course, acquiring Wilberforces and disposing of its assets would still turn a handsome profit for Pusey Associates. A rival company had already agreed in principle to buy the brass manufacturing business, and there were firm undertakings to buy the offices and lesser town centre properties owned by Wilberforces. Assuming the sale of the business could be firmed up, and Wilberforces fell into his hands at the sensible price he now anticipated, he was set to emerge considerably richer. But if he could also develop the land by the canal he would emerge from the deal wallowing in the stuff. He sat with his hands behind his head and stared wolfishly at the ceiling.

* * *

Having brooded on the matter for a couple of days, Pusey went into the office on the Saturday morning with the intention of listening once more to the recorded message from his informant. Failing to find it after a cursory search, he telephoned Miss Goring and insisted that she meet him there, pooh-poohing her offer to explain precisely where it was on the grounds that he had no idea how to work the tape recorder.

Miss Goring was not pleased to have to work on a Saturday. Although the days of the week were hardly differentiated in the eyes of her employer, she treasured her weekends which she lavished on a menagerie of pets at her cottage near Wimbledon. Now, with the goat about to kid, she had had to leave the place in the hands of the neighbours' boy, practically a half-wit, and it was with barely disguised impatience that, defiant in olive green sweater and jeans, she sat across from her employer and waited for him to emerge from his reverie.

Pusey, having registered the fact that for some reason Miss Goring appeared to be dressed like a refugee from the Women's Land Army, ordered her to play back the tape for the umpteenth time before assuming his customary indifference to her presence and continuing to stare out of the window at an ornate office block that appeared to have mutated from a cinema organ.

"I shall be going down to Yorkshire for the rest of the weekend," he said over his shoulder. "I expect to be back on Monday."

Accepting this as a sign of dismissal, Miss Goring plucked her wax jacket off its peg and flashed him a tight smile of farewell.

"*Don't rush back,*" she said, but only under her breath.

"*That jacket smells like a bloody oil slick,*" Pusey said aloud, but only after the door had closed behind her.

Left to ruminate, he considered again the arrangements his anonymous informant had imposed: that Pusey should meet the informant's go-between, agree a suitable reward for the informant, and shake hands on the deal. Far from regarding the proposal as an affront, although it had certain peculiarities that distinguished it from a conventional business meeting, Pusey identified a degree of intellectual rigour which he welcomed. Regrettably, it also required a second visit to a Bradburn now fully alerted to his identity and intentions. Solace, if solace there was to find, lay in the fact that his informant appeared to be no more anxious to be associated with Pusey than Pusey was to be seen in the benighted town. It was their mutual desire for concealment that had led his informant to say that he would be represented by an intermediary and had persuaded Pusey to accede to a meeting place not so much unusual as bizarre.

Which was why, when Pusey set off for Yorkshire, this time by car, he made sure he took his overcoat.

~Chapter 27~

Summer weekends in Yorkshire, provided the wind
is no more than a man can stand up in and the rain
is not actually veiling the bowler from the batsman, are
inseparable from the smack of leather on willow. It was
the smack of leather on Simon, however, that brought a
temporary halt to Bradburn Cricket Club's match
against a touring police side.

It is widely accepted in cricketing circles that
fielding at forward short leg requires the agility of a
Rumanian gymnast and a frame like seasoned teak.
Weaker citizens, and those of a nervous disposition, are
generally encouraged to field at, say, cow corner, where
a thirst for idle contemplation can be indulged while
others get on with the business of ripping the heart out
of the opposition.

Though Simon scored highly in terms of sinew, and
almost as well in terms of agility, he would have been
the first to acknowledge a tendency to daydream. And
to daydream while fielding at forward short leg is
tantamount to performing Swedish drill while acting as
the knife-thrower's assistant. The consequence of
Simon's daydreaming, together with an
unaccustomedly loose ball from Bradburn's first
change bowler, was that the batsman pulled the ball on

the half-volley, Simon took the ball on his shin, the wicket keeper caught the ball off Simon and the police lost one of England's most feared amateur openers. Simon, who was considered to have contributed to the wicket not through mischance but through indifference to self, was carried off to the sort of reception normally reserved for citizens who snatch children from the path of charging bulls. In Spain, Shelmerdine assured him, he would have been awarded both the batsman's ears.

As it was, he saw out the rest of the match from the pavilion and hardly demurred at all when Mowbray called in at the tea interval and insisted that he should spend a few days in the bosom of his family while he recovered.

* * *

"This is jolly," Rebecca said as she picked him up once more at the station. "It's the children's half-term and I was wondering how I could possibly get away with Hazel for a few days. She's running a teach-in for amateur painters at one of the Oxford colleges. She has her own room and I can go along for nothing."

Simon looked stricken.

"I'll shop before I go and you can stay at home and rest your leg," she said comfortingly.

"I've promised to be back on Wednesday," Simon pleaded, "that only gives me four days."

"We'll be back Tuesday evening without fail," Rebecca promised. Drawing up in the car park of a late-night store, she disappeared inside to plunder the freezer cabinets.

~Chapter 28~

Pusey had studied Miss Goring's map of Bradburn at
regular intervals in recent days, unaware that its
age meant that it diverged in some respects from
reality. Now, with the town's topography clear in his
mind, he chose not to drive through the square to
where he could have parked by the canal, but instead to
turn off opposite the cottages just before the
bandstand.

Bradburn's answer to New Bond Street was
suffused in light spilling from behind the security
grilles of shops that appeared to deal chiefly in
jewellery and women's clothing. Pusey parked and sat
quietly in the car for a moment or two, watching in his
wing mirror as a young couple approached arm-in-arm
along the pavement. Twisting in his seat, he angled his
arm to catch the light from one of the shops to check
that his watch matched the time on the dashboard
clock. It was ten minutes to midnight. The young
couple passed by, glancing incuriously at the car. Pusey
averted his face, pretending to look for something in
the glove-box until their footsteps fell away. Satisfied
that the street was now deserted, he slid quietly out of
the car and closed the door with a gentle click. The late
evening air was cool on his face as he retrieved his coat
from the back seat and threw it over his shoulders. His

soft-soled shoes made a gentle padding sound on the worn stone pavement as, seeking the shadows, he stole off towards the Cuckoo Steps.

* * *

It had been remarked on numerous occasions that the only flat piece of land in Bradburn was the cricket pitch, although there were visiting sides who would have been happy to contradict. The fact was that while most of the town was connected by perfectly normal if somewhat steep roads and byways, the roads and byways themselves were in places connected by flights of stone steps where the contours to be surmounted had defeated the early road-makers. Pusey, panting slightly, came to the foot of the most precipitous of these and peered unenthusiastically upwards. Producing a pocket torch from his overcoat, he snapped it on and aimed the beam up to where the ancient steps veered away into blackness. He flinched as some night creature screeched seemingly inches from his ear. Glumly, his free hand clutching the worn iron handrail, he began the ascent and found himself in a world bounded by the pool of light wavering at his feet and the ribbon of starlit sky above.

The steps seemed endless. Having paused briefly to rest against the cool stone walls, he was starting off once more when he stumbled. A flash of his torch showed that the steps had abruptly given way to a gently rising path. Ahead, the shifting beams of street lights flickered through the swaying branches of tall shrubs that now marked the path like sentries. Almost trotting now, Pusey travelled no more than a dozen paces before he came out at a well maintained road where Miss Goring's ancient map had indicated only a footpath. He could, he realised, just as easily have reached the spot by car. Across the road, reassuring under the street lights, was the gate promised by his correspondent. On its far side a rising flight of concrete steps gleamed palely, their edges marked with painted white stripes. Pausing only to get his breath back, Pusey crossed the deserted road and stepped through the open gate. Feeling exposed and conspicuous, he veered from the path and struggled up the treacherously dry grass of the bank towards the dark mass of the building looming ahead. A long way away a clock chimed a tinny, secular-sounding midnight.

Although the night was cool rather than chilly, he paused to slip into his overcoat as he scurried towards the shadows of the darkened building. Within touching distance of its walls he paused for a moment, killing the beam of the torch. The path stretched into the dark on either side of him. Pusey listened to his heart beat and tried to recall precisely what his informant had said. Somewhere - which way? - a door would be slightly ajar. Quivering with anxiety he set off to his left, sleeve brushing the rough brickwork as he felt his way along the wall. He passed a number of rooms, silent behind drawn curtains, then stopped, wondering whether to change direction. On the one hand, reason dictated that if he continued in the same direction for long enough he would be sure to come to the open door, even if it meant stumbling round most of the building's exterior. On the other hand...He set off again and almost immediately stumbled against a door. Pressure from his searching hands was sufficient to send it banging noisily against the inner wall.

Pusey swallowed nervously. The temptation to run was overwhelming as he stared at the grey rectangle of light the open door revealed. Moments passed. Ears straining for the sounds of the challenge he felt surely must come, he produced a handkerchief and used it to wipe the perspiration from his forehead as he tried to conjure up some reasonable explanation he might offer for his presence. Tentatively, panic subsiding, he drew his coat around him and stepped inside.

Risking a quick flash of his torch, Pusey found that he was in a high-ceilinged corridor. It was narrow, with shiny, cream-painted walls. He heard footsteps ahead of him, light and almost certainly female, walking briskly across linoleum. His glasses had begun to steam up and he pocketed the torch for a moment in order to give them a quick wipe with the handkerchief. There was a flash of white and a swish of skirts as the owner of the footsteps, unconscious of the intruder lurking in the shadows, crossed the end of the corridor. The footsteps receded and Pusey steeled himself, ready to bolt at any moment. Nerves jangling, he edged slowly forward in the gloom.

From somewhere on his left the surging gush of a sluice was followed by the sound of a tap dripping into a metal sink behind a half-open door. His eyes were slowly becoming accustomed to the dim light and he hesitated where the corridor gave way to an open area illuminated sufficiently for him to see that it was furnished with plain wooden benches. Off to the right was an untended glass cubicle and two public telephones in front of which a trolley, its white paint chipped with age, supported a tea urn. High overhead a glazed canopy framed stars in a navy sky. To meet his mystery informant he would have to cross the space, pass the wooden benches and enter the corridor opposite. Someone coughed, too far away to startle him. Taking a deep breath, he listened a moment for signs that there might be others in the vicinity until, reassured, he darted across the opening and into the facing corridor. Approaching the third door on the right, he pressed down the handle, thrust the door open and fell into the room. The door, unassisted, swung silently to behind him.

What had been the corridor's mingled smells of antiseptic and floor polish gave way to a single, pungent smell that stung his nostrils and made his eyes water. The room, cold as a meat store, should have been in total darkness. Instead, a table-lamp in a corner office, really little more than a booth, revealed a burly figure in a dark uniform slowly lumbering to his feet from a desk where a drinks flask and sandwiches were set out beside an opened newspaper. Hypnotised, Pusey watched as the figure reached out and pressed a switch. Bright lights flooded the room revealing a décor of stainless steel and white tiles. Miserably, he removed his glasses, wiped the perspiration on his tie then, with trembling hand, replaced them. Unwilling to take his eyes off the approaching figure, he slowly became aware of his surroundings. On his right, so close that he could have reached out and touched them, two steel tables with what appeared to be built-in drainage dominated the floorspace. Opposite, a bank of steel cabinets occupied the wall up to head height.

Pusey watched helplessly as the porter or whatever he was approached. Swallowing and wiping crumbs from his mouth at the same time, and with a voice that suggested nothing more threatening than mild curiosity, the porter said "Now, 'oo the 'ell are you?"

Several things passed through Pusey's mind, among which, as the use of his limbs seemed to be returning, was an almost irresistible impulse to flee. Uppermost, however, was the pressing necessity to provide a suitable explanation before the man decided to summon the police. The porter's expression of stolid enquiry appeared to be edging towards truculence. In an uncharacteristic but inspired move, Pusey opted for the truth.

"I am looking," he said in what he hoped were tones of measured normality, "for Percy Frobisher."

* * *

Percy Frobisher's troubles had stemmed from his monumental cupidity. That, and a fate that had given him Elton Jarvis as a nephew. Jarvis had been born to and promptly abandoned by Frobisher's inaptly named sister, Prudence. Once fate had compounded the insult by removing Mrs. Frobisher and the motherly commonsense with which she had fostered her nephew, the warm-hearted Frobisher had found himself *in loco parentis* and had quickly been reduced to a state where the price of a quiet life appeared to be submission to Elton's every whim. And, as Elton had approached manhood, his chief whim had appeared to be a desire to be the one-man nemesis for capitalism. When Elton decided that a take-over of Wilberforces might be a suitable starting point, Percy, in thrall, had been forced to become his reluctant accomplice. Having first written the letter to Pusey dictated by Jarvis, he had then been bullied into leaving the telephone messages dictated by what he was finally forced to acknowledge was a truly poisonous nephew.

A realist at heart, Elton Jarvis privately conceded that the takeover of Wilberforces would be but a modest step in the overthrow of capitalism. But it would be a start. And if it also resulted in the wholesale dismissal of workers who patronised and despised him at Trades Council meetings, so much the better. He was, he conceded, only slightly less unpopular on Bradburn's Planning Committee, but at least the knowledge gained there had inspired him to approach

Pusey with the prospect of a canal-side development. Even if that might still take some swinging. . .

His masterstroke, Elton was convinced, had been to use his uncle, a lickspittle pensioner of Wilberforces, to act as the reluctant intermediary whom he could disown any time it appeared prudent to do so. It had been his nephew's insistence that he should pen the letter to Pusey and make the subsequent telephone call that had led to Percy's first heart attack, coincidentally freeing his cottage for Shelmerdine's assault on its chimneys.

* * *

"Percy Frobisher!" The porter's tone brightened at the name. "You a relative?"

"Close friend," Pusey muttered, fumbling behind him for the door handle.

"Well, 'e's 'ere alright," the porter conceded. "But," he complained, "someone should've told me you were coming."

Pusey found himself following the man to his cubicle where he produced a clipboard which he tapped with a chewed pencil as he looked down a list of names.

"You were lucky to find me 'ere at all," he said conversationally, a sentiment with which Pusey felt too defeated to take issue, "I normally take my supper to the canteen. Still, let's see..." With a satisfied grunt he stabbed his pencil at a name and approached the ranked steel drawers. "Frobisher...two down, four across."

Grasping a handle, he drew open the drawer that contained the mortal remains of a Percy Frobisher for whom the evening's assignation with Pusey dictated by his nephew had proved the last straw. With a discretion that disguised the fact even from the man in the next bed, Percy had had his second and final heart attack and had expired that afternoon, staring myopically at the fading image of Shelmerdine's sooty-edged get-well card.

Horrified, Pusey stared as the drawer slipped smoothly out on its runners to reveal the waxy features of the late Percy Frobisher. With a yelp that echoed off the glistening walls, he turned on his heel, flung open the door and fled out of the hospital as though all the shades in the mortuary were plucking at his flying coattails, the smell of formaldehyde clinging to him like ectoplasm.

* * *

Ghosts were on Simon's mind, too.

Rebecca had reacted to the purple swelling on her husband's leg by becoming the soul of tenderness. Having first applied a poultice that threatened to add the complication of third-degree burns, she had then removed it in favour of a handful of ice cubes wrapped in a tea towel. These had gone some way to relieving the ache, though at the cost of a large damp stain on the as yet unvarnished floorboards of the sitting room. Now, lying in bed next to a recumbent Simon, she smiled contentedly as she reflected on her ministrations. Indeed, had Simon not convinced her that she should go, she had earlier reached a point at which she would almost have been prepared to cancel the Oxford visit in favour of a few days in her husband's company. Now, having been bested in the argument, she drifted contentedly off to sleep. Despite the renewed throbbing in his shin, Simon was himself approaching the point of warm doziness that precedes sleep when the pillow twitched beneath his head.

"We haven't had a story," Martin said.

Martin had a remarkably deep voice for a six-year-old. Simon struggled wearily to sit up, though even

Martin's voice was hardly likely to wake a Rebecca
capable of sleeping through an artillery barrage.

"It's alright," Martin assured him with
disconcerting intuition, "we won't wake the others - I've
already got them up."

A dimly audible murmuring transformed itself into
the two younger children as they edged round the door,
Katy on hands and knees. Simon winced as he pushed
the bedclothes aside and sat on the edge of the bed.
Martin began to usher his siblings out, casting an
admonitory glance behind to stifle any inclination on
Simon's part to renege.

"Father stopped a cricket ball with his leg," Martin
explained. He had been awake when Simon and
Rebecca had arrived to relieve the babysitter and his
father's ordeal had already acquired mythical status. "It
won the match for his side and he was carried round
the field on a stool."

Simon made to demur, but a glance from Martin
silenced him.

"Hazel says the lady in the bakers couldn't stop a
pig in a ginnel," Nicholas offered. "What's a ginnel?"

Simon, carrying a yawning Katy, followed the boys.
Limping down the stairs and along the hall, switching
lights on as he went, he waited patiently in the sitting
room as Martin consulted the pile of books tottering in
his brother's arms and selected a volume of ghost
stories.

"You can start at the beginning and we'll tell you
when to stop," he instructed.

"The idea of a bedtime story is to send you to
sleep," Simon said, "not to frighten you half to death."

"If we go to sleep you can carry us up," Martin
counselled.

"Slowly," Nicholas piped, "'cos of your leg."

Rebecca was awakened by sunlight.

The cat was kneading the pillow by her ear as she freed an arm from the bedclothes and sent it exploring for her husband. She sat up abruptly as the hand located a space that not only lacked a husband but which was not even warm. Guessing that Simon might be preparing a breakfast tray she listened for sounds of life in the house, but all was still. It was almost nine o'clock by the bedside clock as she got up, careful not to disturb the now recumbent cat, and looked in on the children. All three were deeply asleep. Clutching her robe around her, she padded quietly downstairs.

Simon was asleep on the sitting room sofa where the children, under Martin's direction, had covered him in cushions. Not even Katy had wakened him when, urged towards the stairs between her brothers, she had tottered into her pile of kitchen utensils and sent them racketing across the wooden floor. Three nursery chairs grouped by the sofa, and the book of ghost stories open on Simon's chest, told the story. Tiptoeing out, Rebecca began to prepare breakfast. When the coffee had begun to percolate satisfactorily, and the water was boiling in the pan of eggs, she lit a cigarette and telephoned Hazel to put off Oxford.

"You're behaving like a bloody squaw," an angry Hazel hissed as Rebecca announced that she was forgoing Oxford in order to tend the injured Simon.

Raising her hand as though to stifle a yawn, Rebecca whooped a war cry down the receiver then hung up.

~Chapter 29~

The battle for Wilberforces, safe in the hands of expensive intermediaries, rumbled on. In one of the City's strange courtesies, Pusey's merchant bank sent a copy of the Pusey Offer Document to Wilberforce's merchant bank, prompting a brief call from Kettering to Mowbray. It was, Kettering said apologetically, almost contemptuously brief, doing little more than reiterating Pusey's original assault on the Wilberforce management while restating an offer that comfortably out-valued the target's faltering share price.

"I'm afraid most of the institutions will probably sell," a subdued Richard Causton had told Kettering, as though Ryan & Gilliatt might somehow be held responsible for any defections to the enemy. "I expect most will wait to see whether you manage to smoke out a higher bid when you respond to his Offer Document, but some are already listening to their fund managers and getting out. Let's face it," he said, emboldened by Kettering's silence, "most of them have been sitting on the shares for ages. They'll be happy to get rid of them before they finish up on the Bulletin Board."

For a publicly listed company, the Stock Exchange's Bulletin Board represented a refined kind of ignominy, a knacker's yard for companies whose shares had sunk to the point where market makers were no longer prepared to trade them. It had been left to Kettering to relay the news to Mowbray at one of their now routine London meetings on the Monday morning.

"Not to be *too* dispirited, though," he said, thrust by Mowbray's glum expression into a cheerfulness that was becoming increasingly difficult to sustain. "The Sundays practically ignored his Offer Document, despite their Friday night drop. Our revaluation is beginning to look pretty good and we're putting it about that the very least shareholders will get if they hang on is an increased offer from the other side. That, together with the profits forecast and an increased dividend, should look pretty good."

Mowbray managed a smile. "I know we shan't go under without a fight, but if the institutions prefer cash in hand to promises, well..."

Kettering waved the thought away in a cloud of cigar smoke. "What *is* slightly puzzling is that Pusey came in at a price which, for him, is relatively generous. Are you sure the land by the canal..."

Mowbray shook his head. This was, literally, ground they had been over before.

When Councillor Whitaker had taken him aside after the party, it had been to offer her support should the Wilberforce board wish to strengthen its defence by having the canal-side land rezoned for residential purposes, opening the way for the type of marina the planners at neighbouring Broadbridge had scotched and which had become talismanic in Pusey's eyes. The idea that Wilberforces should apply to have the land rezoned had been an early suggestion from the Palgraves revaluation team.

"The Mayor would support us if we were to apply," Mowbray said tiredly, "but she implied that not everyone on the Planning Committee might feel the same way."

Kettering refused to let the information cast him down.

"Well," he said, "at least we can rely on the family hanging in there."

~Chapter 30~

Julia was at a loose end.

With Simon *hors de combat* and off the scene for several days, and with her father spending much of his time in London, she had been reduced to serving as a spare pair of hands for Harry Temple as he threw himself into the final preparations for Bradburn Show.

The status attaching to Temple's chairmanship of Bradburn Show Committee outweighed by far any that attached to his directorship at Wilberforces. As the final arbiter of space allocation for activities at the Show, his hand in the company's annual wage negotiations was immeasurably stronger than that of the union negotiators whose members were vegetable growers or pigeon fanciers to a man. To goad Colonel Temple to the point where he forgot he was the Wilberforce personnel director and became instead the Bradburn Show chairman was to risk the wrath of wives doing their flower arranging between the clay pigeon traps and the junior brass band contest.

So far Julia had found there was printing to be done, marquee contractors to be visited and innumerable forays to be made to the showground where her uncle would pace out complex distances and angles before making runic marks in the ground with his shooting stick, only to return moments later to scratch them out with the toe of a dusty brogue. Julia trailed tirelessly after him, pretending to herself that she was helping and silently fretting at her impotence in the face of the bid and, occasionally, at her uncle's apparent disinclination to acknowledge its existence. After a couple of days of this she abandoned him to his own devices and started to catch up on the social calls she had been too busy to make when she had first returned to Bradburn. To her surprise, she was welcomed at the Silver Library by a Miss Fitton clutching a handkerchief to her scant bosom and almost fainting with pleasure.

"She's been dying to speak to you but didn't really wish to disturb you, what with that awful business in the papers," said her friend, the stalwart Miss Bertram. She helped Miss Fitton to a flimsy chair which scarcely creaked as her meagre weight collapsed on to it. Clutching an embroidered handkerchief, Miss Fitton stared beseechingly at a thoroughly confused Julia.

"It's the silk crochet thread you brought her from Leeds," Miss Bertram explained. Her tone was subdued, as though to conceal her remarks from a friend who was, Julia reckoned, all of two feet away. "The silly thing spilled ink on it and now she's terrified she won't finish her doily-napkins in time for the Show this weekend."

Miss Fitton flinched as she absorbed Miss Bertram's look of gentle reproof, her tear-filled eyes swimming between her friend and Julia as she managed a tiny nod of contrition.

"You'd been so kind," she sobbed tremulously, "coming all the way from London and then stopping in Leeds to shop for me. I didn't dare telephone..."

"I said you probably had more on your mind than silk thread," Miss Bertram interrupted. "Then I said, if you *were* to call in, and if there was any chance at all that you were going into Leeds..."

Julia bent down and, seeking a spot not yet streaked by tears, kissed the powdery softness of Miss Fitton's cheek.

"I've been terribly busy," she apologised, "but I could easily have popped over there for you. As it is..."

Hope harried anxiety across Miss Fitton's disconsolate face. Miss Bertram, her hand supportively on her friend's shoulder, appeared to be holding her breath.

"...as it is," Julia continued, "I'm going there in an hour or so to collect Simon. If I start a little early I can pop into the wool shop. You'll have your precious thread before the end of the afternoon."

The two older women exchanged smiles of relief, eyes closed in thanksgiving.

"I'll be back shortly," Julia promised as she stepped from the Silver Library's schoolroom smells into the sunlit square, the door closing behind her setting up a celebratory clangour.

"Such a *nice* young man, Mr. Beresford," Miss Fitton said, for Simon had become a regular customer for some of the library's lighter fiction.

"Such a *pity* he's married," Miss Bertram lamented.

~Chapter 31~

The meeting at Palgraves was turning into one of the protracted drafting sessions Mowbray had come to loath. He was surrounded and as often as not ignored by management consultants, bankers, brokers, solicitors and public relations people whose combined fees, he estimated, would comfortably account for a year's profits if the bid ran for as long Kettering was now talking about.

"As we know, gentlemen, posting of the Offer Document by Pusey Associates started the period in which the bid must be completed. They posted their Offer Document last Friday..." All eyes glanced at copies of the document in front of them. "...and that dictates when we must post our defence. We have already made a good start. This morning we will amend it in the light of Pusey's offer, and that will leave us a week or so for due diligence procedures. The Wilberforce finance director and their company secretary are, as usual, at our disposal at Bradburn."

Despite the anticipated longueurs, Mowbray smiled to himself. Although Kettering's pep-talks were liberally sprinkled with 'we,' 'us' and 'our', those around the table knew that immediately roles had been assigned he would disappear and do whatever senior merchant bankers did while matters of detail were being sorted out by lesser mortals. Where the Bradburn defence team were concerned, this meant almost hourly contact with the two lesser mortals who were now sitting opposite Mowbray and staring at him with impenetrable expressions.

One was a portly, morose man in his fifties who Mowbray thought would not have looked out of place on the bench of bishops, the other a pallid young woman in white rimmed spectacles who brought an air of clinical fastidiousness to the drafting process. Nothing, they had impressed on Mowbray, could go into the Wilberforce response until they had scrutinised, dissected and reassembled it into the arid and unchallengeable veracities designed to drive the predator and his advisers to distraction in their search for loopholes.

Kettering ran on for several more minutes before ending his contribution and leaving with the more senior members of the meeting. The lawyers facing Mowbray moved round the table and took the now vacant chairs on either side of him.

"It says here," the female solicitor began in her dry monotone, "that Bradburn is in Yorkshire. I think we might begin by ascertaining that that there are no other Bradburns, or locations that might be confused with Bradburn, within or adjacent the county boundary..."

Mowbray's eyes glazed as, mentally, he began re-planning one of the Bradburn House rose beds.

~Chapter 32~

"How's your poorly leg?" Julia had met the returning Simon at the station and was studying him at arms' length.

Simon beamed. "Practically as new."

Passers-by stared as he lifted a trouser leg to reveal the multi-hued mosaic of his shin and, Julia noted, a much reduced swelling. Fussing like a favourite niece tending an enfeebled aunt, she ushered him into the car and took off into the traffic with nerve-wracking adroitness.

"I spoke to Shelmerdine last night," Simon shouted above the car's well-bred roar, hands cravenly gripping the sides of his seat. "We're going to the nets this evening with Dipstick. Of course, I shall pass with flying colours."

Bradburn Cricket Club's ground was across the lane from the showground, and tradition dictated that on Show Saturday Bradburn would meet Broadbridge in a forty-over match which invariably saw little quarter asked and none given. For Simon, whose place in the first eleven had seemed assured before his accident, it was now a matter of honour to be fit to represent Bradburn on the big day. Julia, concentrating on the road, felt rather than saw the concerned glances Simon seemed to be aiming in her direction.

Julia was aware that, after the initial surge of excitement, the strain of the past few weeks was now beginning to show. But where her own impression was that it manifested itself as no more than a light shadowing under the eyes, Simon's glances suggested he was observing the decline of a terminally sick friend.

"Well?" he prompted as they left the suburbs behind and began to wend their way through the patchwork of fields.

Julia accelerated past a Bradburn-bound bus before replying.

"Not *too* well, I'm afraid," she said. "Father's practically living in London and everyone else is running around answering screeds of idiotic questions from the drafting team there. Except Uncle Harry, of course. I shouldn't be surprised if the Bradburn defence team went out and got drunk every night. Everyone is being very consoling to me, which is sweet but misguided, and the rest, including Bill Pritchard - ha-ha," it was somehow clear the 'ha-ha' attached only to Pritchard, "are getting on with running the business."

"And Hugo Russell?"

Julia's taut expression relaxed into a smile.

"Shrinking fast and behaving like an absolute poppet. Our people couldn't have done without him. I've decided his problem was poor self-esteem. He ate to console himself: being nasty to people was his pre-emptive way of stopping people being beastly to him because he was fat. It was a vicious circle. Dr. Price's pills have stopped him worrying and started him slimming and he's absolutely fine. He's refusing to go home, by the way, until he's achieved his target weight, whatever that is, but Tracy says he's been sending his wife flowers."

Simon digested the news contentedly. He disliked being unable to like people, and the prospect of a rehabilitated Russell appealed to him. What prevented a wider sense of wellbeing, however, was the fact that Julia was looking undeniably peaky, and the golden glow on which her admirers were wont to comment was looking distinctly ochrous. Simon, revitalised after his few days at home, despite a surfeit of hard-boiled eggs, probed for the reason.

"I hope you haven't been overdoing things without me...?" His concerned tone robbed the suggestion of hubris.

Impatiently, Julia denied that she had.

"There's been hardly anything for me to do. The newspapers no longer seem to be bothered, except for the locals, and Monkton Gibbs says even they're losing interest." A sigh escaped as she smacked the steering wheel in frustration. "The consensus seems to be that we shall lose, and that's the end of it so far as almost everyone is concerned. Hugo Russell says bids have their silly seasons when nothing much is happening except for those drafting documents. We have, he says, reached the eye of the storm. You and I can just kick our heels because, frankly, for the time being at least, they don't need us."

There was the suspicion of a tear in her eye as she glanced at him, measuring the effect of her words.

Simon was nonplussed. Upset because Julia was upset, he was totally at a loss what to do about it.

"And," Julia continued, still moist eyed but definitely not blubbing, Simon was relieved to see, "Percy Frobisher died and Elton Jarvis had him cremated practically overnight, poisonous little man."

Simon digested this without comment as Julia drew out to pass a stationary car whose open bonnet concealed the stooping upper half of a human being. Braking suddenly, Julia immediately aimed their car towards the verge and, in a manner uncomfortably reminiscent of Rebecca, threw it into reverse so abruptly that Simon was thrown forcibly against his seatbelt.

"That's Roger Spofforth's car," she said in explanation as she reversed up to it at a speed that threatened to deposit the rest of its owner into the engine compartment. Together they got out of the car and approached as Roger Spofforth screwed his neck round and peered up through oil-streaked spectacles. His expression was one of profound gloom. Even a man of cheerier disposition than Spofforth, Simon conceded, might have been cast down by the spreading pool of foul smelling oil beneath the car. He peered down at the machinery with the comprehension of aboriginal man confronting a thermionic valve.

"Maybe we can help," he said, blushing slightly as his natural humility recognised the offer for the casuistry it was.

"You're standing in the light," Spofforth responded testily.

"And *you're* standing in a pool of oil," Julia pointed out astringently. "I suspect the sump gasket has gone."

Spofforth's head emerged as he drew himself slowly upright. He picked up a rag from the top of the radiator and rubbed desultorily at the black oil covering his hands and wrists. The look of admiration he cast at Julia faded as his glance switched to Simon.

"I was reaching that conclusion as you arrived," he conceded. "The engine has completely seized and the boot is full of the props for our Morris Dance at the Show on Saturday." He quelled the urge to release an Olympic display of tantrum-throwing and merely said pettishly, "We had proposed a full dress rehearsal this evening. I have been chosen to dance the Shepherd's Hey." Spofforth's demeanour changed and he almost blushed at the weight of his responsibilities. "As it is in fact a solo, it is, of course, properly known as a Morris Jig and not a Morris Dance."

The truth, Julia suspected, was that he had volunteered. Readers of superior literature will recall that only a meat-axe could dissuade Poppy Kegley-Bassington from performing her rhythmic dances. Next to Spofforth's attachment to Shepherd's Hey, Poppy would have appeared pusillanimous, it being common knowledge among Morris Men that a Spofforth impaled on every weapon in a butcher's armoury would still have leapt from his coffin and danced Shepherd's Hey unless firmly screwed down.

Julia managed to look suitably impressed while remaining businesslike.

"We'll send Dipstick out for you," she promised, "and we'll get him to bring some sand to put on that oil."

She urged Simon back into her car and they roared off.

Once in Bradburn, Simon went off to the garage to tell Dipstick of Spofforth's predicament and to report his own return to cricketing duty, while Julia, finding the Silver Library now closed, set off for the cottage shared by the Misses Bertram and Fitton. Parking her car on the verge behind their old Morris Minor, she walked down the cottage path past where someone had evidently been interrupted while weeding. A floral print curtain twitched briefly at a downstairs window as she approached. Almost simultaneously the door was opened by a Miss Fitton who stood fluttering on the doorstep, twittering with anticipation.

Miss Fitton's prowess with her crochet needles was legendary, for she plied them with a deftness that had brought not only local but national recognition. Practically the first thing the visitor saw in the over-furnished hall was the framed cover of a national needlework magazine where, at what was quite clearly the foot of the small waterfall in the hills behind the cottage, a crocheted Christening shawl had been spread artlessly across the grass. Alongside, Miss Fitton, her pride of ownership clearly caught by the camera, pointed at it with a proprietorial finger.

Julia stood beneath the picture and handed a small brown paper bag to Miss Fitton. Eyelids fluttering with relief, Miss Fitton plucked out the twin skeins of thread and showed them to a hovering Miss Bertram. Miss Bertram started to extend her hands to grasp Julia's then thrust them into the pocket of her gardening apron as she saw they were still grubby from weeding.

"I'm sure we shall never be able to thank you enough," she said gruffly.

Miss Fitton, possessed by a speechless euphoria, cast an adoring glance at Julia and drifted off into the front parlour. Julia, to her surprise, found herself being gently ushered to the door.

"Miss Fitton simply can't bear anyone to see her work before it's finished, and now there's so much to do before the Show on Saturday." The apology emerged in a conspiratorial whisper as Miss Bertram paused on the threshold. "You wouldn't believe that only a few years ago she started with covered buttons and edgings for linen, that sort of thing. And now..." She shook her head in admiration.

"I'm sure there will be nothing to touch Miss Fitton's doily-napkins," Julia managed as she felt herself being edged over the step. "Mr. Spofforth might just as well give her the first prize right away."

The older woman could not have looked more shocked if Julia had lunged at her with the nearby gardening fork.

"Mr. Spofforth...?" she said weakly.

"He's been asked to organise the handicrafts exhibition; I thought you would have heard...though I don't suppose he'll actually be *judging* it, of course," Julia added quickly.

Miss Bertram relaxed slightly and her expression changed to that of one rising to her feet after a traffic accident to find she had sustained only minor injuries.

"May one ask whose idea...?"

"I believe it was the vicar. His wife..."

Norman Butterworth's wife was pregnant, and though she was known to have a constitution that shrugged off pregnancies as other women contended with dropped hems, her husband had insisted that she should leave organisation of the handicrafts section to someone offering a greater certainty of not actually giving birth during the presentation ceremony. It was, said those who had caught up with the development, just about Spofforth's only qualification. It was also a fact that the Reverend Norman Butterworth, for all his ecumenism, vaguely disapproved of Spofforth's introduction of pagan dancing to Bradburn Show. Sticking him with the handicrafts section would, he told a doubting Connie Butterworth, serve him jolly well right.

Miss Bertram accepted the explanation stoically.

"Mrs. Butterworth has already done the donkey work," Julia assured her, "and I'm sure the judges will all be the usual ones. Practically all Mr. Spofforth has to do is to turn up. What could possibly go wrong?"

Back at Bradburn House Julia drove round the drive to the back, parked the car in its disused stable and walked back round to the front of the house to take in the drowsy evening scents of the garden. As she approached the porticoed porch the scents were replaced by that of her father's pipe tobacco. He was silhouetted against the light from the open door, his face in shadow, but there was something about his posture that made Julia approach him circumspectly. He snapped himself upright at the sound of her footsteps and produced a smile that was clearly an effort.

Julia stopped in front of him, their faces level. "Something's the matter..." she said.

Mowbray stared at her silently for a moment, then reached out and drew her to him. "It's dear old Uncle Edwin," he said. "He's agreed to sell his shares to Pusey."

~Chapter 33~

A lthough the development had so far escaped the
attention of either of the contending parties, Uncle
Edwin had committed his shares to the opposition
fairly early on in the proceedings, though a number of
factors had needed to come together to prompt the
defection.

The first was the fact that when Pusey's financial
advisers had begun to telephone their way through the
list of Wilberforces' private shareholders to establish
their intentions, they had decided to start at the top
with Uncle Edwin whose shareholding dwarfed even
those of the institutions. His call, when it came, was
made by a silver-tongued siren from Pusey's advisers
known to her male colleagues as the Venus de Milo, the
Milo being the square Mile-o which constituted, in City
terms, a pretty rollicking sort of joke. Anything in
trousers, it was believed, was laughably vulnerable the
moment her honeyed tones trickled into its ear. She
could hardly have been aware, however, that Uncle
Edwin's Y-chromosome had withered on the vine long
before she was born. And, so far as there was anything
to be achieved by a telephone call, Edwin would have
been neither more nor less biddable had he been
telephoned from a Bangalore call centre.

The second factor that had led Edwin to defect had been the timing: the bid for Wilberforces had arisen at a crucial time in his bid for immortality.

Edwin's was a strangely reclusive character. It had been formed at the hands of a doting mother and a father whose eccentricity welled from an overdose of whatever it was that coursed in dilution through the veins of Harry Temple.

Many years ago, during his childhood, Edwin had developed an unearthly pallor. Although it was caused chiefly by a diet of debilitating blandness and his parents' reluctance to expose him to the perils of fresh air, it had nevertheless convinced his mother that he would be unlikely to survive the rigours of life at public school. She had therefore engaged a tutor who settled into the Lodge for the remainder of Edwin's childhood and proceeded to cram his pupil with the copious quantities of Latin and textbook botany on which Edwin became inordinately well informed to the exclusion of practically everything else.

Edwin's mother watched with increasing pride as he soaked it all up. His father, Seymour Wilberforce, on the other hand, appeared to be only intermittently aware of the boy's existence. It was Seymour's habit to retire to Pinfold Manor's cavernous cellars immediately after breakfast from where he rarely returned to the bosom of his family before it was time to change for dinner. If, between-whiles, he happened to encounter Edwin in one of the house's seemingly endless corridors, he would step aside politely and gaze abstractedly after the boy as though striving to put a name to him.

Seymour's time spent in the cellars was not wasted. It was spent tending a device he had constructed at great expense and with which he was determined to become the first man to convert coal into diamond. His grasp of scientific principles, however, fell short of his enthusiasm. The result was that shortly after Edwin's eleventh birthday the combination of enormous heat and pressure the experiment required, allied to the increasingly unstable state of the equipment and its operator, led to an explosion that converted much of Seymour Wilberforce to carbon and part of the house to rubble.

Not conspicuously moved by her husband's death, Mrs. Wilberforce had put the house to rights while unwittingly disposing of the world's first synthetic diamonds. She then returned to her sole purpose in life which was to ensure that whatever Edwin wanted Edwin got. Ten supine years after her husband's death, she too expired and, almost on the eve of his twenty-first birthday Edwin found himself heir to a substantial slice of Wilberforce Original Brassworks. Freed by his parents' deaths to wander outdoors, he immediately fell in love with the Cotswolds countryside which had previously registered as something, principally green, on the other side of a plate glass window. He had promptly resolved to dedicate life henceforth to recording its flora for posterity in the form he had so much admired in his personal tutor's illustrated textbooks. Now in his late seventies, and not remotely discouraged by the avalanche of rejection slips that sample pages from his work had so far attracted, Edwin interpreted the bid for his shares as a sign that he should do something he had been considering for some time: he would use a fraction of the money to pay for his work to be published privately.

If the first factor in his decision to sell his Wilberforce shares had been the siren telephone call from London, and the second had been his resolve to publish his life's work, then the third was sparked by a growing resentment of Wilberforces. It seemed to Edwin that on the few occasions his father had condescended, or perhaps remembered, to speak to him, it had been to din into him the fact that everything the family owned stemmed from the good fortune of earlier generations in accumulating a commanding shareholding in the company through a complex series of intermarriages. What he had omitted to add was that their family's attenuating grip on reality probably derived from the same marital conjunctions.

What had once seemed merely a piece of jolly good fortune had, as Edwin grew increasingly reclusive, morphed into a sense of dependency. As time passed, and as Edwin's introspection began to border on paranoia, this had resulted in a heartfelt resentment towards the company, despite the fact that it continued to smother him with an income wildly beyond anything he might ever need. Nevertheless, had he ever had the misfortune to have met Elton Jarvis, they would have been as twin souls in their aversion to the company.

But it had not always been so. After his mother died, his housekeeper, who had half-expected Edwin to wither away in her wake, found instead that his personality began to develop like a bloom borne from darkness into sunshine. Kittens, no longer confined to the disused stables, found it necessary to skitter past Edwin on the parquet in order to avoid being picked up and cuddled half to death. The housekeeper, whose existence had previously rarely impinged on Edwin, found herself working for half the hours and twice the money.

It was at this stage that Edwin decided to learn to play the piano and then fell madly in love with the woman being richly rewarded to teach him. There followed an ill-considered proposal of marriage which she rejected sternly and irrevocably. The damage was done. Almost overnight Edwin succumbed to the Wilberforce family failing and began to retreat into the slough of misanthropy verging on eccentricity that quickly came to define him. Kittens, now cats, were sternly shown the door and the housekeeper's hours were halved with a corresponding reduction in pay. And Wilberforces, the fount of his fortune, became in his imagination the despots with the power to snatch everything away.

The fact that he could have paid to have his book published many times over without even denting a month's income became irrelevant. The pleasure of finally seeing himself in print would be increased immeasurably by dropping the frightful Wilberforces in the cart.

Yet...yet... there remained somewhere in a cobwebbed recess of his memory a vague yet lingering recollection of a time when something – some event - had preceded the tide of resentment; something that had prompted him into a grand and selfless gesture...But that was long ago, before the mist began to descend.

* * *

As the Venus de Square Mile-o had promised, the Pusey Offer Document and a reply paid envelope arrived with Edwin the following morning. Edwin, having signed away his shares with a manic flourish, popped the form in the envelope and propped it in front of the studio clock. Then promptly forgot about it.

* * *

When his advisers relayed to a delighted Pusey the fact that they had received a verbal commitment that would part Wilberforces' largest private shareholder from his holding, Pusey's thanks were, for him, almost fervent. After a couple of days had passed, however, and no material evidence of the transaction arrived, his elation began to flag.

"Ring the old fool up again and tell him to get a move on," Pusey instructed.

* * *

Julia sat opposite her father in one of the easy chairs flanking the morning room fireplace. A single standard lamp provided light that cast the rest of the room into shadows. It suited Julia's mood. Having discovered the concern behind her father's greeting, she had put an arm round his waist and silently steered him into the house before heading for the kitchen to produce the hot drinks they now held as she struggled to understand what had happened.

"I suppose it's not surprising, really," her father was saying, apparently without rancour. "Edwin's never taken a blind bit of interest in the business, and we've done absolutely nothing to cultivate him."

"But he's family," Julia interrupted, "and the biggest family shareholder. He of all people should have stuck it out. And why on earth would he want the money anyway? He must be rich as Croesus."

"I don't suppose for a minute he *does* need it," her father conceded. "Perhaps Pusey's side simply caught him at the right moment. Your mother always said that side of the family is impossible to predict."

"And a company's future, people's futures, can rest on nothing more than his mood!" She sat silently for a moment, then asked, "Why have *I* never met Uncle Edwin?"

Mowbray had started to ease himself out of the deep chair and begin the pottering, pipe emptying routine that preceded his retiring to bed. At Julia's question he sank back into the chair, frowning.

"I suppose there was simply no reason for you to do so," he said. "He is very much a recluse, decidedly dotty, according to your mother. And we, of course, have never made any attempt to involve him in the business. I suppose it was a case of letting sleeping dogs lie, and now we could be about to pay the penalty." He stood up, knocking his pipe out on the side of the grate. "I did speak to him once, though, I'm certain I did. He spoke to your mother, and then to me, but I'm hanged if I can remember about what." He shook his head at his own forgetfulness. "Anyhow, I'm going to lock up."

Bending, he kissed Julia. She smiled up at him and he wandered off, leaving her staring at the flower arrangement standing in the hearth.

~Chapter 34~

Mowbray had found out about Edwin's decision only after repeated prompting from Kettering had persuaded him to telephone their largest shareholder. Balking, Mowbray had protested that takeover rules would confine his conversation to what had already been published so that there was nothing he could use to persuade Edwin to support the company by sticking to his shares.

Besides, everyone knew Edwin was a recluse whose uncertain mental stability was something from which the family had long been content to distance itself. Though no-one could recall how, family members had known for years that he was supposed to be working on some obscure illustrated manuscript, but if they thought of him at all these days it was solely to give thanks that, with the possible exception of Harry Temple, the rest of the family had been spared his affliction. Also, somewhere at the back of Mowbray's mind remained the realisation that some time, what seemed a lifetime ago, he had in fact spoken to Edwin. Why, and what had been said, he had simply no idea, and it was partly in the hope of arming himself by recalling that conversation that he had put off the telephone call until Kettering's prompting made it impossible to do so any longer.

"What if he's absolutely barking?" he had demanded finally, though long ago having recognised that he was no match for Kettering.

"We shall face that when we come to it," Kettering had retorted imperturbably.

* * *

"Gerald Mowbray here," Mowbray said when, after an age, someone picked up the telephone at the other end. "I'd like to speak to Edwin Wilberforce."

Edwin put down the brush with which he had intended retouching the lesser celandine destined to be his life work's frontispiece. He ran a grimy hand through his wisps of grey hair as he stared at the earpiece of the telephone and pouted. It was not one of Edwin's good days, and when the telephone refused to offer elucidation of any kind he dropped it back on its cradle and returned to his palette.

Mowbray's misgivings increased as he listened to the cleared line and was forced to ring again. This time the telephone was answered on the third ring.

"Who's there?"

Edwin's voice was querulous and reedy. Spinsterish, Mowbray thought.

"This is Gerald Mowbray. I'm..."

"Speak up," Edwin commanded petulantly.

Mowbray tried again, louder. "This is Gerald Mowbray, chairman of Wilberforce Original Brassworks; my late wife was Jane Wilberforce, your..." He paused, uncertain of the precise nature of the relationship. "I thought it might be helpful for us to talk. . ."

There was silence for a moment at the other end of the line as Edwin attempted to digest the information.

"Do I know you?" His voice was brittle with suspicion.

"I believe we have spoken some time in the past, though quite a long time ago," Mowbray said. Though no longer quite convinced of the fact, there was clearly a need to establish a bridge.

There was another pause, punctuated by a spitting noise as Edwin licked the tip of his paintbrush to moisten the point.

"From the works?"

"At Bradburn, yes."

"Ah!"

Mowbray sighed with relief at what appeared to be Edwin's dawning recognition.

He began again. "You are one of our major shareholders and I thought it would be useful for us to talk...in view of the bid, that is..."

This met with silence and Mowbray wondered for a moment whether news of the bid could conceivably have passed over Edwin's head; yet Kettering somehow knew from the City grapevine that Edwin not only knew of the bid but was believed to have committed his shareholding to the opposition...

Edwin decided to break the silence. "Was," he said, with what sounded suspiciously like a smirk in his voice.

"I beg your pardon?"

"*Was* a major shareholder." Edwin now sounded almost gleeful. "I've sold 'em. Every last one."

Mowbray lowered the handset for a moment as his worst fears were confirmed. Slowly, he brought it back to his ear. "Could you please say that again," he invited, striving to keep his voice steady.

"Telephoned me. Some City woman." Edwin announced it challengingly, as though she had shown a dash he approved. "Sent me a form to sign."

Having almost no sense of time, and grasping the opportunity to rub a little salt in, he added, "Ages ago. Signed it. Good-bye."

He thrust the telephone back at its cradle. "Can't abide being pestered," he said aloud and turned back to his painting.

Mowbray listened to the telephone being replaced then dialled Kettering's home number, his mind reeling at the enormity of Edwin's defection. Despite an invitation to call Kettering at home at any time, a courtesy the banker rarely extended to his clients, Mowbray had so far found it unnecessary to trouble him.

Kettering's warm reaction to his voice changed to puzzlement as he listened to Mowbray's concerned summary of his conversation with Edwin.

"You are absolutely sure he said he'd signed it?"

Mowbray assured him that yes, certainly, there was no doubt. Ages ago.

"That's damned strange." The line went silent as Kettering thought for a moment. "There's something odd about this, I feel it in my bones. If Pusey had received a formal acceptance from Edwin, he would certainly have told the institutions, the newspapers, too. It would put pressure on the waverers if he could claim not only a major shareholder, but a family one." The sound of Kettering humming tunelessly to himself came down the line as he ran over the possibilities. "No," he said, "something's gone wrong for them. Leave it with me and we'll talk in the morning."

Mowbray, his relief at being in his own home for the night offering a modest counter to the bad news, wandered outside. Dusk had begun to seep into the garden, darkening the grass and investing the paler flowers with a luminous glow. He inhaled the scent of grass freshly mown by young Phillips that afternoon, then lit his pipe and prepared to be reassuring as he heard the familiar note of Julia's car turning into the drive.

~Chapter 35~

"**H**ow do you mean, 'He's not answering the 'phone'?"

Pusey had remained standing, leaning threateningly across the merchant banker's desk. "Have you had the line checked for faults?"

The banker leaned back in his chair to preserve the distance between them.

"There's nothing wrong with his telephone," he said defensively. "The exchange says he's left it off the hook, which he's perfectly entitled to do." He gave the discreet cough of a stage butler nudging his master into complicity in some behavioural solecism. "We have also, as you know, had someone take a close look at the house. They could see the handset lying on a pile of sketches of some sort."

Pusey pondered the information. It had been at his insistence and over the merchant bank's objections that a junior member of its staff had been dispatched to Pinfold Manor to try to winkle Edwin out and establish direct contact. When persistent ringing at the door had failed to produce either Edwin or his part-time housekeeper, their emissary had been reduced to sneaking round the outside of the building and peering through windows almost opaque with grime.

"Damn," Pusey said, his face red with indignation. "What the hell does the old fool think he's playing at?"

He began to pace up and down the office. The banker relaxed sufficiently to lean forward and rest his arms on his desk. "According to the people in the village he's, well, not merely eccentric but practically certifiable."

Pusey rarely showed uncertainty but he did so now. He stopped his pacing and slumped into one of the chairs he had spurned earlier. "You mean, he might not be sane enough to carry out his promise to sell?"

The banker risked a shrug. "I don't know. It has to be a possibility. The chap who went out there to take a look swears there's an envelope leaning against a clock which just *could* be addressed to us. Apparently the window was so filthy it was hard to be certain."

"Get it." Pusey spoke through gritted teeth. "Just bloody well get it."

His adviser studied him appraisingly. "You would not, of course, wish us to do anything irregular? We have already trespassed some way on the far side of..."

"Look," Pusey said, striving to sound reasonable, "he wanted us to have the shares; he said so on the 'phone. We'd simply be helping carry out his wishes."

"Then why not just try again: march up and knock on the door."

"Because he might not answer the bloody door, that's why. Besides, he *might* have changed his mind. Maybe he hasn't posted it because he *has* changed his mind and simply hasn't got round to tearing up the form. Anyhow, we're only *assuming* that the envelope contains the Form of Acceptance." Pusey chewed his bottom lip. "If it does, either he's forgotten to post it, or he thinks he *has* posted it, or he's changed what passes for his mind. All *you've* got to do is to establish that the envelope is addressed to you. Even your people should be able to distinguish between your own pre-paid envelope and a gas bill. If it is ours, we just get in there, grab it and bung it in the nearest letter box. Once the old man gets his cheque he'll assume he'd posted the form and forgotten about it. Us? We'll have the envelope. Damn it! It'll even have his fingerprints on it, not that it'll ever come to that. We'll be in the clear."

He sprang from his seat and loomed once more over the unhappy banker.

"Look, I don't care how you do it. Just get me that bloody envelope."

~Chapter 36~

Two World Wars came and went, leaving the long tradition of Bradburn Show uninterrupted. During the First World War the cricket match had to be represented by scratch teams of land workers and walking wounded from the Cottage Hospital. In the Second, by a children's rounders match. Tradition was observed.

So there is no reason why a speculative takeover bid should be allowed to interfere with employees' enjoyment of the Show this year.

Arrangements for time off in office and factory have been circulated...

Mowbray took in the gist of Simon's draft bulletin, marked a couple of minor amendments and handed it back with an approving nod.

Although there had been no Mowbray around when traditions at Wilberforces first began to accrete, he was a staunch upholder of those he had inherited, even though many of them seemed to have an in-built component designed to reduce the working week.

"People have already been told they can leave at four," Simon assured him. "The bulletin is really to keep the information system flowing when there's not a great deal to report."

Then, instead of loping off to have his bulletin copied, Simon appeared to hover. Mowbray wondered whether he had caught a hint of the previous night's Uncle Edwin development, but Simon was merely awaiting an indication from the abstracted Mowbray that the meeting was over.

"Will that be all," he enquired anxiously, eager to send the bulletins on their way.

Mowbray smiled and waved him out of the office. Swinging his chair round to face the window he observed a square below already *en fête* with bunting and preparations for the next day. It was there that the parade of floats would be serenaded from the bandstand as they assembled for the judging. Following that, and with every float boasting a trophy for something or other, they would process out of the top end of the square, past the cottages and then turn down the lane leading to the showground. Mowbray watched as a van appeared from the direction of the Fox & Chickens. A glimpse of a bald head and luxuriant black whiskers behind the windscreen revealed Sam Harrison on one of the innumerable journeys required to transport the fixtures and fittings for the beer tent. Immediately below, a handful of shoppers had paused in the sunshine to watch workmen hammering and sawing as they erected a platform for the judges. To Mowbray, uncharacteristically sombre, it recalled the preparations preceding a hanging in a Western.

There was a tap at his office door and he swivelled back to face the desk as Hugo Russell stepped in. Russell waved away the offer of a chair and moved behind the desk to look out of the window so that Mowbray had to swing the chair round again to follow him.

"I had no idea of the intensity of these things," Russell said, taking in the activity. Sam Harrison's van had gone and a cleansing department wagon was making the second pass of the morning, its brushes swishing and scraping in a process that would take it up the square on the far side and down the square beneath Mowbray's window and which would continue until there was not so much as a blown straw to offend the eye. The process would, Mowbray knew, be repeated in the morning.

"You'll have been given a job, I have no doubt?" Mowbray enquired. It was impossible not to welcome the change in Russell and Mowbray found it difficult to reconcile today's involved albeit distinctly plumpish figure with the sour-tempered colossus who had arrived in Bradburn clinging to the back of a tractor. "If Harry Temple hasn't roped you in, then Julia will. I don't suppose you're particularly hot on judging small animals?"

Russell grimaced and Mowbray shook his head understandingly.

"Can't say I blame you. Besides, they'd never let me get away with it..."

"Julia has appointed me as steward," Russell volunteered. "Apparently it involves lounging round the beer tent ready to fall upon lager louts; or, if at the cricket match, to fall upon those giving voice for the opposition."

* * *

Julia had been waiting patiently by Russell's desk that morning as he had emerged, frowning, from a meeting in her father's office. He had, she surmised correctly, just been told of Uncle Edwin's defection. For Russell's part, the news had snapped him out of a spell of introspection during which he had found himself mooning once more about the protracted separation from a Constance who was beginning to show distinct signs of melting beneath the avalanche of flowers that seemed to be arriving every other day. It was a deprivation that was thrown into even sharper relief as he regained his office and his eyes lit upon the burnished gold of the legs Julia displayed as she sat on the corner of his desk. One of her legs was raised so that she could clasp her knee in her hands. Russell fumbled for the arm of his chair as he edged behind the desk and subsided into the seat, trying to avert eyes that were reluctant to avert. He compromised by continuing to stare at the legs and adopting an abstracted expression intended to convince their owner that he was not actually seeing them. Though the legs were bare, they gleamed as though encased in silk. It was obviously an effect produced by diet, Russell concluded, and resolved to add fish oil to his regimen.

"What happens," Julia asked without preamble, "if Uncle Edwin has sent off his Form of Acceptance and it's been lost in the post or something?"

Russell steepled his fingers, resting his foremost chin on his thumbs. "Er..." he said.

"What I mean is," Julia continued, neither flattered nor discomfited by the attention, "suppose it never turns up at Pusey's or his bankers - what then?"

"I am not, as you know, a lawyer..." Russell prevaricated.

A touch of exasperation crept into Julia's voice. "Mr. Russell..." Although she had become quite reconciled to the new Hugo Russell, she could not yet bring herself to call him by his Christian name. "...In broad terms, not to the letter of company law."

Hugo Russell had an aversion for the categorical. His senses had been honed in a world where a man's word might be his bond but where, equally, a man's calculated silence could leave him in a position to claim kinship with whichever side of an argument looked like prevailing. Russell, the City said, was not afraid to nail his colours to the fence. Faced with Julia's persistence, he struggled to bring to the surface what little he knew about share transfers.

"So far as I can recall," he began, his voice divested of any inflection that might imply certitude and therefore accountability, "if a Form of Acceptance is properly completed and then lost or mislaid, the owner of the shares must sign a Form of Indemnity which must then be witnessed. He can then get hold of a duplicate form and begin all over again."

"So," Julia persevered, "even if Uncle Edwin has lost the form, he can simply fill in another one, bang that off to whoever it might concern, and we're back where we started..."

"Provided he's signed the Form of Indemnity."

Julia stood up, her skirt falling back to just above her knees. Russell blinked and pretended not to notice. At the door she turned back to him. "Who does the form indemnify, as a matter of interest?"

Russell's grin transformed his face. "I haven't the faintest idea," he said.

~Chapter 37~

Kettering 'phoned Mowbray just before noon.
"Whatever Edwin Wilberforce's intention is, I
would swear that Pusey has received no formal
indication," he began. "Apparently he's been storming
around his banker's office like a bear with a sore head,
and it's my belief that no transfer has been effected."
There were puffing noises as he broke off to light a
cigar. "We've tried 'phoning Edwin but the 'phone's off
the hook. The word is that Pusey's had someone
stalking round the outside of the old boy's house. Only
rumour, of course, but..."

Mowbray was holding the telephone away from his
ear so that Russell could hear both ends of the
conversation. "So, what can we do?" he asked.

"Not a lot, at least for the moment. What we really
need is to give Edwin a good shake and show him the
error of his ways."

"I doubt whether he would detect anything
erroneous," Mowbray said glumly.

"Well, why not forget all about it for a day or two
and get on with that show of yours on the village
green."

Had Kettering ever bothered to conjure up a
picture of Bradburn, which was doubtful, Mowbray

guessed that it would have resembled a nineteenth century Gloucestershire hamlet as visualised by Disney Studios. Despite the depressing trend of events, he was happy to humour the banker. "That sounds like good advice," he said. "Let's speak again on Monday."

He replaced the receiver and the telephone rang again immediately.

"I forgot to ask if I could tell Simon about Uncle Edwin."

It was Julia. From the background noises she appeared to be calling on her mobile from wherever she and Simon were helping with arrangements for the Show. Mowbray repeated the question to Russell who shrugged a 'why not?'

"Put Simon in the picture, but tell him it's not for public consumption," her father advised. "The directors are meeting here for a briefing before some of us get involved in the Show. Uncle Edwin's no longer answering his telephone, by the way, so we shall have to decide what to do next."

* * *

Edwin's failure to answer the telephone resulted not from his aversion to the instrument, which was of longstanding, nor from a more general aversion to intrusions of any kind, but from causes whose results were to be longstanding.

In a way, the failure could be attributed more or less directly to the Venus de Square Mile-o, the siren voice who had convinced Edwin to part with his shares.

Originally Brenda Giles from Warrington, the Venus had long since submerged her provincial origins behind the guise of Ernestine Villiers, an identity that was now as much a part of her as her beautifully rounded vowels and her Dolce & Gabanna suits. Though no frown was allowed to crease the porcelain

brow, it was beginning to occur to her that the
customarily flattering attentions from her male
colleagues had acquired a slightly questioning edge. It
had not taken her long to find out why.

The occasion had been a drinks party in the office
to celebrate the company's successful role in a recent
acquisition. It had been no trouble at all to detach one
of the more vulnerable males from his colleagues and
move him to a quiet part of the room. There she had
backed him against a wall and applied herself to him
like a poultice.

"Why," she breathed into his glowing ear, "are
people beginning to look at me as though I were
somewhat less than the cat's pyjamas? What," she
urged, with a thrust that threatened to permanently
weave her Dolce and Gabanna into his Armani, "have I
done wrong?"

The focus of her attention had swallowed hard,
struggling for a response that would satisfy her demand
for information without terminating a proximity for
which he would have gladly sacrificed his annual
bonus.

"Well?"

"That old boy you 'phoned about the Wilberforce
bid..." he managed.

Ernestine raised a painted eyebrow.

The pinioned man writhed. "He's not come through
with the Transfer Form. There's been a suggestion – no
more than that," he added hastily, "that you haven't
quite pulled it off."

Ernestine detached herself from him, smoothed
her skirt and, without a backward look, set off for her
office. Having retrieved the Wilberforce file from a
cabinet, she sat down behind her desk and picked up
the telephone.

Having moments before hung up on a defeated
Mowbray, Edwin stared at the ringing telephone as
though considering throwing it through a window
whose grime made it barely discernible from the walls.
Then, with the inconsistency that was a feature of his
state of mind, he picked it up and waited.

"Hello?" The dusky greeting from the other end
trickled into his ear like wax-oil.

"Go on," Edwin commanded.

"This is Ernestine Villiers. You remember me?"

"No," Edwin said. .

"About" pause "your" pause "shares..." The dusky
voice was clearly emerging from between gritted teeth.

"Shares?" Edwin countered.

"In Wilberforce Original Brassworks. You were
going to send us your Form of Acceptance..."

Removing the telephone from his ear, Edwin stared
at it before returning it to his ear. "No idea what you're
talking about," he said.

Ernestine's poise was crumbling. Before she could
stop herself she heard herself saying, "Look, you old
fool..."

It was enough. Edwin's free hand clutched his
chest. Dimly, recognition surfaced. The shares... She
was the one who... He stared at the telephone
malevolently. Sibilantly, he said, "What was that?"

Ernestine's heart thumped. "I...I..."

It was too late.

Old fool, was he! Well, perhaps he was. Edwin
rubbed the bristles on his chin and tried to remember...
Anxious Hello's? tripped out of the telephone. Dammit!
These people were as bad as the wretched Wilberforces.
Worse. At least that chap had been civil on the 'phone.
He stared into space, his mind searching for...for what?

It had been years ago. Something...what? Something
preceding his blistering resentment of Wilberforces. . .
and...and...something about a telephone call. Damn
telephones.

"And you, madam, are a strumpet," Edwin barked
into the telephone. He rested the handset briefly back
in its cradle before removing it and throwing it down
beside the instrument. Wilberforces...a conversation
years before...That was it!

Words spoken more than twenty years earlier
returned. It had been during his kitten cuddling period
. . . something had penetrated his resentment and
touched a sentimental streak ...

He thrust a pile of abandoned sketches aside,
provoking a cloud of dust. He coughed as he struggled
to recall events. The cough subsided, leaving a stabbing
pain in his chest and he leaned against the table,
resting on splayed hands for support. All those years
before *he* had telephoned Wilberforces. He had not
only telephoned them but... Events flooded back as he
scowled at a canvas resting on the nearby easel,
watching suspiciously as it appeared to swim in and out
of focus. Memories swirled as he gave the painting a
disapproving prod that sent both it and the easel
crashing to the floor. More dust enveloped him. He
massaged his narrow chest through the tattered
cardigan until a renewed fit of coughing subsided to an
occasional splutter. He set off unsteadily across the
room. Walking at a stoop, hands on hips, his slippered
feet kicked their way through the rubbish strewn floor
until he stopped at the giant partners' desk beneath one
of the grimy windows. The dust was making his eyes
smart and he wiped at them with the fraying sleeve of
his cardigan. Struggling for each breath, he began to
snatch open the drawers, riffling through their contents

and angrily discarding them until he was quickly surrounded by a mound of yellowing paperwork.

Having dealt with one side of the desk he shuffled round to the opposite side and repeated the process, muttering angrily to himself. The physical effort and the clouds of dust his search produced brought back the cough. His grey pallor gained angry pink highlights over the cheekbones as, for a moment, he collapsed against the desk, clenched hands pressed against his chest. He peered around vacantly until one rheumy eye lighted on a roll-top desk, barely visible under a heap of neglected paperwork. Clutching the furniture for support, he edged towards it, his outstretched arm sending the papers on top of the desk cascading to the floor. Fighting a desire simply to rest he grabbed the roll-top shutter and, after a struggle, managed to force it open. As it yielded it revealed a further clutter of papers with others spilling from an array of pigeon-holes. Ignoring those on the desk, Edwin began to pull papers from the pigeon holes. Almost immediately he found himself staring at a slim scrolled document distinguished by a faded pink ribbon.

He clutched the scroll to his fluttering chest and peered around for yet one more thing. There, on the mantelpiece, by the clock... Crab-like, chest heaving against dust searing his sinuses like pepper, he set off towards the fireplace. The journey seemed to take an age and when he reached the mantelpiece he found that he was almost too stooped to reach it. Fighting against a stiffness that kept him cramped almost double, he extended trembling fingers until he managed to grasp the envelope propped against the clock. Tearing open the flap he snatched out the contents and let them flutter to the floor. Then, his vision beginning to fade, he flattened the scrolled pages and thrust them into the now empty envelope. A sudden pain in his chest bent him double. He stayed in that position until the pain subsided then, deliberately and carefully, he eased himself painfully upright until he could replace the envelope in front of the clock.

~Chapter 38~

Bradburn's location at the foot of the dales had ensured a pleasant breeze throughout a summer whose bright sunshine and cloudless skies were now embracing a frantic showground which found Simon averting his face as he tried to avoid a flapping sheet of canvas. His hands held a giant tent peg as far away as the yard-long metal tongs would allow as he tried not to flinch each time the ground shook as a contractor swung at it with a mallet with a head the size of a small barrel. As soon as the peg was secure he was elbowed aside by the mallet swinger who took hold of a rope running through an eyelet in the canvas roof of the tent and attached it loosely to the tent peg.

Simon put the tongs down and eyed the arrangement uncertainly. "Isn't that, er, rather loose?" he suggested. His tone was tentative. As a tent peg holder he was, he recognised, a tyro, having been press-ganged into standing in for a second tent rigger who now reappeared carrying half-a-dozen cans of beer.

A pitying look flickered across the rigger's face as he leaned on the up-ended mallet and flexed the rope with his free hand. "They'll tighten themselves if it rains," he said. "If we leave them tight and it rains tonight, the ropes'll tighten too much and we'll be in trouble." Uncertain of Simon's status, he added grudgingly, "If it stays fine, we'll simply tighten 'em all in the morning."

A whole village of marquees had sprung up since work had begun at daybreak. Volunteers with ladders were busily hanging banners and bunting over the heads of helpers scurrying in and out of tents with trestle tables and chairs, temporary staging, giant tea urns, huge plastic trays of crockery and a whole range of effects without which each custodian was convinced the Show would founder. Edging away from workmen now eyeing him sceptically over the rims of their beer cans, Simon made his way through the maze of canvas, over the ropes and electric cables that snaked across the grass and headed for the embryo press tent where he had arranged to meet Julia. They arrived together, Julia having carried a cardboard box from where the labyrinth of tents and delivery trucks had forced her to leave the car.

"It's mostly catalogues and stationery for the results service," she explained breathlessly, lowering the box on to one of the trestle tables set out in an L shape on the bruised grass inside the tent.

Although Bradburn Council sponsored the Show for the benefit of its citizens, it was also open to local businesses to sponsor individual activities. Wilberforces, in accordance with tradition, were sponsoring the gymkhana, which took place outside the natural amphitheatre occupied by the Show, plus the Small Animals section, a competitive pet show which for years had forged rivalries of Sicilian fervour. It had been Simon's idea that this year, in the interests of furthering press relations, the company should also sponsor a press tent offering a results service for the handful of yawningly indifferent reporters who traditionally managed to glean all they required to know from their corner of the beer tent. There had been ready assent from the Show Committee who would be relieved of the responsibility for providing each of them with a completed results programme at the end of the day.

"The Cub Scouts can provide runners in the marquees to bring results back to the press tent," Simon had explained. "We'll have a pigeon-hole for each of the local media which we'll keep fed with the latest results. They can spend their time doing the colour stuff and enjoying themselves."

Simon stood aside as two workmen from the factory entered with a box with sufficient pigeon-holes to have serviced the Washington press corps. Fewer than a dozen bore the names of local media organisations. The men rested it on a trestle table and Simon and Julia followed them out.

"It will be a real family day tomorrow," Julia said as Simon accompanied her to where she had left the car. She looked at him with a half-smile. "You won't be able to move for sticky children."

The smile Simon returned was tinged with guilt. "To be honest, it's the cricket I'm really looking forward to."

His leg, as he had been called on to demonstrate that morning, had made dramatic progress.

"Moves like a gazelle," Splasher had mused as Simon tore round the boundary of the cricket field.

"'As swift as the roes upon the mountains'," the Reverend Norman Butterworth had concurred happily.

"I shall pop over and keep an eye on you," Julia promised.

They stopped for a moment as they reached the car, watching the activity around them. Colonel

Temple appeared through the bustle, pausing occasionally to scowl at whatever fixtures and fittings caught his attention. His usual expression of confused amiability was absent for once.

"What a day to call a board meeting," he huffed. He raised his shapeless tweed hat to his niece but glared at the car she was about to step into as though considering having it wheel clamped.

"Hardly a board meeting, Uncle," Julia placated. "Father just wishes everyone to be in the picture before we break for the weekend."

"Did you know," Simon asked, tactfully changing the subject, "that the tent riggers have to leave the ropes loose in case the weather breaks?"

Temple beamed at him. "Always do, m'boy, did it in the mob," he assured him. "'S just good order and discipline, not a weather forecast. Take a look at that sky."

Together, the three tilted back their heads and stared at the sky, a vast parabola of blue blemished only by the darting shapes of starlings.

* * *

The bar in the Fox & Chickens was quiet. It was not, however, without atmosphere.

"Are you absolutely sure you have left nothing to chance? Shouldn't you be up there now to make sure everything is ready for morning?"

The Reverend Norman Butterworth's tone was fretful. He knew he was expected to have more time to spare than the idlest loafer in the parish, while idlers like Spofforth seemed loath to carry out even the modest tasks for which their limited skills qualified them. If his catechism was intended to galvanise Spofforth into action it appeared to be failing. Spofforth, already traumatised from finding himself car-less when he needed it most, was feeling further crushed by his new responsibilities. He leaned against the bar and waved a limp hand. "I have done everything a man can do..."

"Are the exhibits being put out tonight or in the morning?"

"Tonight...that is...in the morning, er..."

"The *large* entries go in this evening, the *smaller* ones in the morning. Mrs. Butterworth has explained this to you already..."

"That's not Christian, that ain't." Isherwood's challenge was launched from his customary place by the smouldering fire.

"I beg your pardon?" Butterworth's tone was disarmingly mild.

Bolstered by the nodding heads of his cronies, but betrayed by the receding tide of memory, Isherwood ploughed on.

"It's a smear on the people of Bradburn, that is."

Apparently nonplussed, Butterworth sought enlightenment.

"*And* un-Christian?" he queried.

"They only puts out at night them things that's too big to pinch," Isherwood announced triumphantly. "That's because they don't trust us, an' if that's Christian charity I'll eat my 'at." He turned to his supporters, several of whom, with better memories than their erstwhile champion and an inkling of the direction the argument might take, were now concentrating on their drinks.

"You have a point, Mr. Isherwood," Butterworth responded reasonably. "It is true that, with limited funds to spend on security, we take whatever measures are open to us to protect the work of the people of this town from sneak-thieves and hobbledehoys who know not mine from thine. We also, you will not be surprised to learn, put great faith in the Good Book when it tells us, 'Blessed is the man that endureth temptation; for when he is tried, he will receive the crown of life.' You will recall, however, that when your nephew failed to endure temptation he was tried and received six months."

There was much baring of gums by those surrounding Isherwood. The matter disposed of, Butterworth returned to Spofforth as though the interruption had not taken place.

"Relying on the good nature and experience of the people of Bradburn, let us assume for a moment that all is well at the showground, that exhibits are where they are supposed to be, displaying the numbers they have been allocated, and that nothing has gone astray. You feel comfortable with that assumption...?"

Spofforth fiddled with his spectacles and nodded miserably.

"Then I suggest a less cavalier attitude to events tomorrow when, as you know, the small handicrafts and the children's entries have to be in place by ten o'clock. I would earnestly advocate an early night to foster the utmost concentration, Mr. Spofforth."

Although it was unspoken, those present registered the un-churchly implication that otherwise Spofforth, who had eased off his stool and was now edging towards the door, would be dancing Shepherd's Hey with his legs in plaster. On his way out of the door he narrowly missed colliding with Shelmerdine on his way in. Something of what had passed was evident from the way Butterworth stared after the vanished Spofforth.

"Handicrafts section?" Shelmerdine enquired innocently, his eye on Kitty as she reached for a glass and began to pull him a pint of beer.

"You can safely leave Spofforth to me," Butterworth said sternly, "as Mrs. Butterworth has threatened to rend me limb from limb if he makes a mess of the job tomorrow. Now, in your guise as skipper of Bradburn first eleven, let us give final thoughts to tomorrow's match..."

* * *

To have acquired a vicar who could keep wicket with the best of them and then come in at a comfortable number six was something Bradburn had accepted with an equanimity verging on smugness; yet, if asked, few if any of his parishioners could have explained how that benison came about.

Norman Butterworth's calling had arrived some years before with an abruptness that made Paul's conversion on the road to Damascus appear tardy. While the circumstances had been mundane in the extreme - as an employee of the Gas Board he had been delivering the wrong appliance to a house in Huddersfield - his conversion had been total. Theological college had been followed by an inner-city curacy in which he had demonstrated his principles by threatening to punt anyone who produced a guitar through the nearest stained glass window, while generally declining to take part in any act of worship that threatened to reduce the liturgy to pier-end entertainment. It was an independence of mind that had failed to commend itself to some of those set above him. These included the Rural Dean whose silky grey waves and soigné manner inspired the racier element in the Mothers' Union to refer to him as the Rural Dream. A rural sojourn for Butterworth eventually became inevitable when the Dean called on the Bishop and suggested, not for the first time, that it was time for him to move.

The Bishop, who rather liked what he had seen and heard of Butterworth, faced the meeting without enthusiasm. Then the Dean played his trump card.

"I believe," he said, shuddering with distaste, "he has recently been preaching sermons about bishops who have been assassinated."

The Bishop perked up visibly. "But my dear Archie, how interesting..."

The Dean's eyelids fluttered. "I am afraid, Bishop, he appeared to be advocating it."

Had he been wearing one, the Bishop's eyebrows would have disappeared inside his mitre.

"Then..." he said reluctantly.

"Bradburn, Bishop?"

It was not true that Butterworth had advocated assassinating Bishops. What he had been at pains to point out to his congregation was that some of them had left the world by that route; and, as the reference had been merely one of the asides he occasionally used to snap their eyelids open, he had never actually got round to condemning the practice. And, though his move to Bradburn had been conveyed to him in emollient terms, Butterworth's muscular soul had rejoiced at the chance to contend with the ruggedly non-conformist spirits that flourished there. The native reserve with which his initial arrival had been greeted disappeared almost magically when it was discovered that he had hands as safe as the Bank of England and was a resolute number six in the batting order.

And nothing, short perhaps of the personal intervention of the Archbishop of Canterbury, would have kept him from the annual Broadbridge confrontation.

* * *

Shelmerdine drained his pint and leaned across the bar to deliver Kitty a frothy kiss. Other than moving among his men like Henry V before Agincourt, which would have involved a pub crawl of some dimensions, there appeared nothing left for the captain of Bradburn's first XI to do. Happily, he set the glass down on the bar and set off home for an early night.

~Chapter 39~

The day of the Show dawned flawlessly.
Fairground showmen slumbering in chrome-encrusted caravans smiled in their sleep as they dreamed of the day to come. Scores of others, volunteers and pressed men, crept silently out of their homes and spilled into the still cool streets. At the showground the gum-boots of early arrivals kicked up arcs of sparkling dew as Harry Temple, flushed with energy, settled the problems of stewards in gruff monosyllables, breaking off occasionally to refresh himself from a thermos of coffee that gave off a fragrant hint of rum.

In the town square the riot of coloured bunting had been supplemented by a giant 'Hands Off Wilberforce' banner slung beneath the office balconies. Workmen on the reviewing stand were using staplers provided by Miss Varley to fix the swags of red, white and blue muslin that would complete it. Signs were being erected to debar all but Show traffic while children broke away from adults to dash through the artificial rainbows created as a municipal cart watered the flower arrangements in their giant concrete tubs.

* * *

A dog fox hiding in the long grass surrounding the cricket field pricked its ears at the sound of the sneck lifting on the door of the groundsman's hut. Cautiously, his nose testing the soft morning air, he hesitated for a moment before turning and melting into the undergrowth. Across the pitch, on the roof of an Edwardian pavilion gleaming with fresh white paint, ring-necked doves strutted and cooed mindlessly. Cub Scouts marshalled by gestures from Ted Ellingham carried wooden benches from the hut and set them out around the boundary. Satisfied with their progress, Ellingham returned to the hut and emerged bearing a skeletal wooden frame. A youth carrying a slopping bucket of whitewash trotted dutifully after him across an outfield mown in broad contrasting stripes. Setting the wooden frame down at one end of a playing strip shaved to the colour of straw, Ellingham took a brush from the whitewash bucket and set about marking out the creases with the solemnity of a warlock drawing a pentacle.

The sound of an engine and a squeal of brakes broke the morning's hush as Shelmerdine's van halted just inside the gates. As Shelmerdine and Simon emerged to take in the scene, a schoolboy with sleep in his eyes plodded patiently past, pushing a squeaking wheeled device that left a snail's trail of whitewash designating the boundary. A horn sounded and they skipped aside to admit Sam Harrison and a van with the staff who would man the green and white striped beer tent. Sam, as befitted his status, would supervise the bar in the pavilion now being swarmed over by helpers setting out chairs: cushioned cane for the guests, scratched bent-wood for the players. Two small boys emerged from the groundsman's hut struggling under the weight of a box containing numbered tins for the scoreboard. A third emerged with the wooden stool they would need to reach the nails on which the tins would hang.

Shelmerdine shook his head in wonder. "You know what we are?" he asked an abstracted Simon, "we're gladiators."

* * *

Simon, however, was in a strangely joyless mood. His normal sunny expression had been replaced by a brow creased by the weight of unaccustomed troubles.

Until the previous evening he had considered his relationship with Julia to be one of affectionate friendship and unshakeable trust. If Julia had tended to take the lead when decisions were made, all well and good; it was her family's business that was at risk, not his. And now...

Over the past few days his worries about her wellbeing had disappeared and he had watched delightedly as she had regained her customary glow and good humour, as though Edwin Wilberforce's defection had tapped a fresh spring of resilience. Their relationship, he would have sworn, had never been warmer. Why, then, had it seemed to unravel on the Friday afternoon? He could not even begin to guess.

Having accompanied Harry Temple on yet another tour of inspection, the two of them had been sitting in a corner of the refreshment tent used by officials and fairground workers alike. Julia had been toying with the spoon in her teacup when Simon, *a propos* of nothing, said, "Perhaps we could take a stroll around the fair this evening."

Julia had taken the teaspoon out of her cup and placed it carefully in the saucer, her attention apparently absorbed by a pair of sparrows hopping hopefully between the tables. "I'm afraid I shan't be able to," she said. She continued to avoid looking at him. "There's...something's come up. I've..."

As Julia fumbled for the right words, it dawned on Simon that for the first time in their relationship she was avoiding his eye. More than that, she was clearly holding something back. Of course, she had every right to turn him down; but Julia, the Julia he knew, would not have hesitated to say why; would not have left him with the dreadful feeling that she was cutting him off, that for some reason their relationship was entering a new, cooler phase. He found himself blushing. Probably, even now, he was intruding. He stood up, pushing back the folding wooden chair so abruptly that he had to grab it to prevent it collapsing.

"It's only for this evening," Julia was saying, "there are so many things..."

Simon was not listening. Her apologies became submerged by his.

"I was being selfish." His words tumbled out. "I should have realised..."

Just what he should have realised he would have found it hard to say. Somehow, though, he knew he must have trespassed beyond some point at which he was not welcome. To Julia the misunderstanding had descended so quickly that her mind panicked into numbness. Her eyes pricked at her clumsiness as Simon, backing away in confusion, clipped the chair again and sent it crashing to the duck-boards. Conversations around them stopped. Crimson-faced, Simon picked up the chair, replaced it by the table, then turned and hurried out with a mumbled goodbye.

Left alone, Julia sighed then blinked away an incipient tear so that she could consult her wristwatch.

* * *

Shelmerdine took a final glance around the cricket field then turned and headed for the van, Simon at his side.

"If it stays like this and we win the toss, we'll bat first," he said.

The prospect lifted at least some of the gloom from Simon's shoulders.

~Chapter 40~

Bradburn Show ran along the greased lines of custom. Custom dictated that the last of the carnival floats should turn into the showground ten minutes before eleven o'clock; it was the customary careful timing that allowed the cricketers to watch the floats arrive and welcome the VIPs before crossing from the showground to the cricket field, and it was the same timing that allowed any of those on the floats who wanted to watch the cricket to jump down, cross the lane to the cricket field and find their places around the boundary before the first ball was bowled.

It was now ten forty-five. There was a stir in the ranks lining both sides of the lane as the procession, its approach long signalled by the spirited tones of the brass band, came into sight round a bend in the lane. Behind the band, stretching back out of sight, came a cavalcade of spaceships, dinosaurs and tableaux whose ingenuity would have flattered the Lord Mayor's Show. Children hanging on the bars of the opened gate to the cricket field yelled with glee as a television cameraman, concentrating on the trade unions and their 'Hands Off Wilberforce' banner, tripped and stumbled as he scuttled up the grass verge to avoid a police car. The car, headlights blazing, overtook the procession on the wrong side of the road and swung past them into the field. The council's limousine, purring sedately, turned in smoothly after it. Councillor Whitaker, a smiling Mowbray at her side, waved through open windows to spectators crowding behind the honour guard of Bradburn players immaculate in their whites. The mayoral car bumped slowly round the outfield in the direction of the pavilion as the Broadbridge team, grim-faced and aloof, watched unmoved through the windows of their changing room.

* * *

The assertion that cricket was invented to give a non-spiritual people some notion of eternity would have been greeted with incredulity at Bradburn where the game was played with a fervour to make a Samurai blench. Yet, despite the fact that they played the game with single-minded ferocity, the Bradburn club's concern for the courtesies attending the game was meticulous and the hospitality extended to visitors was legendary throughout the league.

Where rival Broadbridge matched Bradburn's commitment, they fell short of their standards both as hosts and as visitors. It was at Broadbridge, legend had it, that a southern team's coach had decamped with a smell of burning rubber after encountering nothing more than the Broadbridge wives preparing sandwiches. And, though a number of friendships bridged the two sides, it was accepted by all that the annual 'friendly' admitted of no quarter. For opposing friends to have exchanged anything more fulsome than a sullen nod on match day would have smacked of disloyalty.

* * *

"What *really* separates us," Shelmerdine was explaining to his team in the changing room, "is our pride, our ability and our dedication, and their inability to tell a bat from a possing stick."

Outside, the pavilion clock showed two minutes to eleven. Every seat creaked under an occupant and the territory between the boundary and the benches was dense with sprawling children. There was a final flurry of activity at the foot of the pavilion steps as a baker's van discharged wooden trays of warm bread and cakes. Then, as the minute hand of the clock touched eleven, the van scooted away and Shelmerdine appeared at the top of the pavilion steps in whites that were almost iridescent. Half a pace behind him came Millington, Broadbridge's blue-jowled skipper and a fearsome striker of the ball. There was a roar of applause from the crowd and polite hand-claps from the VIPs. Following the captains came two grave-faced umpires, their membership of a rival league guaranteeing desiccated impartiality.

Solemnly, Mowbray rose from his seat in the front row. Producing a coin from his pocket, he showed each face to the opposing captains. Millington, as visiting captain, was invited to call and Mowbray handed the coin to a cerise-hatted Councillor Whitaker. The crowd grew silent as she flicked it inexpertly into the air and allowed it to fall to the ground at her feet. The captains stooped to study it and there was a howl of support from sections of the crowd as Millington punched the air in a signal to his supporters. Giving Shelmerdine a look of menacing contempt, he turned to the umpires.

"We'll bat," he said, and stalked back into the pavilion to pad up.

* * *

Despite Spofforth's increasingly plaintive requests, it had been impossible to extract from the Show organisers anything other than the most approximate

indication of when his men would be performing, and
it was the prospect of having to dance at a moment's
notice that had persuaded Spofforth to rise from his
bed that morning and step not into the jeans and
vaguely agricultural smock which had been his original
intention, but into the white shirt, socks and matching
knee-length trousers that were the foundation of his
Morris costume. He had stared at the result in his bed-
sitter's only mirror, set so far above the empty
fireplace that it required an athletic leap to be able to
see anything below thigh level, and concluded that the
effect was perfunctory rather than thoughtful. A
further irritation was that the trousers, instead of
buttoning where they met his stockings at calf level,
flapped hopelessly in that general area as a
consequence of having lost their buttons during
successive launderings. Shuddering at the barely
thinkable prospect of waking his fearsome landlady to
borrow her sewing kit, he pulled on the green garters
and tucked the flyaway trousers into them. The
problem then became what to do about the half-dozen
bells attached to each garter. No matter how many
different walks he practised between the wardrobe and
the window he could find no way of walking without
setting them jingling. Spofforth sat on his unmade bed
and pondered the prospect of sneaking through
Bradburn's early morning streets sounding like the
muffin man. For once, irresolution yielded to resolve.
The garters, and their bells, would stay. Casting
caution to the winds, he slipped into the two broad
green bands which crossed his chest to complete the
outfit. There would be no half-measures. Like it or not,
the arts and crafts lot were going to be supervised by a
Morris Man in full fig. Looking as much the part as it
was possible to do without leaping around like a

dervish, he tinkled out of the house and down the garden path.

Whether it was fate or coincidence that led Simba to emerge into the street at the same moment was known only to the gods.

Simba was a lurcher whose normally equable temperament could on a bad day make Isherwood's Spot appear companionable. What was more, Simba had not had a good morning. Firstly, he had been evicted at the crack of dawn from his place on the kitchen mat as George, Bradburn House's head gardener, had set off for his fenced-off section of the kitchen garden to select vegetables for the Show; he had then been excluded from operations by having the gate closed firmly in his face, and when he had tried to clamber over the fence and got stuck halfway he had been returned to the path by a push from the business end of a rake. Whether he now regarded Spofforth's appearance as a sop from some canine providence, or whether the sound of the bells on Spofforth's garters reminded him of the Post Office cat, the fact was that Spofforth had taken barely half-a-dozen strides in the general direction of the showground before he became aware of the sinister grey blur streaking in his direction. Emitting a screech of pure terror, his legs pumping practically to his chest, Spofforth shot off along the street with the frenzied jingling of a troika pursued by wolves.

It was testimony to the speed of Spofforth's reactions that Simba managed only a single lunging snap before one of his quarry's flying heels caught him under the chin and stopped him in his tracks. Spofforth, having concluded that he was in for a fairly severe mauling, heard Simba's yelp with mixed emotions. Uppermost was the hope that he had

loosened every tooth in the dog's head, while beneath
that was a palpitating panic in case he had merely
spurred his pursuer to greater heights of malevolence.
For his part, Simba sat on the pavement and reviewed
events with an expression rendered poignant by the
piece of Spofforth's trousers hanging from his mouth.
After a moment or two he stood up and stared after the
retreating Spofforth before shaking his head
philosophically and trotting back to Bradburn House
reasonably pleased with the balance of his morning's
work.

Spofforth drooped against the wall he had been
about to scramble over, his hollow chest rising and
falling as he fought for breath and watched anxiously
as his assailant wandered off into the distance. A
grazed sensation and a sudden access of fresh air told
him immediately that his Morris suit was damaged
beyond repair, but the real horror of his situation only
struck him as he attempted to return to his digs: each
time he placed his right foot on the ground it repaid
him with a fiery stab from his ankle which brought
tears to his eyes. Morris dancing, it was clear, was off
the agenda. But walking was still possible, just, and
Spofforth limped back to his digs with the assurance
that he could at least use his injury as an excuse for
abandoning the Handicrafts section to their own
devices. Sitting with his injured ankle in a bowl of cold
water, he had proceeded to try to telephone first
Norman Butterworth and then anyone else he could
think of who might be remotely connected with the
event so that he could hand in his resignation on what
were irrefutably medical grounds. When no-one
answered, he consulted his watch which indicated that
anyone with the remotest interest in events should
now be at the showground. Briefly, he considered

simply not turning up, but the thought of the effect this would have on Norman Butterworth prompted him to bind his ankle in strips of cloth torn from what remained of his Morris trousers, change into smock and jeans, and limp off to the showground.

To his relief, by the time he arrived at the handicrafts marquee the exhibitors were happily milling around. A dispute concerning the propriety of an entry in the 'Not more than five vegetables arranged in an amusing fashion' had been resolved, and an early encounter with Miss Fitton and her partner had, he felt, concluded reasonably. Now, satisfied that events were at last under control, he consoled himself with the thought that the day could have little left with which to afflict him.

That was before he heard a spine-tingling shriek from elsewhere in the marquee.

Stifling an urge to shriek back, he hobbled towards the commotion just in time to see an apparently lifeless Miss Fitton being lifted on to a row of folding chairs while a distraught Miss Bertram fanned her ineffectually with a copy of the Show programme.

* * *

Broadbridge's opening pair consisted of Millington and a young farmer called Carter who looked to have been cast from the same considerable mould. There were encouraging shouts from the Broadbridge contingent and expectant applause from around the ground as, side by side and unsmiling, they stumped down the pavilion steps and stalked across the immaculate green of the outfield towards the wicket.

Carter's youth and prowess, allied to his captain's reluctance to risk being out first ball, dictated that he should take strike. This involved a considerable pantomime during which he studied the sky with the absorption of a meteorologist, took guard with almost maidenly fastidiousness, then removed his cap and spent a long moment studying the way in which Shelmerdine, having consulted with his opening bowler, had disposed his fielders. Satisfied that he had read Splasher's intentions he replaced his cap, gave Millington a satisfied nod and settled down to face the bowler, his bat tapping the ground an inch or so behind his back foot.

There were those in Bradburn who maintained that Brice, their opening fast bowler, lacked the fire of his youth; that too many years confined behind the counter of his butcher's shop had diluted the speed and venom required of an opening bowler. In that fabled youth, the oldsters claimed, Brice would appear to quaking batsmen as no more than a florid dot somewhere in the region of the sight-screen, then as an avenging demon at half the distance, and finally as a tremor in the ground followed by the arrival of a ball that was the last thing many of them saw before waking up in the pavilion. He was nevertheless, they conceded, still a bit quick. Brice was in fact capable of winding himself up to a daunting speed over a couple of overs, after which he was content to rest until he could be let loose among the tail-enders.

So far the bowler's end umpire had observed the preliminaries with hawk-like attention. Now, as Carter completed his assessment of the field placings and Brice paced out his thirty yard run, the umpire slowly raised his left arm. He held it out from his side for a moment, savouring the expectancy of the crowd; then, satisfied that rituals had been observed, he allowed his arm to drop.

The hush around the ground became total.

Brice, stationery at the beginning of his run-up, lowered his head in some secret communion. After a moment he raised it, exhaling slowly. Then, inhaling deeply and executing a strangely dainty hop, he set off on his run up to the wicket, forefinger and middle finger gripping either side of the seam of the gleaming new ball. His first few strides appeared almost tentative, as though unsure of the terrain. Then he began to accelerate. As he approached the wicket in full stride, his right arm came up briefly in front of his chest before windmilling round in a great arc until, back arched, front foot thumping down across the crease and with Carter clearly in his sights over his left shoulder, his cocked wrist lent a final spasm of energy and the ball was released towards the batsman with a whirring noise audible at long leg.

* * *

Somewhere, beyond a lush green fold in the dales, a breath of wind nudged a pair of idling clouds together and sent them drifting gently in the direction of Bradburn.

* * *

Roger Spofforth could have placed his hand on his rapidly beating heart and sworn that, whatever impression his increasingly hostile audience might have gained, he had most certainly not deliberately redirected Miss Fitton's doily-napkins to the White Elephant stall. Had his voice been capable of carrying above the general clamour, he would perhaps have explained that, after Miss Fitton had reluctantly entrusted them to him only moments before, he had put them down *temporarily* in order to deal with a display table threatening to collapse under the teetering wares of Bradburn's amateur potters. It was hardly his fault, he might have continued, that the nearest adjacent surface also accommodated the mean and jumbled bric-a-brac of the White Elephant stall. So far, however, he had failed to utter a word that could be heard above the angry accusations of a milling mob of exhibitors.

Miss Bertram, her bulk amplified by a billowing saffron robe, caught at the waist, Spofforth noted with a nervous blink, by a plaited rope that would have restrained a drifting tanker, loomed over her shrinking victim and fixed him with bitter eyes.

"I think," she began in tones that produced an expectant hush around them, "that you have made a *very* serious mistake, Mr. Spofforth."

Spofforth was not disposed to argue, other than over the nature of the mistake which had actually been to allow himself to become involved in any aspect of their wretched Show in the first place. The air beneath the marquee's primrose and white drapes appeared to him to be thickening. He found he was perspiring profusely as his thoughts escaped to the sequestered calm of academe.

"Perhaps if we were to take Miss Fitton into the fresh air..." he suggested timorously.

There was a murmur of excitement from those at the front as Miss Fitton, recumbent and pallid on her litter, opened fearful eyes. They flickered briefly to a point above Spofforth's head before she re-entered her swoon and attention returned to the verbal drubbing about to be handed out to her assailant.

"You are a stupid, cruel and incompetent man," Miss Bertram began. If at that stage Miss Fitton had levitated and hovered above them it is doubtful whether it would have distracted the crowd. "We visited the handicrafts stall to see whether you had laid the doily-napkins out properly, only to find that they were missing. And now what do we find?" Her eyes dropped to where the napkins lay crumpled between a souvenir egg-timer from Whitby and a Clarice Cliff teapot without a lid, then lifted so that they could canvass an audience whose heads were shaking in uniform condemnation. Satisfied that she had their attention, Miss Bertram transfixed Spofforth once more, her voice dropping an octave as, very slowly, word distanced from word, she spat, "Yours - was - a - despicable - act."

Dark looks assailed Spofforth. The crowd frowned supportively at Miss Bertram, but her voice had broken on her last word and she was reduced to a forlorn hand gesture that told the crowd that that was all. Disappointed that events had stopped short of a public thrashing, they reluctantly accepted what they evidently regarded as a thoroughly anticlimactic dénouement and began to drift away. Miss Bertram, a forlorn figure now that her anger had dissipated, turned her back on Spofforth and joined those ministering to a Miss Fitton now slowly being helped into a sitting position.

"It was the doilies..." Miss Fitton said tremulously, her white-gloved hand plucking imploringly at her friend's robe, unaware that the point had been more or less grasped by all concerned.

Had it not been for the unmistakable scent of trampled grass, Spofforth would have concluded that he was in the middle of a particularly ghoulish nightmare. As it was, he grabbed the doilies from the White Elephant stall and, followed by a Miss Bertram quivering with suspicion, limped between the laid-out tables and dropped them carelessly among the frog fasteners, covered buttons and miscellany of Irish, Tunisian and Turkish lace on the embroidery stall.

"Frankly," he said to a Miss Bertram rendered mute by the realisation that she was to be offered yet another affront, "I wouldn't give any of it house room."

* * *

Brice's first delivery flew towards Carter with the venom of a nest of scorpions. The ball pitched on off-stump a couple of feet in front of the popping crease, reared towards his head like a live thing and then, quite simply, seemed to disappear.

Whether at that point Carter's feet twinkled or shimmered was a nicety with which Monkton Gibbs would toy later when he came to write-up the game. So far as the crowd was concerned there was a noise like an axe striking a log and Carter was gazing serenely in the direction of deep mid-wicket where the fielder was leaping sideways to avoid a ball that appeared to have been propelled from a cannon. Pitching briefly just inside the boundary rope, it whistled over the heads of the seated spectators, ricocheted around a clump of birch saplings and finally returned to earth to nestle harmlessly in the long grass. The umpire, face impassive, signalled a four.

Shelmerdine's expression was thoughtful. Oblivious to the cheers and howls from the crowd, he strolled in from mid-off for a word with his bowler. For his part, Brice was staring down the wicket with an expression that suggested he was having difficulty reconciling what he had seen with the laws of physics.

"Well," Shelmerdine said, his eyes fixed on the smirking Millington, "it looks like we're not going to tweak 'em out."

Silence descended on the crowd once more as Shelmerdine and Brice made minor adjustments to the field. Brice again paced out his run, scored a line in the grass like a bull about to charge, accelerated up to the wicket and, without any discernible change in his action, delivered a ball at scarcely more than medium pace.

Carter read it faultlessly and, refusing to play early, despatched it along the ground in the general direction of Simon at deep mid-on. His sprint to intercept it ended in a skid that failed to reach the ball by inches before it raced over the boundary. The umpire signalled another four, the numbered tins rang against the scoreboard and the noise of enthusiastic clapping washed over Simon as he lay on the grass and thumped his fist against the ground. Somewhere above him a spectator picked up the ball and lobbed it to a fielder.

As he started to rise Simon halted in mid-press-up. His face was inches away from a pair of familiar white shoes, the neat ankles above them held primly together. The scene assumed a dreamlike quality as, still practically prostrate, he raised his flushed face to see Rebecca smiling down at him from her wicker chair. Simon stared speechlessly, his expression that of a man who finds himself magically debagged.

Eyes sparkling, her hair making dark wings for her face as she lowered her head, Rebecca whispered, "Julia invited us; we'll see you later."

Mind whirling, Simon returned to his fielding position. At some point the children's faces had managed to impinge on his vision and he had a somewhat clearer impression of Martin saying, "If you'd gone more to your left you could've stopped that." He shook his head in bewilderment and tried to focus once more on the match.

The limited duration of Brice's venom was well-known throughout the league and Carter contented himself with playing the next three balls back to the bowler. When Brice began his run-up with the last ball of the over there was a drawn-out yell from the home supporters which reached a crescendo as the ball was released. Sensing the first truly loose ball of the over, Carter attempted a showy reverse sweep and was still rolling his wrists as the ball struck the edge of the bat and looped neatly into the Reverend Norman Butterworth's gloves.

'The umpire's finger stabbed skywards,' Monkton Gibbs wrote later that afternoon, 'as a crestfallen Carter began his lonely trek back to the pavilion.'

* * *

The roar from the crowd that greeted the fall of Carter's wicket carried easily to the showground where Miss Fitton, her pink smock creased as though she had slept in it, which in a sense she had, dabbed cologne on her temples and limply accepted the compliments on once more having won the embroidery class. Miss Bertram, having watched Spofforth totter off in a cloud of sulphurous resentment, was restored to her normal good humour and displayed her friend's doily-napkins with as much pride as if she had made them herself.

Elsewhere, within earshot of the flat crack-crack of the clay pigeon shoot, Bradburn's leaderless Morris Men skipped and jingled and waved and fluttered before an audience of bemused youths and their giggling girlfriends. The Green George, crimson-faced after having been compelled to dance Shepherd's Hey when all he wanted was to do was down another pint, execrated the missing soloist and, casting an anxious eye at a darkening sky, encouraged his men to greater speed.

* * *

Weary, but now smiling the smile of one who has reached and acted on a momentous decision, Roger

Spofforth sat on his suitcase at the bus stop outside his digs and contemplated his return to academe. The thought of leaving Bradburn for ever caused not a single pang; indeed, he felt positively light-headed at the prospect of never having to set foot there again. He had done the just thing so far as his landlady was concerned, having left on the hall table a cheque for outstanding rent, less the sums he had meticulously noted over the months as being charged to him for imaginary breakages. And, although he had no particular grievance against Ibstock, he felt no qualms at leaving him with a car whose value was almost certainly insufficient to cover the cost of its repair.

As he stepped carefully on to the platform of the bus, shaking the dust of Bradburn off his feet for ever, his final thought became a wish: that Miss Fitton might one day be carried away screaming for having woven a silken cord and used it to strangle the Reverend Norman Butterworth.

~Chapter 41~

Applause greeted Bradburn's fielders as they
accompanied Broadbridge's perspiring batsmen
towards the pavilion for lunch, yet it sounded only
faintly in Simon's ears. Though his concentration on
the game had never wavered, he was still struggling to
come to terms with a looking glass world in which it
seemed a man's family could appear and disappear at
will. Though his impression of having seen Rebecca
and the children remained clear, the next time he had
looked in that direction he had seen Connie
Butterworth in what he thought of as Rebecca's chair,
and though he had subsequently caught a glimpse of
Martin's school blazer, he could not escape the thought
that perhaps some existential fuse had blown.
Troubled and preoccupied, he followed on the heels of
Shelmerdine and Butterworth who, hands clasped
behind backs, heads together, were teasing out the
problems of captaincy. Edging between them, and with
a note of apology in his voice at distracting them,
Simon said, "I know this sounds silly, but Rebecca and
the children were here earlier and now there's no sign
of them."

The two had stopped suddenly so that Simon
found himself half a pace ahead. Shelmerdine spoke as
though noticing Simon for the first time. "Would you

say the ball was starting to swing in that last over?" he demanded.

Butterworth, lips pursed, peered heavenwards. "The sky is definitely darker," he said. Simon transferred his own gaze to the sky and agreed that the darker blue over the hills could be more than an effect of distance.

"The last two came in a bit," he conceded, falling in once more behind his friends.

All three peered towards the horizon where plumper clouds than Bradburn had seen for weeks pursued their undulating shadows over the gentle slopes of the dales.

"It's definitely getting muggy," Shelmerdine said, head shaking in vexation as they set off again for the pavilion.

For the first time, Simon became fully aware of the applause. For some reason Shelmerdine and Butterworth had allowed themselves to be overtaken once more and he found himself being nudged forward. The scattering of applause gained in volume as he trotted up the pavilion steps immediately behind the Broadbridge batsmen. Although it had been left to others to dislodge the Broadbridge openers, Simon had bowled well to take two early wickets and, although the first ball of his last over had been despatched to the boundary by a textbook cover drive, his next ball had made amends by sending the batsman's off stump cartwheeling.

The applause petered out as spectators turned to their picnic baskets or disappeared in search of lunch. Simon reached the head of the steps and felt himself thrust into the pavilion by a final pat from Shelmerdine. One side of the longroom's club-style lunch table had already been commandeered by the

Broadbridge players. Lunch, judging by the coolness
of their expressions, would offer little remission from
the dour events on the field. Simon began to pull a
chair out opposite one of the Broadbridge batsmen and
was struggling to detach it from where it had caught on
a trestle-leg when it was snatched from his hands by
Shelmerdine who promptly sat on it. Seeing that he
would have been sitting opposite a player he had
earlier dismissed following a questionable decision -
the clink of coins as the umpire toyed with them in his
pocket before raising his finger had had the
preternatural clarity he recalled after having once had
his ears syringed - Simon paid silent tribute to his
captain's tact and drifted along the table. The seat
opposite Millington had predictably been left empty,
the Broadbridge skipper's less than sunny nature
having become positively stygian after being clean
bowled one run short of his half-century. Simon
headed for it with what he hoped was a consoling smile
only to find himself pushed aside once more, this time
by Norman Butterworth.

"You're lunching in there," Butterworth informed
him, "orders from Mowbray." Grabbing the sleeve of
Simon's sweater, he pointed to the door at the end of
the longroom through which the VIPs were
disappearing. Grimacing, Simon joined the line of
blazers and summer dresses and patiently followed
them into the hospitality room. Inside, he stepped to
one side of the door and looked across the assembled
heads for a familiar face. A plumply eel-like Hugo
Russell shimmied past with a tray of drinks and
beamed companionably. Simon ventured into the wake
Russell's bulk was still capable of creating and edged
through the chattering guests. He smiled vaguely
around him, conspicuous in his whites, and caught a

happy smile from Julia before he almost stumbled as
he was gripped firmly round the legs. Nicholas
remained there for a moment, beaming up at his father
as Martin proffered a hand which Simon grasped
delightedly. Then, it seemed to Simon, Rebecca
appeared from nowhere, leading a tottering Katy by
the hand. Those around them became preoccupied by
their own affairs as Simon stooped and clutched
Rebecca with a grip that threatened to lift mother and
daughter into the air simultaneously.

"I was beginning to think I'd imagined it," Simon
whispered into Rebecca's hair.

Before she could respond, a hand reached out and
guided them to where they meekly took their places at
the lunch table.

* * *

Having seated Rebecca and Simon, Julia righted the
chair she had tilted against the table and took her
place between Hugo Russell and a Martin already
probing his salmon mousse with a critical fork. Katy,
secure and beaming in a highchair set between her
parents, played happily with the cutlery as Nicholas,
between his mother and Hugo Russell, politely hid a
yawn as Russell conjured a fair representation of a
rabbit from his paper napkin. Though serious
conversation was effectively extinguished by the
hubbub arising from the cramped tables, Julia was
happy to see that Rebecca and Simon were chatting
animatedly above Katy's preoccupied head.

Her decision to invite Rebecca and the children as
a surprise for Simon had produced concerned clucking
from her father.

"What is intended as a friendly gesture towards a
couple you have become fond of could be seen as
interference," he had counselled, his pink face worried.

"What if Simon would rather wait to see them at home? Suppose, for some reason, there's been a rift in the lute...?"

Julia pooh-poohed the concerns. "Rebecca was thrilled at the idea," she countered.

Her resolve had not weakened until, wishing to free the Friday evening to meet her guests at the station and settle them into Bradburn House, her feeble attempts at dissimulation had reduced Simon to his stumbling retreat and brought her to tears of frustration.

For Simon, whose life often included descents into confusion, the dénouement crowning the morning's events held a radiance that explained and then banished the shadows of the past twenty-four hours. He gazed at Rebecca adoringly.

"Julia felt dreadfully guilty," Rebecca was saying, "but she did want it to be a surprise and, well, it was worth it, wasn't it?"

Before Simon could respond Shelmerdine appeared at the door. He peered around the room until his eyes caught Simon's, preventing what Martin was convinced would have been the wholly unacceptable sight of his parents kissing in public. Shelmerdine was making his way to Simon's table.

"We're going out ten minutes early," he said. "The weather could break and we've agreed to get a move on."

As he spoke, someone near the door put the lights on to dispel the gathering gloom. The kiss Martin had feared manifested itself as the merest peck on the cheek for Rebecca as Simon grimaced his regrets to the rest of the table, grabbed a bread roll off his side-plate and followed his captain out and on to the pitch, chewing contentedly.

* * *

The threatened change in the weather had arrived subtly. During lunch the uninterrupted sunshine of recent weeks had slowly turned into a fitful interplay of light and shadow as clouds scudded across the darkening sky. Heavier clouds, thickening and filling as they loitered above the moors, now loomed over the dales as wives and girlfriends emerged from the curtailed lunch and despatched menfolk to their cars to retrieve cardigans they had not expected to need before evening.

'Broadbridge confidence evaporated on resumption,' Gibbs noted as the Broadbridge tail-enders, eyes terrorised behind visored helmets, survived with an over of speculative prodding as Brice's thunderbolts hurtled from the deepening gloom. The declaration negotiated over lunch that should have allowed Broadbridge another half dozen overs before yielding the strip to Bradburn became redundant. The umpires held brief colloquies with the batsmen and the rival captains before hurrying towards the pavilion as the first heavy drops of rain fell from the darkening sky.

* * *

Generators coughing into life at the showground, filled the grounds with the reek of diesel. Artificial lights sprang on, glowing through canvas speckled black with the first splashes of rain. Spectators at the show ring watched glumly as anxious owners led fretful ponies snickering to their boxes. A wind, warm and ominous, shook the branches of the surrounding trees before rushing away to leave an unnatural stillness. A reflective balloon, trapped in the branches of a swaying poplar, tugged helplessly at the end of its string.

Then the lightning came. It was, Shelmerdine
swore later, as if the world had stuck its finger in a
socket. Children shrieked as eye-searing flashes
speared earthwards pursued by crackling explosions of
thunder. Ears rang with shock as the rain began in
earnest, spearing down and shooting horizontal
torrents off canvas roofs which moments before had
been hot to the touch. Unable to squeeze into now
crowded marquees, those marooned outside found
themselves cut off from each other by an impenetrable
curtain of water. Beneath their feet, parched grass
streamed like hair in rushing rivulets. Near the edge of
the showground, at the end of the showmen's caravan
encampment, Isherwood's dog, thwarted by the hated
walking stick as it strove to join its master beneath the
raised shutter of a hamburger stand, exorcised years of
bile by nipping him on the ankle before disappearing
into the warm dry grass beneath the vehicle.

* * *

The onset of the storm had trapped Julia during a
routine visit to an almost deserted press tent. Now she
stood by the sodden flap and watched in disbelief as a
procession of bedraggled women approached through
the abating rain. Without exception they appeared to
be accompanied by children being dragged, carried or
pushed along in her direction. And there, beckoning
the convoy on from beneath a giant golf umbrella with
which he was simultaneously trying to protect those
nearest to him, was Harry Temple. Immediately
behind him, Sister Brennan from the factory clinic was
almost invisible behind what was clearly identifiable as
a giant bale of disposable nappies. As Julia watched,
one of the mothers hanging on to Temple's arm came
to a sudden stop as mud sucked off a shoe. Thrusting
her baby at Temple, she retrieved the shoe before

removing its companion and resuming her course in stockinged feet. Temple, a bemused baby tucked absently under his arm like so much laundry, hurried ahead of his charges. Collapsing the umbrella with one hand while contriving to pass the baby to Julia, he ushered his niece further into the tent.

"Got to commandeer your resources, m'dear," he said, stepping aside as Sister Brennan and her train of dripping adherents piled past them, "nappy station's flooded out." Release from the storm appeared to have released the children from their stunned silence. What had begun as a gentle whimper from one direction was taken up by others until conversation disappeared behind a communal wailing. The scents of summer disappeared beneath a cloud of ammonia and worse as helpers staggered in with buckets whose contents sloshed threateningly beneath their lids. Temple cast a single horrified glance at his charges, raised his hat to Julia and, turning on his heel, squelched back towards his saner responsibilities, umbrella bravely at the slope.

* * *

Grudgingly, with much sinister flickering and rumbling, the storm retreated. Thunderheads that had turned day into night slowly dispersed. The sun appeared, pale and tenuous at first then with a conviction that brought steam from clinging summer dresses. The last of the thunder retreated grumbling to the hills, leaving a legacy of dripping canvas and marshy footpaths.

* * *

The cricket ground's almost uninterrupted expanse of water reflected the clearing blue of the sky. Mowbray, standing at the foot of the pavilion's concrete plinth, conferred with the umpires as water eddied around his brogues. Dipstick hovered at their elbows as they reached their decision. He looked up and gave Shelmerdine a thumbs down as Mowbray detached himself and returned to the pavilion with a disappointed shake of his head. Ellingham passed him on the way out and, with water lapping at his ankles, set off to retrieve the wickets whose reflections bobbed in the wake of a mallard and his mate as they paddled contentedly from gully towards short leg.

Shelmerdine lounged on the players' balcony, chair tilted, feet on the veranda rail. Millington, jaw knotted in frustration, stared after Ellingham's retreating back, his fist slowly thumping the rail beside Shelmerdine's feet.

Splasher fumbled for the bottle of beer beside his chair. Waving it idly at the flooded pitch, he shook his head admiringly. "I'll say this for you Broadbridge lot," he said, "you'll stop at nowt to avoid a thrashing."

* * *

In the hospitality room, players' wives and girlfriends helped Sam and Hetty Harrison clear what remained of an afternoon tea largely ignored by guests, most of whom had not waited for stumps to be drawn before getting their things together and departing while still digesting lunch.

~Chapter 42~

Once Simon's motives had been tested and judged allowable on compassionate grounds, and once he had drunk a token pint, he had been granted leave from the post-match carouse and had already changed out of his whites and into blazer and slacks by the time young Phillips arrived in Julia's car to take him to Bradburn House.

He found Julia and Rebecca taking tea on a terrace already dried out by a sun restored to a sky which had resumed the flawless blue of that morning. Empty glasses still littered a glass-topped cane table, a souvenir of the visit by the Wilberforce directors and their wives who had called in for an aperitif on their way to rest and change before that evening's dinner for the show organisers.

"It will be either a wake or a celebration," Julia explained as she poured Simon a glass of wine from a cooler whose ice had turned to water, "depending on how the show has gone and on who has won what for doing what. Uncle Harry will make a speech thanking officials and judges, someone will make a speech thanking Uncle Harry, and no-one will dare go home until everyone who wants to has had a say." She stood up. Rebecca followed, casting Simon a glance he recognised as being pregnant with a meaning he was unequipped to decipher. Approaching her husband, Rebecca pulled his head down and brushed his cheek with her lips.

"You have been excused the dinner," she explained, smiling. "Mrs. Benson will feed us and the children and then we can take them to the fair." She disappeared after Julia into the deep shadows of the house, leaving Simon looking out over gardens sparkling in the sunshine.

Apart from a few snatched words with Rebecca at lunchtime, and little more than a glimpse of the children, it seemed to Simon that his family's descent on Bradburn might hardly have taken place. Now, with the need to go to the show dinner removed and the prospect of an evening together, he felt reconciled to Rebecca's confession at lunchtime that she and the children would have to return to London the following day; that, or forever be anathematised by the wretched Pownall for keeping Martin away from Rosehill Infants' School without an *exeat*. With the shadow of an evening apart from his family lifted, he fell into a reverie in which familial tenderness bumped against the realisation that the enjoyment and prosperity Bradburn represented, while welcome, would be no more than an interlude. Once the bid for Wilberforces was resolved, whichever way it might go, he would again have to address the problem of finding a more permanent means of putting bread in mouths.

"Have you thought what you're going to do once we've sorted this business out?"

Simon started so violently that wine spilled from his glass on to the terrace. Mowbray's appearance at his elbow, and the uncanny way he had boarded his train of thought, produced a sensation that left him incapable of speech for several moments.

Mowbray, conscious of the effect his remark had produced but uncertain why, peered vaguely around in a search for George as he waited for Simon to recover. George, in the meantime, having spotted his employer emerging from the house, had retreated to the certain cover of the walled garden where he proposed to do whatever could be achieved in the few hours that remained before he knocked off for his annual holiday.

"It could all come down to what Edwin decides to do," Mowbray mused.

Simon, though visibly struggling towards speech, remained mute.

"If he has really decided to throw in with Pusey, which must be a distinct possibility, then it could be practically all over. If he doesn't, then we must suppose we're in with a chance. You could be back with your family in days if we lose." Mowbray smiled at the irony. "Not that we're going to, of course."

"I hadn't really thought about losing," Simon eventually succeeded in saying. "Either way, it will be strange to be unemployed again..." Anxious to dispel any impression of angst, Simon added quickly, "I'm sure there'll be lots of opportunities..."

He broke off as young Philips passed by on the path below, his barrow already filled with clippings from storm damaged roses. Mowbray raised his pipe in greeting and Simon waved. Phillips, encumbered, managed a deep nod.

Mowbray's eyes returned to quartering the garden. Without particular emphasis he said, "I don't suppose you've thought about moving the family up here?" He had begun filling his pipe and the question was punctuated by the sucking and tamping that accompanied the application of a match before a fragrant cloud embraced the pair of them. "I'm not sure we can occupy a full-time public relations man, but I know Harry would be glad of a hand. Something for you to bear in mind, anyway." Mowbray glanced at Simon's face then looked away again.

Aware that, inexplicably, he appeared to be being offered a job, all Simon could manage was, "I..."

Mowbray waited a moment, then said, "It's possible Julia's mentioned something of the sort to Rebecca. Thought perhaps you ought to know." He gave a sudden start and stared hard in the direction of the walled garden. "Cigarette smoke," he exclaimed happily. "That'll be George." Turning once more to Simon, he said, "Just you think about it," and cantered happily down the steps in pursuit of the head gardener.

It had been Julia's early warning of her father's intention to sound Simon out about a job that had prompted a warmly approving Rebecca to follow her new friend into the house as soon as she had seen Mowbray hovering inside the shadows of the house awaiting his opportunity.

"Obviously, father would like you to have time to talk about it before you have to go back to London," Julia had explained to Rebecca. "Not that there's any need for you to decide in a hurry, especially with this Pusey business hanging over everyone's heads."

Having glanced back solely to confirm that Mowbray was indeed engaging Simon in conversation, or at least attempting to, the girls had retreated upstairs to the nursery where Nicholas sat blissfully astride the rocking horse, now sanitised and restored to its rightful place. Martin was reading to a Katy whose presence had to be largely assumed as she was almost obscured by a veiled straw hat from the room's burdened cupboards. Rebecca and Julia sat on either side of one of the broad windowsills and gazed out over the freshened green of the dales.

"It's all very tempting," Rebecca said wistfully, "but it just depends on so many things..." She wound a lock of hair round a finger then let it spring back into place. "On winning this wretched bid, on Simon..."

"You deal with Simon, I'll deal with the bid," Julia said. Absently, she wandered over to Katy and tied the hat's chiffon scarf under the child's chin. "That Pusey man seems to be able to do what he likes while everything we do has to be taken apart and reassembled by some wretched committee in London. There really ought to be something we could do."

Her expression had been abstracted, Rebecca reported to Simon, but resolute.

* * *

The sight of Rebecca's clothes hanging in the wardrobe of one of Bradburn House's guestrooms cast a shallow illusion of home over Simon as he sat on the bed and pondered the exciting but dislocating possibilities revealed by his conversation with Mowbray. Rebecca, having confided her faith that he would reach the right decision, had left him contemplating the contents of a hold-all containing sufficient of his belongings from the Fox & Chickens to allow him to spend the night at Bradburn House. Earlier she had listened to his account of his conversation with Mowbray as nearly non-commitally as she could manage, secure in the knowledge that her wishes would prevail. There was therefore nothing to be lost by allowing him to undergo the mental agonising he would undoubtedly feel such a watershed merited.

"I'm sure you'll arrive at the right decision, darling," she had assured him and had disappeared happily to help Julia dress for the show dinner.

So far, Simon had mused to the point where he was considering to what extent his improvements to the Ealing house had altered its saleable value, and, unfailingly honest as he was, in which direction. When Rebecca returned and greeted him with a hug that sent them both sprawling across the bed, his face had been wearing the preoccupied expression that can be seen in certain lights on the face of the Sphinx.

"There would certainly be economic advantages in moving North," Simon conceded once they had disposed themselves against the pillows.

Rebecca gave his mental steering wheel the Jesuitical twitch she felt it needed. "We'd make lots of money on the house, considering everything you've done to it..."

"Schools might be a problem..."

"Martin starts junior school in September. Julia is convinced we could get him in here. It's where Julia went, and Kitty..."

"...and Shelmerdine," Simon brooded.

"...and Shelmerdine," Rebecca conceded.

"It would mean leaving your London friends."

"Name them," Rebecca challenged, mentally apologising to Hazel.

"You wouldn't have Julia. She normally spends most of her time in London."

Tyres crunched on the gravel below their window. Rebecca urged Simon off the bed and hurried him down the wide sweep of stairs and across the hall to catch Julia and her father as they prepared to drive off to the dinner. Julia shooed her father into the car ahead of her as they approached. She was wearing an ivory creation that left her arms and back bare. As her friends approached she held her skirt out and looked at Rebecca.

"You're quite sure it's not too Glyndebourne?" Reassured, she gathered her skirts and joined her father in the back of the car. Simon closed the door gently after her and they watched hand in hand as Julia waved through the window. The Phillips boy, scrubbed and wearing a tie, slipped the car into gear and eased it slowly round a bend in the drive.

"She really is beautiful," Rebecca said, not for the first time.

"But Julia hasn't got me and the children," Simon chided.

Rebecca, whose normal inclination would have been to squelch the conceit with something mordant, smiled as she took his hand and led him back into the house.

* * *

Katy was compelled to spend most of her time at the fair observing events from the arms of whichever parent was not accompanying the boys on the more tranquil rides available, but the boys themselves suffered no such deprivation. Avid for new thrills, they squirmed through the heaving crowds, squelching through the cloying mud and dragging protesting parents from attraction to attraction until they were prepared to concede that they had ridden on everything within their compass. Now, with Katy on Simon's shoulders and the boys clutching their parents' hands, Simon and Julia resumed the discussion of their newly presented future against a background of throbbing diesels and music from a dozen contending attractions. Only Martin, watching first one and then the other, concluded that something momentous was afoot.

"They're probably discussing a divorce," he shouted to Nicholas. "It's because daddy's been away so much."

For once he had misjudged his man. Instead of being thrown into terrified silence, Martin dug his heels in by the hook-a-duck stall and let out a howl that managed to penetrate the surrounding din. Picked up and reassured by Simon, and Martin having scowled through a largely inaudible talking-to, candyfloss was awarded all round and Simon and Rebecca continued their speculations in a heady atmosphere of spun sugar, diesel exhaust and the aroma of boiling frankfurters. The kiss that ended the discussion and sealed the decision to abandon Ealing for Bradburn was exchanged shortly after Simon had relinquished Katy long enough to strike the test-your-strength machine with a force that split the head of the mallet and threatened to send the bell chasing the factory's smoke into the next county. To Simon, normally impervious to fanciful imaginings, the blow symbolised a punctuation mark beyond which life would be richer and more purposeful. For Rebecca, the kiss confirmed her wisdom in having telephoned to add their names to the books of Bradburn's leading estate agent.

~Chapter 43~

What Julia hoped to achieve by paying a visit to Uncle Edwin, who as far as she was aware had never heard of her, was something which, as things turned out, she was never asked; although, had anyone thought to put the question, she would have found the greatest difficulty in providing a satisfactory answer. To the extent that she ever attempted to rationalise her actions that day, she concluded that they were probably prompted by nothing stronger than the recognition that whereas the problem, in the shape of Uncle Edwin, was in the Cotswolds, she, quite patently, was not; and it was possible that deeper analysis might have found a fragile justification somewhere along the line that unites 'nothing ventured, nothing gained' with 'she who hesitates is lost'.

It was true that the Sunday morning had found her lonely and quite distinctly at a loose end for once, an unforeseen consequence of having the Beresfords roaming around the district looking at properties which they would continue to do until it was time for Rebecca and the children to leave. All she knew was that she felt restless and adrift in currents that were taking Wilberforces heaven knew where. The only prospect that offered any certainty was that the

Wilberforce defence document would be posted the following day, after which Pusey could let them stew for at least another week before deciding whether to revise his offer. Following that, the whole mad business would start again: there would be yet another opportunity for Pusey to revise his bid until, eventually, the fate of Wilberforces would be decided by its shareholders.

Including Uncle Edwin.

Freeing herself from the mess she had made of the Sunday papers, she telephoned Russell to check her understanding of how events would now transpire.

"That is correct," Russell had said, attempting to sound consoling. Then, with his ineradicable desire to cover all options, he added, "Unless something happens in the meantime to upset their apple cart."

She spent the rest of the morning struggling to interest herself in the newspapers and drifting in and out of the kitchen for coffee. Her father fussed in once or twice, urging her to accompany him to the post-Show cocktail party. Harry Temple threw these each year in his efforts to make the transition from one Show to the next as seamless as possible, and she was secretly relieved when the company secretary arrived shortly after noon and carried her father off to the revels.

Left to moon around the empty house she made herself a light lunch, prepared something for her father's supper and was strolling disconsolately around the garden when she remembered Simba.

Arrangements concerning Simba had been made as a routine aspect of George's last minute decision to spend a couple of weeks with his daughter and dog-hating son-in-law. Having left young Phillips with a list of jobs Hercules could not have accomplished in a fortnight, he had confirmed with Julia that Simba could be housed in the stables for the duration as usual. Now, a glance at her watch showed that the agreed time for collecting Simba was about to pass. By the time she reached the lodge, breathless and apologetic, George had locked the door and was in the process of stepping into a car where his glum son-in-law sat behind the wheel drumming his fingers on the dashboard. Simba, looking restive and anxious and distinctly unlike the dog that had put Spofforth in fear of his life, was tethered to the bootscraper.

"I knew you'd not be more than a few minutes," George said, a sentiment his tone belied. "There's a bag of meal in the stable for him and I've put his water dish there." He clambered into the car, fumbling theatrically for the seatbelt. His son-in-law got out, nodded at Julia with averted eyes, picked up George's suitcase, threw it into the boot and slammed the lid.

"I won't be gone long," George said, though whether to Julia or Simba was unclear as the driver got in and the car shot off with a jerk that pitched George's cap over his eyes.

Simba whined, holding a mournful expression as long as it took the car to disappear, then turned his huge brown eyes on a Julia he had known since puppyhood. His look was clearly meant to say that he was now at her disposal and what, if anything, did she propose to do about it?

"I suppose, silly dog, you want a walk," Julia said. Then, because she told herself the fresh air might blow away her discontent, she unfastened his lead and, with Simba high-stepping sedately beside her, set off down the road towards town.

* * *

The sky was a washed, cloudless cobalt. Had it not
been for the occasional puddle at the side of the road,
and the fact that the gurgle had for the first time in
weeks been restored to the narrow brook that ran
between the road and the walls of Bradburn House, the
previous day's storm might have been imagined. Julia
and Simba stuck close to the grass verge beside the
stream, Simba adding spirit to the occasion with a
disconcerting prancing gait that had Julia hurrying to
keep up. There was a languid, drowsy air to the early
afternoon. The crawling line of motor cars that usually
brought much of Bradburn to a standstill at weekends
was absent, and as Julia and Simba passed the factory
and crossed the canal bridge they might have been the
only two creatures in the world. Even the town square
proved to be only languidly busy as people sprawled on
benches or strolled aimlessly around, peering at their
tanned reflections in the windows of shops that were
mostly closed. Only the children expended energy,
clustering round the ice cream vendor by the
bandstand or ignoring half-hearted reproaches from
sun-dazed parents as they clambered over the Show's
judging platform and trampled its bunting on the
stone setts.

Bringing Simba to heel, Julia approached the
offices and pressed the illuminated night bell. Since
the bid, the office had been manned on a twenty-four
hour basis and she waited impatiently for whoever was
on duty to let her in. Despite the languorous warmth of
the square, an atmosphere of crisis seemed to emanate
from the building like a cold grey cloud.

The bell echoed again inside the deserted lobby.
The frosted glass in the huge doors concealed what was
happening within until there was the sound of bolts
being withdrawn and one of the doors was opened by a

spectacle-less Miss Varley, slimly elegant in pastel sweater and slacks. She stood aside to admit Julia, one hand fluttering in a gesture that indicated and at the same time disparaged the informality of her clothes.

"I had no idea..." Abstractedly, Miss Varley patted Simba on the head. Simba, accustomed to more circumspect behaviour, put his head on one side and stared at her.

"You look lovely," Julia said.

Miss Varley managed to blush, smile and shake her head at the same time. "I'm to be relieved at three. I hadn't expected..."

"I shouldn't have disturbed you," Julia apologised. "I was simply at a loose end."

"There's not a great deal to do here, in fact," Miss Varley confided. "The company secretary was in earlier. I faxed something to the London solicitors for him, but he left before noon to pick up the chairman. I believe they're going to Colonel Temple's."

Julia nodded. "I cried off, I'm afraid." She stopped, uncertain how to go on. Miss Varley was looking at her expectantly. Still without any clear purpose, Julia said, "Perhaps, if you'd look after Simba for a few minutes, I could just pop upstairs."

Simba looked baleful as Miss Varley took his lead and, with a gentle tug, led him firmly in the direction of reception, his lolling tongue leaving a trail of saliva on the tiled floor.

Left alone, Julia walked up the stairs in the grip of the building's crypt-like coolness. She hesitated outside her father's office and then, seeing an open door further along the corridor, headed instead for the company secretary's room.

The office was furnished sparsely. Ben Bartlett regarded anything other than a desk and chair as mere frippery, although there was, by necessity, a second chair facing the desk where his secretary sat. There was also a large oak table with a scuffed leather top. Open on the table was a stiff-bound volume of computer printouts, the register of shareholders he had abandoned once it had answered that morning's enquiry from London.

Julia approached and riffled it pages aimlessly. It was a moment or two before it dawned on her what the book represented; then, her forehead wrinkling in a frown, she began searching the entries under W.

Edwin Wilberforce stood out from the slim ranks of Wilberforces by the simple fact that the number of shares registered against his name had two more digits than any other entry on the page. Providentially, there was a pencil and pad by the register. Feeling unaccountably nefarious, Julia copied down Edwin's address which she recognised as being somewhere below the Midlands and put it in the pocket of her jeans.

Back in the telephone exchange, Simba had drunk most of a bowl of water provided by Miss Varley and was sitting with his head in her lap and gazing soulfully into her eyes.

"I suspect he's rather stupid," Miss Varley said, handing the lead to Julia, "but he is rather sweet." It was an epithet never before uttered in his hearing, but Simba wagged his tail approvingly and cast slavish glances back at Miss Varley as Julia bade her farewell at the door and hurried him down the steps to the square.

Miss Varley slid the bolts back into place. Turning, she leaned with her back against the door and stared at the bust of Albert Wilberforce.

"That young woman's up to something," she told him. "I should have known all along it would take a woman."

* * *

While Julia's demeanour might have appeared purposeful to Miss Varley, and continued to appear so to those she recognised and smiled at as she dragged Simba through the square, she had left the office no nearer to deciding a course of action than when she had left home. But, slowly, an idea was beginning to crystallise.

* * *

Pusey's emissary to Edwin Wilberforce, on the other hand, was perfectly clear what the situation required and he was dutifully recalling his instructions as he donned a black roll-neck sweater and examined the effect in the mirror. Short of rubbing soot on his face, a course that failed to commend itself for cosmetic reasons as well as through lack of the raw material, he expected that, as the shadows lengthened and night fell, he would be as near invisible as was aesthetically acceptable.

"Pusey is an impossible client," Pusey's banker had explained to the junior analyst whose uncritical allegiance had marked him out for the assignment. "He is quite without scruples and expects everyone else to be so, too. Fortunately for him..." The young analyst's eyebrows rose in anticipation of an admission that could hardly avoid aligning his firm's morals with those of the client, though doubtless in terms through which the association would be rendered innocuous. "...Fortunately for him," the banker continued, "we have a moral commitment to conclude the Wilberforce business on his behalf..." *And pocket the fat success fee*, the young analyst said under his breath. "...Even if

the only means at our disposal are highly irregular."
He dabbed at his brow with a lawn handkerchief and
fixed his junior colleague with a glower that suggested
he had brought the whole thing on himself.

"The envelope you saw on your initial visit to
Edwin Wilberforce must be secured," he said
magisterially. "We have, of course, allowed him time to
post it, but..." His outstretched palms and pained
expression suggested a bishop about to offer a
benediction only to find he had forgotten the words. "It
is almost certainly addressed to us, or intended for us,
or would have been addressed to us or intended for us
had he known what his best interests were. It is, one
might say, ours in all respects other than that we do
not yet possess it." He lowered his hands to the desk
and paused to reflect on the case so far. Finding that it
satisfactorily impugned the client's motives while
casting those of the bank in a light of manipulated
loyalty, his expression lifted. "In short," he concluded
brightly, "you really cannot afford to come back
without it."

The rest of what was intended remained
unspoken, yet each understood it to run along the lines
of, "*Of course, this conversation has not taken place.
If you should be caught at some compromising point
in the venture, your actions will be disowned by the
bank. Our own reputation will be preserved by
dismissing you in terms of disapproval that will
resound around the City and render you henceforth
unemployable.*"

It was the phantom conversation rather than his
instructions that echoed in the young analyst's ears as
he got into his motor car and pointed it once more
towards the Cotswolds.

* * *

By the time she had turned Simba loose in the stableyard to refamiliarise himself with his new base and its smells, Julia found herself brooding in the echoing emptiness of the house. What had been merely the seed of an idea earlier had, she found, become an irresistible desire to climb into her car and beard Uncle Edwin, as it were, at source; and, as she was incapable of letting 'I dare not' wait upon 'I would', she penned a comfortingly evasive note to her father, propped it against his wilting salad and set off towards the Cotswolds.

~Chapter 44~

Only the muffled roar of the car's restored exhaust disturbed the sleepy Cotswolds as Julia followed instructions she had coaxed from an evening stroller and headed through the descending dusk towards Pinfold Manor.

"He'll not let you in, you know," her informant had cautioned. "Only the housekeeper goes in, and that's only to leave his meals and collect his dishes." He had sniffed disapprovingly. "He used to leave his clothes to be washed, but she says he rarely bothers these days. The garden's a jungle and the house smells like a mausoleum. He should be committed, you know. Still..."

Whatever other revelations he might have intended were lost to the night air as Julia, her face glowing from the open-topped journey, hair streaming like fluttering silk, waved her thanks and sped out of the village. The directions took her briefly through winding country lanes until eventually she drew up across the road from the rusting gates and tumbledown lodge which, she had been told, would identify Pinfold Manor. She switched off her lights, stopped the engine and studied the looming walls of the house where they curved away into the deepening dusk on either side of the lodge. She stayed in her seat for a moment, listening for what should have been the reassuringly normal squeaks and rustlings of the night, but they were absent. If there was such a thing as an air of menace, a concept she would have dismissed as nonsense in daylight, then Pinfold Manor, invisible behind the crumbling masonry of its walls, seemed to exude it in invisible clouds.

Then, chiding herself for her timidity, she thrust open the car door and hurried across the deserted road to the gates. Pale moonlight penetrated the surrounding trees to reveal an overgrown drive filled with patches of deepening shadow. Nettles smothered in road dust thrust at her as the light from her torch probed past the gates' ornamental ironwork and washed over the outline of a decrepit lodge. The gates themselves stood slightly ajar and Julia grasped one by an upright and pushed. The gate resisted, rusted into place as securely as if welded.

Stepping back, she used splayed fingers to dim the torch, playing its beam over huge stone gateposts topped with urns scabbed with faded moss. A nest, unkempt and long abandoned, drooped from a hole where a bell-pull had once been. She re-crossed the road to the car, rubbing her upper arms to dispel goose bumps. Resisting the urge to jump in and drive away, she locked the car, crossed the road once more and, exhaling a deep breath, forced herself through the gap where one of the gates leaned away from its fellow. A cloud moved slowly across the moon, casting all around into darkness except for the pale pool of light from her torch. She flicked the beam ahead. A drive rank with coarse grass stretched beyond the weak beam of the torch. Horses' tail sprouted from verges no longer distinguishable from the knee-high grass of the grounds that stretched away beyond them. Shrub roses, barren and misshapen, marked the sites of long abandoned flowerbeds. Trees flanking the drive stirred and murmured in a rising evening breeze, their gnarled branches seeming to claw at the darkening night sky. Switching off the torch to preserve the battery, Julia followed the dimly perceptible line of trees in what commonsense said had to be the direction of the house. Goose-grass, treacherous and unseen, clutched at the legs of her jeans. Untended shrubs reached out invisible branches to pluck at her hair then became precious sanctuary as, once, she fled to hide in them when the weeds ahead appeared to sway with the passage of some large animal. The threat evaporated and she stepped back on to the drive, forcing herself to quicken her pace, stumbling over obstacles and wishing desperately she had provided herself with a more powerful torch. At last, despite the darkness, she sensed that the drive was widening to a more open aspect, perhaps even to the house itself. Risking a few moments of her precious battery, she flicked its light around her and saw the edge of what had once been the gracious sweep of the Manor's forecourt. Dousing the torch, she pressed slowly forward to where the house must lie, hands extended to probe the darkness.

The next moment she was plunging face downwards into the weeds, her feet grasped in what felt like a poacher's snare. More affronted than afraid, she sat up, her hands searching the darkness for the fallen torch. She almost groaned aloud with relief as she found it and shone it accusingly at her feet. Somehow they had become entangled in a discarded loop of wire which she untangled and threw into the bushes. As she did so the cloud passed from the moon. Julia froze. The great bulk of the house towered above her, windows recessed in crumbling stone staring blindly down. She shivered and stood up, flicking her hair back over her shoulders in a gesture of defiance.

"Presumably, Uncle Edwin," she said to the night air, "the absence of lights suggests you live at the back of this excrescence."

Above her, a door creaked.

Stifling a squeal, Julia doused the torch once more and fled into the darker shadows of the building's massive portico, heart thumping. Once more clouds snuffed the moon and plunged the world into uniform darkness. Although she was for all practical purposes invisible, Julia had to concede that so were the steps and whatever was responsible for the creaking door. Heart pounding, she sidled along the portico wall until she could peer round it. She could see nothing. She withdrew her head and considered her position. The creaking of the door could simply mean that Edwin had absent-mindedly left it open, in which case it was not remotely menacing. Equally, it could have been a guest arriving from another direction, in which case it could only have been the housekeeper referred to by her informant earlier that evening. Again, not menacing. On the other hand...On the other hand, it could have been the noise made by somebody leaving the house, in which case...where was he now and, what's more, what had happened to Uncle Edwin?

The situation had the predictable effect on someone with Julia's temperament.

Taking a deep breath, she flung herself round the corner, took up the crouch favoured by New York's Finest, thrust the torch in the direction of the door and pressed the switch.

The torch flickered and went out.

Before doing so, however, it had briefly revealed steps devoid of any lurking presence and, at the top, a door whose dilapidation and sprung joints appeared to account for the fact that it was ever so slightly ajar. Her adrenalin still pumping, Julia bounded up the steps, put her shoulder against the door and charged headlong into the pitch black interior.

* * *

Pusey had a sense of foreboding.

What caused it, or what it meant, eluded him. But no matter how he tried to shrug off the feeling, a worm of unease worked within him so that he found himself going about his business with an unfamiliar tentativeness, as though any precipitate action on his part might trigger events beyond his capacity to manage.

"I don't like the feeling that matters have moved out of my control," he complained menacingly, having dragged his merchant banker to the telephone from his evening snooze in front of the television. "You're sure your man has gone for the envelope?"

"Certainly," the banker said stiffly. "He is a young man with more spirit than intellect and will undoubtedly carry out his mission successfully."

Pusey grunted, unconvinced.

"What if he's caught?" he probed, anxious to explore possibilities but fearing to unleash whatever his foreboding threatened.

There was a sigh at the other end of the line. "He is totally, inescapably deniable. Have no fear. "

"He *will* post the letter locally, so that it appears the old man had posted it?"

"He has already identified the nearest post-box to Pinfold Manor."

"What if the old man denies having posted it?"

"The likelihood of his knowing whether he is Edwin Wilberforce or the Emperor of Ethiopia is, I gather, extremely remote. If he *does* deny having posted it, who's going to believe him?"

There was a precarious edge of asperity creeping into his voice and he stifled it. There were accounts still to be rendered and there would be little point in providing a honing stone for Pusey's notorious niggardliness.

"Then we're more or less home and dry...?"

"Providing the institutions honour their commitments..."

Pusey gnawed a knuckle, a rare display of inner turmoil. "It's just that I feel..." He shook himself and stared irritably at the handset. "It's nothing," he said abruptly, "we'll speak in the morning."

Banging the telephone back into its rest, he flung himself into an armchair and scowled at the shadows lengthening on the wall.

* * *

Crashing through the door, Julia shot full-tilt along the hall only to come to a full-stop against what was undoubtedly a fellow creature.

There was a startled oomph! as breath was driven from a body, followed by a combination of noises as hard and soft things bounced off some invisible item of furniture and tumbled to the floor. What Julia surmised was a brass tray rolled interminably on its edge before subsiding with a ringing clatter somewhere along the hall. Before that, however, she had added to the cacophony with a shriek that still rang in her ears. The thought of what impact she might have had on one who was certainly geriatric and conceivably osteoporotic made her shudder.

"Uncle Edwin?" Her voice was tremulous. To the side of her something stirred. "Uncle Edwin? It's me,

Julia, your..." She hesitated, uncertain, for the moment, of the relationship.

Nigel Scrope-Stewart's contribution was not so much an interjection as a vocal spasm. "What on *earth*," he hissed, fixing her in the beam of a torch against which hers had been as a scintilla to a supernova, "are *you* doing here?"

Julia's relief at not having flattened Wilberforce's principal shareholder collapsed into confusion as she shielded her eyes and tried to imagine how the voice of Scrope-Stewart could conceivably be emerging from a point around three feet above floor level in Uncle Edwin's hall.

Wondering whether for the first time in her life she was about to have hysterics, she said weakly, "Nigel...?"

Scrope-Stewart flashed the torch briefly at his face, revealing him to be sitting with his back to the wall, his expression of injured confusion given a somewhat diabolical cast in the light of the torch. He looked, Julia thought, like a clubbable Mephistopheles. Then he plunged them back into darkness.

"How do you mean, what am *I* doing here?" Julia hissed back. She was surprised to find herself mildly comforted by his presence, yet there had been a proprietorial edge to his tone which she resented. "What on earth are *you* doing here?"

"Keep your voice down." Nigel's voice was hoarse with anxiety.

"Why should I? It's *my* uncle's house." Pricked by a pang of conscience, she added, "I hope your head's better. I didn't really mean..."

Nigel gave a reflective grunt. "I didn't open the blasted bathroom door, I fell through it." His whisper somehow managed to convey his sense of injury. "Actually, I had been on my way to apologise."

"Oh." The single syllable managed to sound contrite.

"It ruined that suit," Nigel added reflectively. "It was dry clean only."

Recovering, Julia giggled. The dazzling effect of Nigel's torch had faded. Now sufficient moonlight crept through the door and filtered along the hall for her to pick out his shape as he began to stand up. He rubbed his elbow gingerly, his shadow bobbing on the wall.

"You came charging in like a wildebeest," he said. He risked another flash of the torch to examine himself for damage which appeared to be confined to a generous coating of dust.

"I shall ignore that, Nigel," Julia promised, taking Nigel's extended hand as she stood, "provided in the next five seconds you come up with a reason for lurking in my uncle's hall."

"Your uncle?"

"Great uncle, actually," Julia added, having had time to mull over the matter, "on my mother's side."

Nigel digested this. "But you are Julia Mowbray."

"Mother was a Wilberforce."

"I'd no idea."

"That is no excuse. Now...?"

There was a pause during which Nigel, had he been able to read the expression on the pale oval that was Julia's face, would have quailed. The twin creases of concentration between her eyes were becoming an accusing frown as realisation dawned.

"You," said Julia, "were something in the City."

It was an epithet many might have accepted without shame, but not Nigel. He jerked away as though struck.

"You're not working for any of our advisers, or you'd have come out of the woodwork before now."

Julia was thinking out loud. "Therefore...therefore, you're working for that dreadful Pusey man."

Nigel's hands emerged from the gloom, placating. "Please, keep your voice down."

"What have you done with Uncle Edwin?" Julia closed in on the cringing Nigel, a looming Nemesis. Then, "Where's your car?"

"Pardon?"

"Where've you put your car? Or did some accomplice drop you off. "

"Old girl..."

"Start again, Nigel."

It was impossible to transmit placating body language in the darkness. Nigel did his best to appease with his voice, his *sangfroid* in tatters. "Julia, I have done nothing with your uncle. He is nowhere to be seen. So far as I am concerned, he is *non est*. My car is at the back of the house. I came in through the gate the daily uses. I'd only just got through the door when you came in and knocked me flying."

"You seem to know an awful lot about my uncle's home..."

"I...I've been here before," Nigel admitted, then wished he had been more reticent when Julia's stabbing forefinger found his chest.

"You're after Uncle Edwin's shares."

Nigel's face said everything as, briefly spotlit by moonlight now streaming through the open door, he manoeuvred for a position beyond Julia's reach.

"Something in the City? A snake in the grass, more like." Finding that less than satisfactory, she added, "Have you *no* loyalty?"

Nigel gulped. He gazed at Julia with hangdog eyes, knowing that, come what might, unless he was prepared to betray the girl for whom he yearned his

City career would be history. He opted for prevarication. "I don't think there can be anyone at home," he said, no longer lowering his voice. "There are no lights on anywhere and I haven't heard a sound since I got here - apart from you." They listened together in silence. "Perhaps he's gone to bed," Nigel suggested, "or fallen asleep in a chair."

"It's a waste of time for you to speculate," Julia said with a return to her former asperity. "Whatever you came for, you're obviously up to no good and you might just as well go back to London. Now." Her finger pointed imperiously towards the door.

Nigel temporised. Rapid thought was not his forte but it was clear to him that by some means or other he had to snaffle the envelope which, if he recalled Pinfold Manor's topography correctly, was in the room before whose door Julia now stood. "I can't just leave you here," he wheedled, inspiration adding, "what if he's completely off his trolley and attacks you?"

Slightly taken aback at the revelation that Uncle Edwin's mental state appeared to be common knowledge, Julia hesitated.

Bolstered by her uncertainty, Nigel said, "We might at least see if we can find him. The very least we can do is make sure the old boy's not come to any harm."

He edged towards the door. Julia stepped aside uncertainly, allowing Nigel to slip eagerly into the room. With his back shielding his actions, he flashed the torch ahead of him and stifled a sigh of relief as it illuminated the pale oblong of the envelope on the distant mantelpiece. Julia edged in behind him and fumbled for the light switch. Nigel kept the torch on as a single bulb in a cobwebbed chandelier sprang into life. Most of the room remained stygian. Julia gasped at what she could see of the scattered drawers and heaps of strewn paper. "He must have been burgled," she said weakly.

She advanced into the room and stared disbelievingly at the daubed efforts on the canvases stacked against the walls. Nigel followed, then, executing a neat flanking movement, managed to finish up ahead of her as she rounded the table. Julia stopped, distracted by something on the floor as Nigel oozed in the direction of the fireplace. He glanced towards Julia, awaiting his opportunity.

It came as Julia collapsed against the table and pointed speechlessly at something that lay in its shadow. In a very small voice, she said, "I think I've found Uncle Edwin," and with a shriek that made Nigel's scalp prickle she threw herself into his traitorous arms. But not before he had taken advantage of the distraction to trouser the envelope.

~Chapter 45~

The funeral oration that followed what had been certified as Edwin's heart attack was short, grudging, and could have broadly applied to almost any man in the congregation, of whom there were few. Apart from a few curious villagers, attending, the vicar suspected, chiefly to see in what form and to what degree Edwin's madness might have manifested itself in other members of the family, which naturally led to a fair degree of interest in Harry Temple, the only mourners were the Wilberforce directors and their families. They, having observed the niceties in a minimalist manner, set off back to Yorkshire as soon as was decently practicable. Even Mowbray found himself totally unmoved by the death of a man whose last act might well have been to consign Wilberforces to heaven knew what sort of future and he was striding into his office before Minnie Emmett had finished the afternoon tea round.

He was surprised to find Miss Varley breathless with anxiety and a Hugo Russell who picked up the telephone and began to dial at the sight of him.

"Mr. Kettering asked if you would telephone immediately you got back," Miss Varley explained anxiously. "He telephoned after you had left for the funeral but wouldn't have you disturbed." She smothered a moue of concern as Mowbray's face clouded. He gave her a strained smile of reassurance as Russell handed him the receiver.

"Kettering," Russell mouthed.

Mowbray announced himself and waited for the other to speak.

"We're not quite sure what's going on down here," Kettering said after a brief exchange of politenesses. "I had the oddest call from Pusey's bankers this morning, and they have now sent me a document that appears to put a completely different complexion on the whole business. Our lawyers are looking at it now, but the implication seems to be that you could soon be in the sunny uplands."

Mowbray beckoned Russell nearer. "I'm putting you on the speaker," he told Kettering, pressing the button so that when Kettering resumed he could be heard throughout the room.

"I gave Russell the headlines while you were at the funeral, but at that stage I hadn't seen the actual evidence..." He spoke for several minutes. As he did so Mowbray's expression passed through bewilderment, past realisation to stunned relief.

At last Kettering's voice ground to a stop. Mowbray, his thoughts in ferment, thanked him almost absently and listened to the sound of the receiver being replaced before slowly replacing his own.

"I knew it," he said to the world in general, "I was absolutely convinced I had spoken to Edwin."

* * *

Ignorant of the nature and extent of Nigel's betrayal, Julia's first reaction once she had recovered her wits had been to suggest that the best thing he could do would be to get back to London in short order, or face the prospect of explaining to the police exactly why she had found him in her uncle's house. Nigel, delighted to find beauty allied to such generosity of spirit, had kissed her cheek with a fervour meant to indicate there was lots more available from the same department before scooting back to London, pausing only to check the address on the envelope before sealing it and popping it into the post-box he had already identified as being closest to Pinfold Manor.

Julia, having telephoned the police, found a space among the strewn papers that was as far away from Uncle Edwin as possible and, in order to distract herself, filled the time until they arrived by idly examining them by the light of the torch she had forced Nigel to forfeit. When the police arrived, followed shortly by an ambulance, she gave them a short statement accounting for her presence after which she was clucked over by a matronly policewoman before at last being allowed to return home. So far as the world was aware, all she had achieved had been to ensure a prompt interment for Uncle Edwin who might otherwise have lain undisturbed until his housekeeper made one of her regular visits.

But that was so far as the world was aware.

At Bradburn she had found her father warming a bowl of soup in the kitchen. Making him sit down to drink it, she added what she could to the telephone call she had made earlier, stifled tears at the death of a lonely old man, was consoled, and stifled them again. Later, when her father had telephoned Kettering and retreated to the terrace with his pipe, she allowed a tear at last to crawl down her cheek when she found the salad she had left for him wrapped in a newspaper business section and imperfectly concealed in the waste bin.

Nigel, in the meantime, had returned to London cock-a-hoop with success and wasted no time in conveying the good news to his employer. The banker, having produced a warm glow in Nigel by congratulating him fulsomely, promptly passed on the good news to a Pusey whose enthusiasm seemed distinctly muted.

"If he posted it to you as late as that," he complained, "it's not going to reach your office until Tuesday."

Used as he was to his client's ill-humour, the banker bridled slightly. "There was no possible means of getting it here by post any sooner," he said, risking a hint of tartness. "Sending it through the post was, you will recall, part of the stratagem."

"I'm out of town on Tuesday," Pusey responded flatly. "That means I can't be there when you open it."

"I am sure we can be trusted..."

"I would have liked to have been there," Pusey insisted. "Get hold of me through my office immediately you've got the letter."

* * *

On the Tuesday morning Nigel arrived at the office while even the most assiduous postmen were probably still in bed and waited impatiently for the mail to arrive. His employer, hardly a whit less anxious, popped his head round the door every five minutes or so, eyebrows raised, only to retire frowning each time as Nigel sheepishly shook his head.

When at last the mail arrived Nigel fell on it and then practically howled with a frustration not untinged with terror when a repeated riffling through the pile of envelopes failed to produce the one from Pinfold Manor. It needed no more than the sight of Nigel slumped at his desk among the litter of the morning's mail to convince his employer that things were not going entirely to plan.

"You are absolutely sure...?" he began, his voice icy.

Nigel nodded miserably. "It was impossible to make a mistake. The collection time said the following morning, and the letter went in the box. Even *I*..."

His employer unfroze slightly and gave a judicial nod. Even Crope-Stewart...

"We shall await the second post, after which I must have a word with our client," he said. "I do not suppose he will be overcome with joy."

The second post brought no reprieve.

There is a gulf between the understatement beloved of Englishmen and raw verbal inadequacy. To suggest that Pusey was less than thrilled on hearing of the letter's non-arrival would be to trifle with the very roots of the language. Pusey was incandescent. Having at last banged the telephone down on a banker holding his own receiver as far away from his ear as the length of his arm allowed, Pusey attempted to call him back only to hang up each time as he found the vehemence of his rage had left him literally speechless. At last he allowed the call to go through and, in a voice squeezed dry of all emotion, said, "Get that letter. Get it, or I shall explain to the City exactly how you attempted to do so."

* * *

"No panic, Harry," the postmaster had said forgivingly on the Monday morning, "anyone can miss a box on a new round. There's never anything in that one near the Manor, anyway. No, don't go back. You can take a look in the morning. Here, I've just brewed this..."

* * *

On the Wednesday morning, as the Wilberforce board were *en route* for Edwin's hastily arranged funeral, the banker and Nigel met on the steps of the office and ascended them in silence. Half-an-hour later, still silent, they sat on either side of the banker's desk as an office junior delivered the stack of mail and retreated. As usual many of the letters were in the bank's own reply-paid envelopes and the banker's face fell at the prospect of having to open them and examine their contents one by one. Nigel, however, having fanned them into a shallow pile across the desk, pounced on one that bore a dozen dusty fingerprints and handed it over like a spaniel returning a particularly testing catch.

The banker's attempt at imperturbability was betrayed by hands that shook as he picked up a crystal-handled paperknife, slit the envelope while taking care not to damage its contents, and removed the pieces of paper it contained. He unfolded them, noting the pink ribbon and its timeworn appearance, studied them for a moment with a look of growing puzzlement, then handed them to Nigel without comment.

Nigel, terrified at the appearance of papers that were certainly not the Form of Acceptance, pretended to study them while his head spun in search of an excuse that might exonerate him of responsibility for a development he could not even begin to comprehend. His employer, with an expression Nigel could not read, picked up the telephone and dialled Pusey's number.

Pusey greeted his voice with gloating certainty. "Well?" he snapped.

He listened in silence as his adviser droned smoothly on. At last, when the banker had come to a stop, there was silence for several seconds until Pusey recovered his voice. At last, so hoarse with emotion as to be almost unintelligible, he snarled, "You're fired."

The banker sighed the sigh of one relinquishing an intolerable burden, joggled the telephone rest and, when the line cleared, dialled Richard Kettering.

* * *

Pusey sat alone in his office, hands flat on the desk in front of him, and tried to think with his customary calm. He stood up and wandered over to the window. Old Wilberforce's room had been ankle deep in papers, the banker had said. He struck the window frame with his fist as the thought came to him. The man was a blind fool. Picking up the telephone, Pusey dialled the number of the man he should have used in the first place.

~Chapter 46~

H aving exhausted the attractions of copying out
Mr. Pitman's short forms, Tracy turned her
attention to Simon's back as he stood at the window
and stared blankly down at the glass roof of the arcade.
"The meeting in the boardroom begins in a couple of
minutes," she chided, "you'd better get a move on."

Simon nodded absently and Tracy frowned at his
absorption as he moved round the desk and out of the
door. The early evening meeting had been called at
short notice, allowing just sufficient time for the
cousins to arrive. To Simon, that was ominous. Not
merely ominous, but as it almost certainly presaged the
revelation of some lethal masterstroke by Pusey, it
threatened to disrupt the bright new future for the
Beresfords the weekend had held out before them. Not
that Saturday's euphoria had survived the departure of
his family. Simon had awoken that night soaked in
perspiration after a dream in which Pusey had won the
battle for Wilberforces, Rebecca had sold the house for
a bag of beans and he had been left scouring the streets
of Ealing for a doorway to sleep in with his family
crocodiling behind him.

Earlier that evening, Rebecca had leaned out of the
window of the carriage that would bear her and the
children back to London and attempted to disperse the

gloom their departure had provoked. "You are not to worry about anything," she assured her husband. "Pusey's not going to win, you will have a lovely new job and I'll find us a cottage with roses round the door."

That had been Sunday. Since then, so far as Simon could see, absolutely nothing had happened to move events in any direction. Julia, bearing up wonderfully after the shock of finding Uncle Edwin's body, nevertheless seemed preoccupied. Today, with Julia and the directors at Edwin's hastily-arranged funeral, he had been so distracted that Russell had taken pity on him and used his newly restored Jaguar to drive him to an inn in the country where he had treated Simon to a nourishing organic salad.

The board's return shortly before teatime had prompted an explosion of activity in which, it appeared to Simon, he was irrelevant. Mowbray's telephone had never stopped. Simkiss, the little lawyer, fussily involved at last, had held long conversations with his opposite numbers in London. Julia, having changed out of her funeral weeds, had been her warm self yet unforthcoming when they bumped into each other as she emerged briefly from a meeting with Simkiss and her father. Simon was still pondering the meaning of events when he bumped into Julia once more outside the door to the boardroom.

"What...?" Simon began.

Julia, her eyes bright with excitement, put a finger to her lips, grabbed him by the hand and pulled him into the boardroom where Temple intercepted them and led her to a place on the left of her father's vacant chair. There were curious glances from a number of the other directors as Mowbray broke off a conversation and moved towards his place. One of the cousins, Simon noticed, was still dressed for the races, swing tickets dangling from his binoculars case. Collectively, the directors managed to look both pessimistic and apprehensive. Hugo Russell, slimmer now and, Julia thought, resembling a mature Rubens cherub, waved a cheerful hand as she and Simon took their places. Irrelevantly, Simon noticed Russell's suitcases standing near the door, their expensive pigskin patched with exotic labels.

Mowbray said something to Miss Varley and, with an expression that was difficult to read, stared around the table until the hum of conversation subsided.

"I hope you don't mind my having invited Julia," he began, "the reason will become clear." There were assenting murmurs from the others and he continued. "I have news for you all, and it is important that you should hear it promptly. It is, I hasten to add, good news."

Harry Temple, already in the loop, beamed at Julia then at the room in general.

"Pusey and Associates are to withdraw their bid for our company," Mowbray said. He raised his hand to stifle an outbreak of startled comment. "A consequence will be a number of changes here, of course, but that had become inevitable in the light of the events of recent weeks. These should not be too painful and it may even be that one or two of us will be able to retire gracefully."

Temple harrumphed. The others remained silent.

"I said Pusey Associates were to withdraw their bid," Mowbray resumed, "but that is not technically correct. What has happened, in fact, is that Pusey's advisers have become aware of a development I shall come to in a moment that will have that effect. They telephoned Palgraves while most of us here were at the funeral to say that, in view of that development, they will now be unable to obtain the acceptances they need and their client will therefore have no option but to withdraw." He stretched out a hand and cupped Julia's hand on the table. "As we all know, one of the greatest uncertainties since the bid arrived has been how Edwin Wilberforce would react. Up to the time of his death he had led us to believe that he had agreed to sell to the bidder. His holding was so substantial that it would almost certainly have convinced any waverers among the institutions that we could not win and they, too, would have sold. And that would have been that. Wilberforces, certainly in the form we know it, would have ceased to exist."

He broke off for a moment and looked at the faces around the table. Bill Pritchard, the marketing director, looked bored. As the youngest director he had listened without comment when, in the early stages of the defence, Palgraves had first suggested that, if Wilberforces escaped Pusey's attentions, the City would almost certainly demand changes in the way it was managed. If that meant getting rid of the old buffers who had got them into this predicament, it was a prospect Pritchard faced with equanimity. As the youngest member of the board, any such moves would inevitably ratchet him in the direction of the driving seat... He met Mowbray's eyes with a complacent smile.

Fleetingly, Mowbray recalled what Kettering had said about him. "Although that young man performs entirely to his own satisfaction, he appears to be almost single-handedly responsible for the company's poor sales record. He will certainly have to go if the City is going to take us seriously when we talk to them about the future."

Mowbray squeezed Julia's hand and continued. "As neither Pusey nor his advisers had confirmed receipt of

Edwin's commitment, we were somewhat at a loss. The way in which events have now turned out is, well, simply remarkable."

To Simon, who was watching Julia closely, it appeared that she coloured slightly at this point, though her eyes were directed demurely at her lap.

* * *

Harry Temple was not entirely unhappy with the prospect of retirement, although his feathers had been considerably ruffled at the fact that it had been proposed by outsiders. "Like to see *them* running this place as well as Bradburn Show," he had huffed.

This morning he was, Mowbray noted, paying more attention to events than was customary. Like Simon, the colonel enjoyed a good thriller and, although he had already read the last page, as it were, old Gerry's tale had all the makings. Removing *The Times* racing pages from his lap, he folded them and stuck them in the pocket of his tweed jacket, the better to concentrate.

"As some of you know," Mowbray was saying, "when most of us went to Harry's on Sunday, Julia took it into her head to call on Uncle Edwin. Without quite knowing what she might achieve, she..."

Ben Bartlett, the company secretary, gripped by the unfolding story but anxious to address the backlog of work the bid had left him with, watched the animation in Mowbray's face and offered silent thanks for the lifting of the weight from their shoulders. He and Aneurin Williams, the finance director, had dealt with the brunt of the research called for by those working on the defence in London. They, together with the production director, were to be what Kettering had described as the grit in the oyster from which the new management team would emerge. His attention returned to his chairman.

"So," said Mowbray, "Crope-Stewart disappears with what he has every right to believe is Edwin's Form of Acceptance and in the firm belief that it's all over bar the shouting. And then, this morning, they opened the envelope and found that what they had finished up with was not the Form of Acceptance but..." He allowed himself a short pause for effect. "...but Edwin Wilberforce's will, signed and witnessed more than twenty years ago."

There was a stunned silence until the Broadbridge GP asked, with a brusqueness he normally reserved for the consulting room, "And who does it all go to?"

Not yet prepared to be drawn, Mowbray smiled and held up a hand. "I have mentioned to one or two people during our battle with Mervyn Pusey that I had spoken to Edwin at some time, years ago, but that I couldn't for the life of me recall what I had called him about. His will, gentlemen, is dated exactly a week after Julia's birth announcement appeared in *The Times*, and it leaves everything to my daughter – Wilberforce shares, Pinfold Manor, everything. "

The only sound in the room was the ticking of the boardroom clock.

"I was wrong in one respect. I had never telephoned Edwin: *he* had telephoned Bradburn House to find out whether the 'née Wilberforce' in Julia's birth announcement in the press did indeed refer to Jane." Ignorant as he was of Edwin's kitten-cuddling phase, he continued, "What persuaded him to make over a very considerable fortune to our daughter and then subsequently ignore her existence..." He shrugged. "He had no relatives of his own of, course. He was, we know, eccentric, and became increasingly so from then on..."

Stunned silence gave way to expressions of relief and disbelief as the import of his words sank in. Simon and Harry Temple almost collided as they converged on Julia until the older man stood aside as she first hugged Simon then threw herself into her uncle's arms.

Hugo Russell was pumping Mowbray's hand and beaming at the room while the rest of the directors pushed their chairs back from the table and shook their heads at one another in varying degrees of astonishment.

Only Miss Varley remained seated, though a pink glow of pleasure spread slowly from her face to her neck and thence discreetly out of sight as she smiled shyly in the direction of a breathless Julia.

* * *

Rebecca, having been unwilling to contemplate anything other than a successful defence by Wilberforces, had listened to Simon's telephone call calmly. Hazel was now sitting on the Beresfords' bed pouting as Rebecca rummaged in cupboards for the cases that would soon begin transferring the family's belongings north.

"You must continue to do under your arms, you know," she was saying. "People up there just let themselves go."

Rebecca broke off from her packing and stared fondly at her friend. Words rose unbidden from some Sunday School corner of her mind as she fought and failed to swallow them. Sitting down beside Hazel she placed a tender arm round her friend's shoulders.

Solemn faced, forcing a puzzled Hazel to meet her eyes, she recited solemnly, "'And they called Rebecca, and said unto her, wilt thou go with this man? And she said, I will go.'"

Hazel's eyes widened in disbelief. Then, as Rebecca's lips began to twitch, they both began to laugh.

~Chapter 47~

A suitably bland press statement announcing the successful bid defence was agreed and rushed out by Brightlings. Simon produced and distributed a celebratory bulletin in record time while the directors telephoned their contacts in the community to give them a discreetly edited version of events. At last Mowbray, elated but tired, got back to Bradburn House and joined Julia and Simon in toasting the London-bound Hugo Russell in champagne. There, a chastened and more tractable man, Russell planned to restore himself to what would no doubt be an appropriately cautious Constance from behind a veritable thicket of red roses. As Mowbray and the youngsters basked on the terrace in the late summer sun there was a crunch of gravel as Shelmerdine's disreputable van drove up and deposited Kitty; then, with rare sensitivity and in a cloud of diesel fumes, he roared off and parked it in the stableyard.

Once everyone had been given a fresh glass of champagne, and then a second, and Shelmerdine and Kitty, having answered Julia's summons, had been put fully in the picture, Mowbray sat in his favourite garden chair, lit his pipe and puffed contentedly. "You know," he said, "there is just one thing that still puzzles Kettering."

Wandering over to her father, Julia sat on the arm of his chair and lifted his spectacles so that they rested on his forehead. He wrinkled his forehead until they slipped back once more on to the bridge of his nose, completing a charade she has used as a child whenever she wanted to distract him.

Smiling but undeterred, he said, "When Kettering first telephoned us about the will, he quite rightly said that, so far as Pusey's merchant bank was concerned, the will was sufficient to make their side withdraw. Pusey evidently didn't think so, however. The police telephoned shortly before I left the office. According to them, Pusey sent some petty criminal to Pinfold Manor to sift through all the paper Crope-Stewart had reported finding on the floor. Pusey reckoned the old man had dug out the will when he felt ill and stuck it in the first envelope he could find. To use the envelope, he would have had to dispose of the Form of Acceptance. That, presumably, therefore had to be somewhere among that mess on the floor. . ."

Julia had wandered behind Simon and was resting her hand on his shoulder. As Mowbray teased at the puzzle, Simon had the fleeting impression that her hand delivered a nervous squeeze.

"No doubt Pusey reckoned that if Edwin appeared to have kept every other piece of paper sent to him, why would he have disposed of the Form of Acceptance?" Mowbray continued. "If Pusey's man could have found it, Pusey could have claimed, though it would have been a lie, that it was in his hands before Edwin's death. He could then have used it to win his bid: Edwin's shareholding would have carried the day."

His audience, drinks forgotten, were transfixed.

"What Pusey didn't know was that his bank had already told our side about the will. However, when

Pusey's man was arrested by a patrol keeping an eye on the empty house, he admitted that he'd been through the papers thoroughly and that the Form of Acceptance simply wasn't there. He, incidentally, was more than happy to implicate Pusey who will have some awkward questions to answer before he's ever let loose in the City again." Mowbray looked around at his rapt audience. "It certainly makes you think," he said, and began once more the serious business of attending to his pipe.

Julia, who had arrived home from Pinfold Manor covered in dust up to her elbows, relaxed her grip on Simon's shoulder and shook her head wonderingly.

Raising her glass to them all, she kissed her father on the top of his head. "It certainly does," she said.